S

I

L

K

Edited by
Lesley Ellis Miller and Ana Cabrera Lafuente
with Claire Allen-Johnstone

S I L K

*Fibre, Fabric
and Fashion*

With over 600 illustrations

Thames
&Hudson | V&A

Front cover: (top to bottom) details from
p. 307, p. 295, p. 456 and p. 157

Back cover: detail from p. 388

Spine cover: detail from p. 389 right

Frontispiece: detail from p. 476
pp. 4–5: detail from pp. 176–7
pp. 6–7: detail from p. 163
pp. 8–9: detail from p. 473
pp. 10–11: detail from p. 328
pp. 12–13: detail from p. 349
pp. 66–7: detail from p. 94
pp. 104–5: detail from p. 195
pp. 224–5: detail from p. 247
pp. 274–5: detail from p. 350
pp. 372–3: detail from p. 424
pp. 492–3: detail from p. 450

First published in the United Kingdom in 2021
by Thames & Hudson Ltd, 181A High Holborn,
London WC1V 7QX, in association with the
Victoria and Albert Museum, London

First published in the United States of America
in 2021 by Thames & Hudson Inc., 500 Fifth
Avenue, New York, New York 10110

Silk: Fibre, Fabric and Fashion
© 2021 Victoria and Albert Museum, London/
Thames & Hudson Ltd, London

Text and V&A photographs © 2021 Victoria
and Albert Museum, London
Design © 2021 Thames & Hudson Ltd, London

Designed by Roger Fawcett-Tang
Edited by Caroline Brooke Johnson

British Library Cataloguing-in-Publication Data
A catalogue record for this book is available from
the British Library.

Library of Congress Control Number 2020933625

ISBN 978-0-500-48065-6

Printed in China by RR Donnelley

MIX
Paper from
responsible sources
FSC® C144853

Be the first to know about our new releases,
exclusive content and author events by visiting
thamesandhudson.com
thamesandhudsonusa.com
thamesandhudson.com.au

V&A Publishing
Supporting the world's leading
museum of art and design,
the Victoria and Albert
Museum, London

Contents

Introduction

'Ever since Antiquity, the love and longing for silk textiles has fostered connections across Asia, Europe and the Atlantic ... Sericulture and silk manufacturing ... propelled both peaceful interchange and cross-cultural competition, generating wealth and power, and transforming economies and societies.'[1]

INTERNATIONAL SILK CONGRESS LONDON September 1951

The International Silk Association held its congress in London in 1951, just three years after its establishment. It was keen to assert the renaissance of silk, commissioning a poster design from the illustrator and fashion photographer Cecil Beaton. He conjured up the glamour of a fabric long associated with luxury: Venus, goddess of love and beauty, emerges from the waves bedecked in silks in many colours and patterns, leaving post-war austerity behind (1).

In the early twenty-first century, silk is still very much to the fore, with few synthetic fibres able to match its allure and cachet. For ceremonial and traditional festivities or rites of passage, it retains its long-established role in royal and official robes, ecclesiastical vestments and regional, traditional and wedding dresses. It graces the catwalk (2), ballroom, opera house and red carpet. It is also available as smart workwear, party dress, kimono, *qipao*, saris and sumptuous, seductive underwear.

1 (LEFT)
Renaissance of Silk, poster advertising the International Silk Congress in London, by Cecil Beaton, London, England, 1951. Colour process engraving

V&A E.1924-1952

2 (OPPOSITE)
Evening dress of embroidered silk organza and tulle by Oscar de la Renta, New York, USA, Spring 2015

V&A T.44-2017

3
Ceremonial hunt from the
Akbarnama (*Book of Akbar*) by
Miskina and Sarwan (makers),
Mughal empire, about 1590–5.
Watercolour and gold on paper

V&A IS.2:55-1896

Over the centuries, silk has also furnished interiors, allowing for lavish display through coordinated wall hangings, upholstery and rugs. It was a firm favourite in Europe, the Middle East and the USA well into the twentieth century, often commissioned rather than bought off the shelf because of its expense. Climatic conditions and cultural preferences informed decisions about colours, patterns and types. In India and the Middle East, silk awnings, cushions, floor covers and hangings provided rich colour, warmth and privacy in palace interiors. They travelled with their owners when they went on campaigns and diplomatic missions or visited residences in other places. During the Mughal empire (1526–1857), royal tents usually had plain red outer walls, but might have rich velvets inside (3).[2] In Europe and America, wealthy patrons of the arts posed in silk dresses in silk-accoutred interiors redolent of their means and style. Elfrida Ionides rests elegantly on a velvet upholstered sofa, set against a kimono mounted on a screen (4).

Silk was used to a lesser extent in Japan and Korea. In Korea, for example, silk cushions and mattresses were sat on in the cold season, and screens might be made of silk (5).

4 (RIGHT)
Portrait of Mrs Luke Ionides, née Elfrida Elizabeth Bird, by William Blake Richmond, London, England, 1882. Oil on canvas

Purchased with support of the Art Fund and the Friends of the V&A.
V&A E.1062-2003

5 (BELOW)
A bedside folding screen with *gung-su* embroidery with floral design and auspicious phrases, Korea, 1885–1910

Conservation supported by the Overseas Korean Cultural Heritage Foundation and Mir Dental Network of Korea.
V&A FE.29-1991

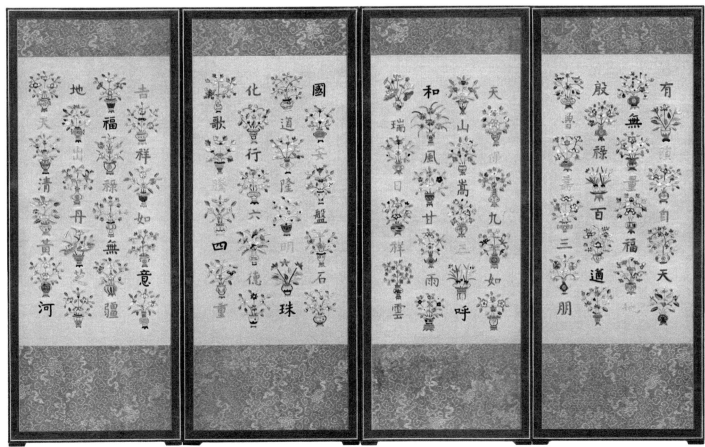

6 (ABOVE)
Queen Victoria's Saloon, railway carriage, London and North Western Railway, built by Wolverton Works, England, 1869, recently conserved

7 (LEFT)
Serenity Phantom interior with embroidered and painted silk, designed by Cherica Haye for Rolls-Royce, England, 2013

Luxury transport such as sedan chairs, barges and carriages, trains and ocean liners, cars and private jets, echoed the richness of silken interiors, conveying messages about their occupant's or owner's power, position and taste. Queen Victoria ordered a dazzling electric blue watered silk for the saloon coach in her royal train in 1869 and enjoyed it until her death in 1901 (6). Those of high rank in nineteenth-century India travelled in elephant howdahs and bullock-drawn carriages bedecked in silks with gold trimmings (8), and as recently as 2013 Rolls-Royce commissioned silk for the interior of its opulent bespoke Serenity Phantom car (7).

8
Carriage drawn by bullocks,
photograph from the Gordon Gift
Album, vol. 5, India, 1891
V&A PH.1267-1908

9

Bedstead with hangings of Italian cut silk velvet and Chinese satin linings, trimmed with braid and fringe, designed by Daniel Marot, upholstered by Francis Lapierre, London, England, about 1700

Given by the Rt Hon. the Earl of Melville.
V&A W.35:1 to 72-1949

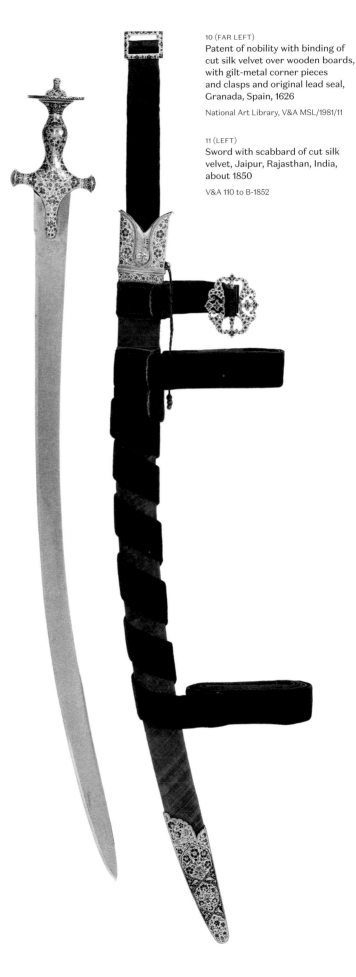

10 (FAR LEFT)
Patent of nobility with binding of
cut silk velvet over wooden boards,
with gilt-metal corner pieces
and clasps and original lead seal,
Granada, Spain, 1626

National Art Library, V&A MSL/1981/11

11 (LEFT)
Sword with scabbard of cut silk
velvet, Jaipur, Rajasthan, India,
about 1850

V&A 110 to B-1852

Not surprisingly, silks became heirlooms, preserved
intentionally for future generations of the same family
or institution – adorning prestigious state beds (9),
binding official documents such as letters of nobility (10)
or enveloping ceremonial equipment (11). Repurposing
or recycling was common, for reasons of thrift or as an
expression of sentiment, creativity or faith: consider the
conversion of postulant nuns' trousseaux of silk gowns
into priestly vestments or church ornaments, silk kimono
and *Nō* robes gifted to temples to be turned into Buddhist

robes or altar cloths, the passing of silk saris from mother
to daughter, the wartime transformation of silk parachutes
into blouses or dresses (12), the crafting of favourite frocks
into a patchwork quilt (13) and the designing of a unique
high-fashion evening gown from a historical coverlet (14).
These actions speak of the longevity and versatility of silk as
well as its economic and emotional value. They reveal, too,
its potential to contribute to the twenty-first-century quest
for ethical and sustainable fashion.

These examples of fashion and furnishings are merely
among the most visible current and historical faces of
silk, which has also been employed for medical, military
and scientific purposes. They act as an appetiser for the

selection of sumptuous objects in this book, which come from across the globe and were used in war and peace, in places of worship and at home between 600 CE and the early twenty-first century. These silks reveal creativity and technical virtuosity, so the focus is on their physical qualities, including their techniques of embellishment. But what exactly is silk, where does it come from and how is it made? A mid-nineteenth-century educational illustration (15) helpfully sets the scene for a brief introduction to the properties, origins and preliminary steps in preparing silk for use: at its heart is the *Bombyx mori* silk moth, its lifecycle represented by caterpillar (larva), cocoon, chrysalis and moth, all posed against luscious mulberry leaves.

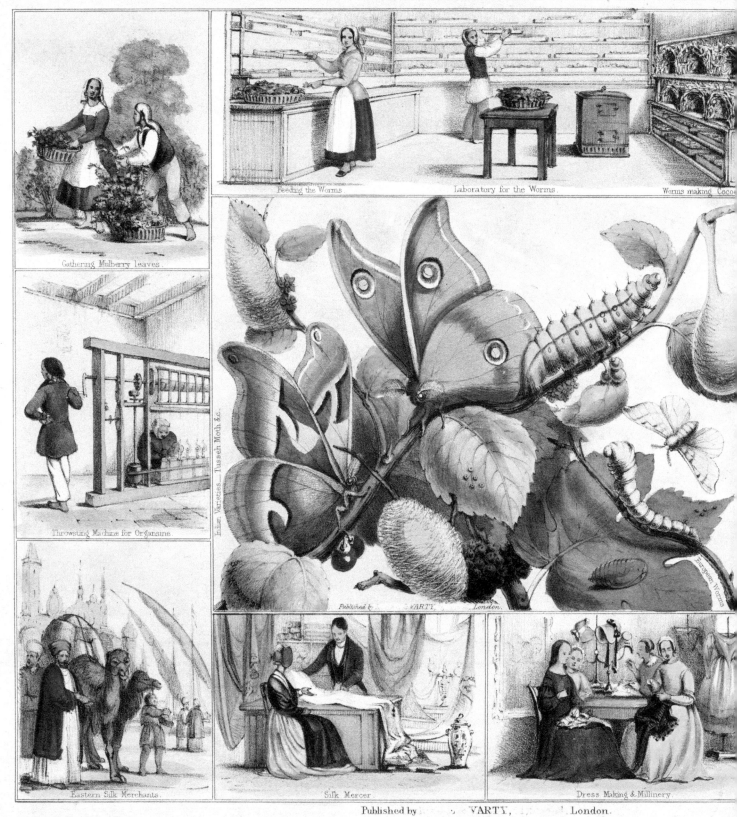

Gathering Mulberry leaves.

Feeding the Worms.

Laboratory for the Worms.

Worms making Cocoons.

Throwsting Machine for Organsine.

Indian Varieties.—Tusseh Moth &c.

European Worms.

Published by VARTY, London.

Eastern Silk Merchants.

Silk Mercer.

Dress Making & Millinery.

Designed & Drawn on Stone by W. Hawkins.

Published by VARTY, London.

THE SILK-WORM.

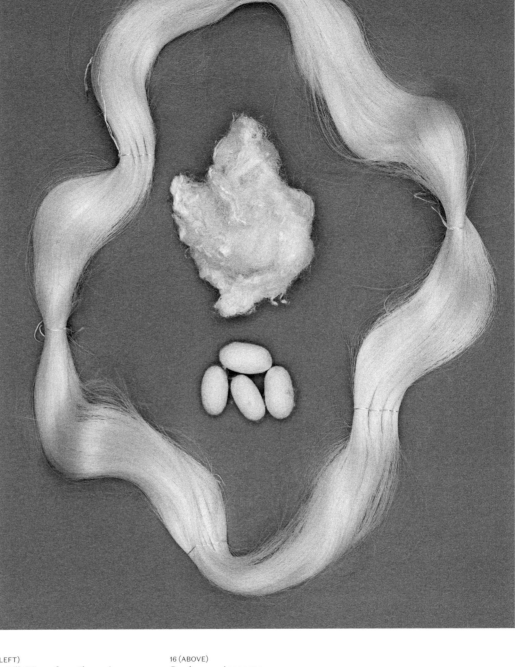

15 (LEFT)
The Silk-Worm, from the series
Graphic Illustrations of Animals
by Benjamin Waterhouse Hawkins,
published by Thomas Varty,
London, England, about 1850.
Coloured lithograph print on paper

V&A E.305-1901

16 (ABOVE)
Bombyx mori cocoons,
fibre and reeled silk

Private collection

MOTHS AND SPIDERS

Silk is an animal fibre that comes from different species of moths and spiders. The best-known and most widely cultivated is the *Bombyx mori*, whose native habitat is China. In north-east India the indigenous *Antherae mylitta*, *Antheraea assamensis* and *Philosamia cynthia ricini* provide the 'wild' silks tasar, muga and eri/endi respectively. In Africa the *Borocera madagascariensis* in Madagascar and the *Anaphe infracta* and *Anaphe moloneyi* in Nigeria are their equivalents. The silk fibre, or filament, originates in the cocoon that the silkworms build around themselves as they prepare for their chrysalis state, from which they emerge as moths (16).

Bombyx mori thrive on a diet of mulberry leaves, and sericulture – the farming or cultivation of silkworms – involves providing them with massive quantities of foliage as they lie on aerated shelves in sheds. Having eaten, the larvae extrude a gummed filament and wind it around themselves. Over the following month, as the chrysalis matures into a moth, it eats through the cocoon, breaking the filament. Silk farmers must ensure that the moth does not munch its way out, in order to guarantee the longest, strongest and finest filaments for making thread. They do so by suffocating the chrysalis, or by placing the cocoons in boiling water. This second process also removes the sericin, the gum substance that keeps the filaments together, facilitating their reeling from the cocoon. The *Bombyx mori* moth is now entirely domesticated, while India's indigenous 'wild silks' are domesticated to lesser extents (17).[3] Broken filaments, or staples, from any species are commonly called waste silk. They may be spun into a coarser and weaker silk.

17
Group of silk skeins. Left to right: mulberry silk waste, eri, two qualities of muga, four qualities of tasar, Madhya Pradesh and Assam, India, 2015
V&A IS.16 to 23-2015

Spiders also produce silk, and the *Nephila madagascariensis* is cultivated in Madagascar. Farming has had limited success, though Europeans were already pondering commercial exploitation in the early eighteenth century, with the Académie des Sciences in Paris evaluating a report on the subject in 1710. M. Bon of Montpellier had managed to make a pair of stockings and a pair of mittens from spider silk, both being strong and naturally mouse-grey.[4] The dingy colour evidently contrasted unfavourably with the brilliant white of mulberry silk (16), and is quite different from the golden yellow of *muga* silk, or the yellow colour of Madagascar spider silk, a cape of which dazzled visitors to London in 2012 (18 and 19).[5]

Raw silk has many properties that contribute to its desirability as a fibre. It is lustrous, strong and lightweight, qualities not replicated in any other natural fibre and eagerly sought by those attempting to create the artificial silks that became commercially viable in the first third of the twentieth century.[6] The characteristic continuous filament of each species is physiochemically distinctive: *Bombyx mori* filament has a triangular profile so it reflects light, while wild silks have a spiral or flat profile, so are relatively matte.[7] Filaments are very fine (about one denier) and may be as long as 1,200 metres.[8] This length contributes to their great strength, which is enhanced by twisting filaments together to form a plied thread. Such threads are strong enough to act as warp threads stretched taut on a loom and subjected to the action of beating bars and shuttles. They can also bear the impact of block or copperplate printing or the pressure of pleating. Indeed, their strength is such that they have been used for fishing lines, mountaineering ropes, parachutes and medical sutures.[9] In addition, in common with other animal fibres such as wool, silk absorbs liquids easily, so takes a variety of natural and synthetic dyestuffs well. It is also warm in cold weather conditions and cool in warm ones, so highly suitable for use in high-performance underwear.

Visual inspection and physical handling alone are seldom sufficient to identify the silk type used in textiles beyond the shadow of a doubt, though the smoothness of mulberry silk and its warmth to the touch are indications.

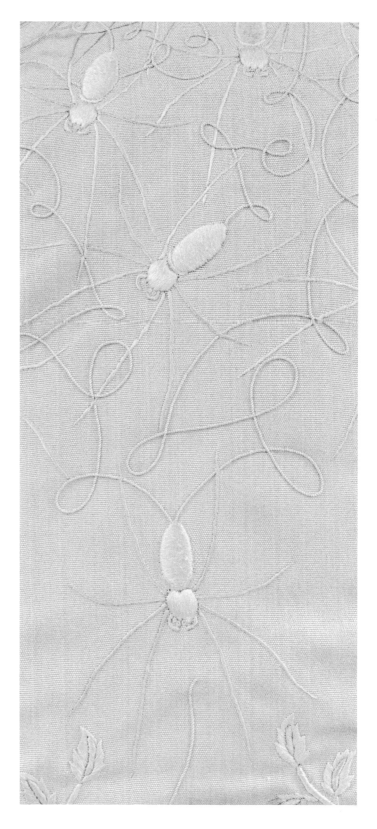

18 (ABOVE) & 19 (OPPOSITE)
Woven spider silk cape by Simon Peers and Nicholas Godley, Peers Workshop, Antananarivo, Madagascar, 2011

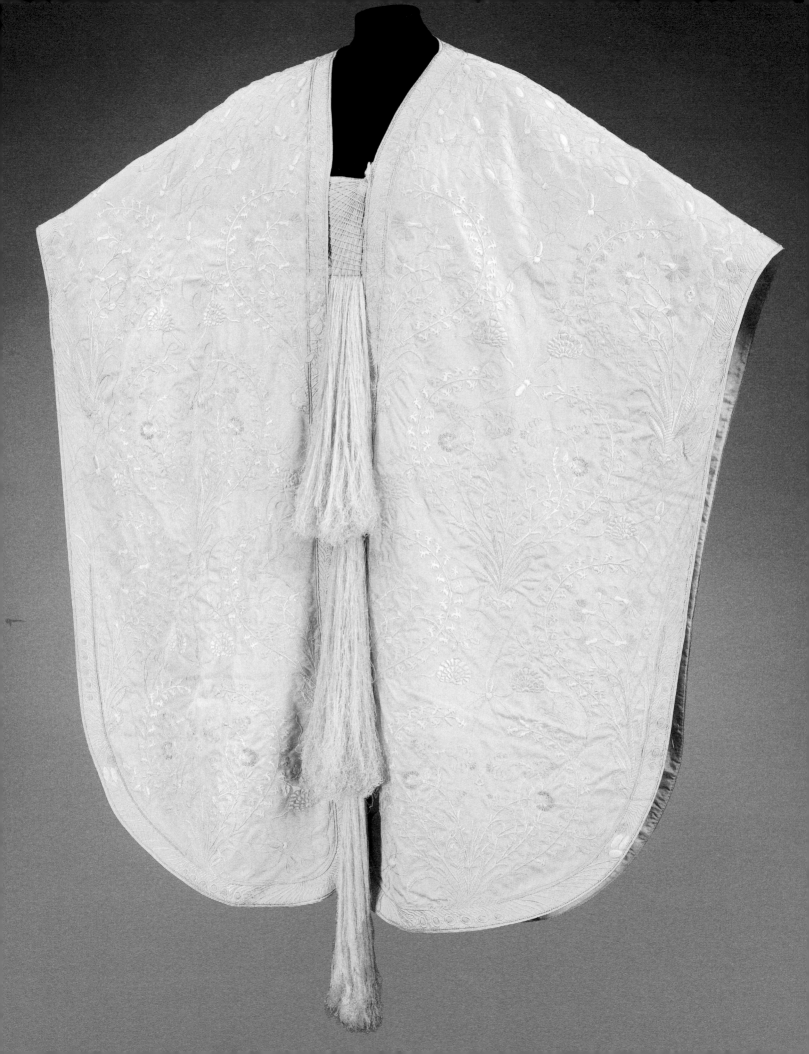

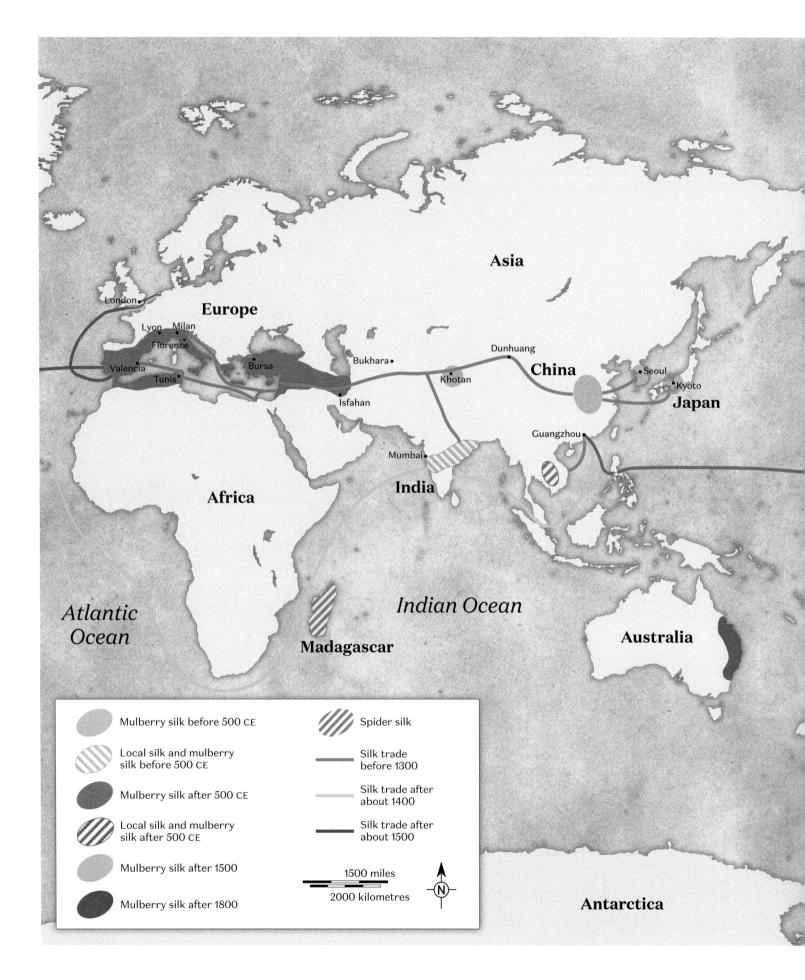

Asia

Europe

London

Lyon Milan

Florence

Valencia

Tunis

Bursa

Bukhara

Isfahan

Dunhuang

China

Khotan

Seoul

Kyoto

Japan

Guangzhou

Africa

Mumbai

India

Atlantic
Ocean

Indian Ocean

Madagascar

Australia

Antarctica

Mulberry silk before 500 CE

Spider silk

Local silk and mulberry
silk before 500 CE

Silk trade
before 1300

Mulberry silk after 500 CE

Silk trade after
about 1400

Local silk and mulberry
silk after 500 CE

Silk trade after
about 1500

Mulberry silk after 1500

1500 miles

Mulberry silk after 1800

2000 kilometres

N

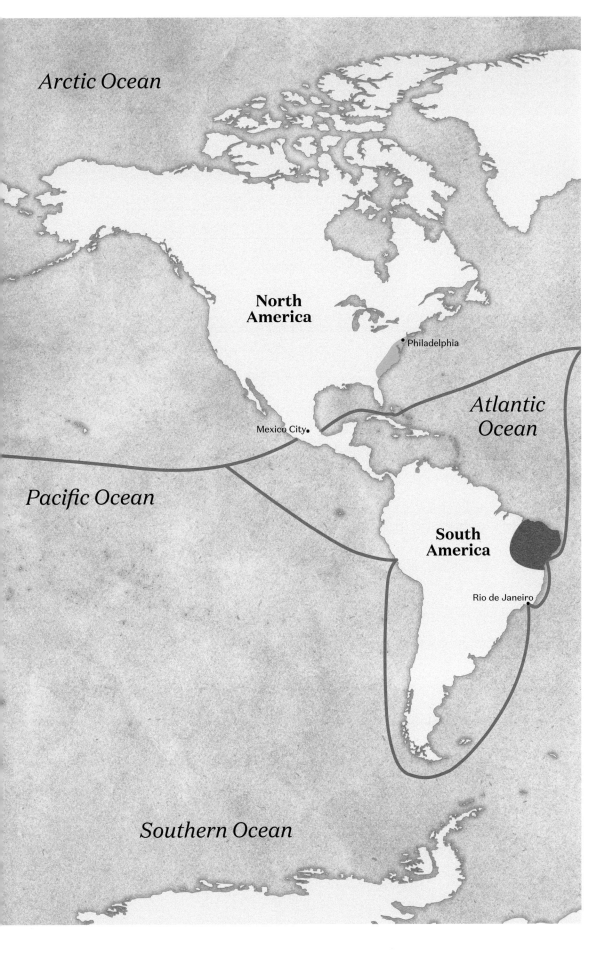

Arctic Ocean

North
America

Philadelphia

Mexico City

Atlantic
Ocean

Pacific Ocean

South
America

Rio de Janeiro

Southern Ocean

SILKWORMS, MULBERRIES AND MIGRATION

A very large number of silkworms are needed for the production of fabric and they have particular food requirements. One hectare of land planted with mulberries feeds about 400,000 silkworms, whose cocoons spin into 100 kg of raw silk, enough to make about 500 blouses of a type common in western fashion in 2019.[10] Thus, moriculture – the cultivation of mulberry trees – has been key to the successful breeding of silkworms.

The journey of *Bombyx mori* silkworms along trade routes from China to the Middle East and Europe has long been mythologized (21).[11] Archaeological and historical evidence now clarifies that sericulture originated in China and was already firmly established in the third century BCE. By the fifth century it had arrived in Khotan (present-day Xinjiang, China) thanks to the marriage of a Chinese princess to a governor of that oasis, which was one of the main cities on the trading routes now commonly known as the 'Silk Roads' (20).[12] Cocoons were brought to Europe in the sixth century to Constantinople (present-day Istanbul), capital of the Byzantine empire.[13] From there, they reached Anatolia, Greece and Syria, which flourished as an area of cultivation from about 900 CE. By the same date,

sericulture was already fully established in Iberia. More or less concurrently it reached North Africa and Sicily from where it spread to the south of the Italian peninsula. It was flourishing in both the Iberian and Italian peninsulas by the thirteenth century. In Asia sericulture extended from China to Korea and Thailand by about 100 BCE. It had extended to Japan (22) by the third century, about the same time that the *Bombyx mori* probably arrived in India, complementing local wild silk production.[14]

From the ninth to the fifteenth centuries, in the Iberian peninsula and Sicily, the cultivation of *Bombyx mori* was organized in farms within a system of irrigated orchards that had been developed by Muslims. Italy dominated European sericulture from the thirteenth century, in particular stimulating the economy of the later industrialized areas of the north, the Veneto and Piedmont. From the mid-nineteenth century decline set in, due to epidemics among silkworms, competition from synthetic fibres and lower-cost Chinese imports (23 and 24) decimating production in Italy by the 1970s.[15] Forty years later in 2015, the revival of small-scale sericulture in the Veneto was mooted.[16] In France, a similar situation pertained. The Cevennes became the major area of production, flourishing from the thirteenth century

SER, SIVE SERICVS VERMIS.

Iustinianus oua vermis accipit Serinda ab vrbe, fila qui net aurea. 9.

Ioan. Stradanus inuent. Phls Galle excud.

23
Gathering *jinsang* mulberry leaves
by Wu Jun, Guangzhou, China,
1870–90. Watercolour and
ink on paper

V&A D.911-1901

24
Feeding the silkworms by Wu
Jun, Guangzhou, China, 1870–90.
Watercolour and ink on paper

V&A D.914-1901

to the mid-nineteenth century, when it declined dramatically as a result of the same epidemic and similar forms of competition. The last mill closed in 1965, and new initiatives in the late 1970s and 1980s could not compete with cheap imported Chinese raw silk. The tradition and cultivation of worms is still, however, promoted in the area through educational institutions and there have been new initiatives in three-dimensional spinning since 2015.[17]

Japan closely paralleled European states in the Tokugawa period (1603–1868) during its isolation from the outside world, with sericulture becoming one of the most dynamic areas of its economy. The first handbook on silk production was commissioned by the government of the Tsugara Domain in 1701, with more than 100 such manuals published in Japan over the next 150 years. Uekaki Morikuni's *The Secrets of Sericulture* was printed in Japanese in 1803 and was later translated into French by the Dutch government's interpreter (Paris and Turin

1848), with an introduction and commentary by the French expert Matthieu Bonafous. Significantly, it was reissued as the European silkworm blight worsened. It revealed that the Japanese had promoted labour-intensive techniques of production: they had lavished attention on the preparation of mulberry leaves to tempt the worms at different stages in their development, and on ensuring good temperature control in the sheds and high standards of hygiene. They also purchased new eggs each year and bred selectively (five types of silkworm were reported in the early eighteenth century, and over 200 in the 1860s).[18] Raw silk was to become a major export to Europe, interrupted during the Second World War but restored thereafter.[19] Since the 1970s, Japanese production has been largely devoted to supplying its own kimono-making weavers.

Many other initiatives to develop the moriculture necessary for sericulture were made, despite apparently unpromising climatic conditions. In early seventeenth-

century Britain, James I (r. 1603–25) encouraged sericulture on English soil, while later monarchs revived the idea during wartime shortages. Largely unsuccessful as a major commercial enterprise, sericulture did continue in small-scale private ventures such as that at Lullingstone Silk Farm in Kent in the 1930s, then in Hertfordshire and between 1975 and 2011 at Sherborne in Dorset.[20] Ireland managed limited production into the mid-twentieth century.[21]

The opening up of trade routes and imperial expansion provided further opportunities in more propitious climes, in Australia as well as the Americas (25 and 26). In North America, royal incentives, first from Sweden and then Britain, from the seventeenth into the eighteenth century, anticipated profiting from the native American red mulberry tree. Some silk was exported from seventeenth-century Virginia, South Carolina and Georgia, and a 'wave of American sericulture … washed across the more northerly regions of Pennsylvania and New England' between the 1750s and the 1800s, 'seduc[ing] into its orbit willing

25 (OPPOSITE)
Sericulture in Australia: the South Yarra Rearing-house, Victoria, Australia, 1874. Engraving

26 (ABOVE)
Women feeding silkworms with mulberry leaves, published in Henrietta Aitken Kelly, *The Culture of the Mulberry Silkworm* (Washington 1903), p. 16. Engraving

27
Feeding silkworms in Paraná, Brazil, published in the *Gazeta do Povo*, 2019

experimenters: naturalists and botanists, Enlightenment associations, and entrepreneurs, as well as ordinary farmers and working women'.[22] By the late nineteenth century, the demand for raw silk far outstretched the returns of local sericulture, and China and Japan became the main suppliers. The building of railways connecting western and eastern coasts in the 1880s hastened the demise of North American sericulture: steamships crossed the Pacific from Yokohama in Japan to Seattle, Vancouver and San Francisco where the privileged 'Silks' – the name by which the trains were known – sprinted to New York in under 90 hours, all other traffic held up to allow them to pass.[23]

Australia nurtured ambitions for and experienced the vagaries of sericulture in a country with the right climate but a small potential consumer base. The Australian Agricultural Company first speculated on the viability of sericulture in 1825, announcing its intention of planting mulberry trees. Small private ventures followed, contributing to the establishment of the Silk Committee of the Agricultural Society of New South Wales, which actively promoted sericulture by disseminating information and lobbying government from 1869. This move was timely as mulberry leaves were by then readily available and Australian silkworm strains free from the blight suffered by European and, to a lesser extent, Chinese and Japanese silkworms. Government funding did not, however, follow, though an 1893 New South Wales government report reiterated that sericulture was ideally suited to the then colony.[24] Over 100 years later, a report for the Australian Rural Industries Research and Development Corporation in 2000 took up the cause, recommending suitable strains of mulberry, silkworms, methods of cultivation and government support for a breeding and development centre at the University of Queensland.[25] Funding ceased in 2005 and the plantation was destroyed.[26]

The great success story has been Central and South America, to which the Spanish introduced sericulture in the early sixteenth century when the crown offered financial incentives to plant mulberry trees and employ the indigenous population in rearing silkworms. From the 1540s to the 1580s, sericulture flourished in certain areas of Mexico (or New Spain), but thereafter imports of Chinese raw silk via the Manila galleons from the Philippines hindered further development for over a century.[27] The mulberry trees survived and small quantities of silk apparently continued to be produced mainly for local use as thread. Since the late 1990s, the Mexican government has encouraged the commercialization of sericulture through subsidized centres by introducing new types of cocoons from Japan that yield two to three times longer filament than the variety brought by the Spaniards. It is also introducing new varieties of mulberries,[28] and early in 2019 an announcement of major investment encouraged families to stay in the country, rather than move to the cities in search of work.[29]

In contrast, Brazil did not promote sericulture until after gaining independence from Portugal in 1825; the first private entrepreneur built sheds in Itaguaí in the province of Rio de Janeiro between 1838 and 1839 and received government support from 1844. His business became the Imperial Companhia Seropédica Fluminense in 1854, boosted no doubt by the needs of an imperial court and the Neapolitan silk weavers who arrived with the new empress in 1843.[30] Expertise was drawn from Italy and France, as

was this model of state sponsorship.[31] Sericulture activities followed in 1912 in the province of Minas Gerais and in 1921 in São Paulo. The latter subsequently received injections of human and financial capital which laid the foundations for the success of silk farming in Paraná: first, Japanese immigrants brought expertise in 1940, establishing the company that has become the major supplier in Brazil. In the 1960s industrialists in São Paulo invested further.[32] By 2014 Brazil had become the largest silk producer in the West (27), and between 2001 and 2019 ranked fifth in the world – substantially below China, India and Uzbekistan and roughly on a par with Thailand and Vietnam.[33] Government support has been fundamental.

As the South American examples reveal, the fact that sericulture is low tech, takes up little space and lends itself to flexible family working in rural areas where it may supplement other income makes it attractive in the twenty-first century. Since 1948, the International Sericulture Commission has brokered international cooperation by providing training, undertaking research and development and disseminating its findings. Its 20 member countries include representation from provincial governments, research and development institutions, universities and commercial companies. Tellingly, only France and Greece represent Europe, and the commission's office moved from France to Bangladesh in 2011. The commission has ambitious sustainable development goals that include tackling poverty and promoting gender equality. It is keen to introduce sericulture to poverty-ridden areas of Africa, South Asia and South America.[34] Africa, in contrast to the other two areas, still produces only a very small amount of silk, although there was some evidence of activity in Burkina Faso, Kenya, Madagascar, South Africa and Uganda in 2007 and Botswana and Namibia by 2019.[35]

In valuing the opportunities sericulture offers to empower women, the commission is reinforcing a long-established tradition worldwide that caring for silkworms is suitable work for women. Not surprisingly, they dominate images of collecting leaves and feeding the hungry insects, although the male head of the household often acted as manager. Women also feature prominently in recent reports on new projects, having been enterprising champions of sericulture from the eighteenth century – no doubt partly because farming is work that can be done from the home while looking after extended family.

FILAMENT TO FABRIC

Silk processing usually begins where the silkworms are being reared, especially the drying, sorting and reeling of silk cocoons (28 and 29). It has to be done quickly or the cocoons will spoil. This, too, has often been women's work, organized to fit in with agricultural or other tasks. In the past, reeled silk was often sent to other places for the later stages of processing. These tended to take place close to courts or cities where there was a demand for silk fabrics. Spain, Italy and France developed both sericulture and powerful silk industries – the latter from the ninth century in Iberia and Sicily, from the eleventh on the Italian peninsula, and, in a sustained way, from the fifteenth in France. England largely failed at sericulture but succeeded in manufacturing and finishing. By the mid-twentieth century, China and India were the main producers of raw silk and have remained so, while Europe and the USA had become the main silk processors.[36]

28 (ABOVE)
Silk cocoons being removed from mulberry branches by Utagawa Yoshikazu, Japan, 1849–50. Woodblock print on paper

V&A E.13729-1886

29 (OPPOSITE)
Women reeling silk by Utagawa Yoshikazu, Japan, 1849–50. Woodblock print on paper

V&A E.13726-1886

The sequence in the conversion of fibre into fabric has altered little over time, though methods of processing have changed as a result of scientific and technological research, innovations in art and design education, and the promotion of ever faster seasonal change in fashion to wide markets. In general, after the silkworms have been suffocated or boiled, the cocoons are dried and sorted, the filament is reeled from the cocoon, and then thrown or spun into threads (30 and 31).[37] Thereafter, the silk is washed, degummed, bleached and dyed. Some is destined for sewing or embroidery threads, some for the warps and wefts of the fabric to be woven or knitted (32) and some for industrial or medical purposes. Waste and wild silk may be used as wadding or padding or spun into thread. Once the fabric is constructed, it is finished – for example, dyed, printed or embroidered. Each task requires specialist skills, and a division of labour has long existed in the industry, with knowhow in different countries transferred along traditional and new Silk Roads.

It was often women who made the threads, spinning them with a distaff or wheel, plying or twisting together filaments according to the fineness required. Twisting filaments together gives strength – the tighter the twist, the stronger the thread. In general, strong threads are necessary for the warps held taut on the loom because they have to withstand tension. Looser twists work for wefts. Organzine, a silk yarn made of two or more twisted threads, doubled and twisted in opposite directions in the plying, is often preferred for warps. The twist can also create a variety of aesthetic and textural effects. Spinning in a clockwise direction produces a 'Z' twist and in an anti-clockwise direction an 'S' twist.

30
Drawing silk filaments by Wu Jun, Guangzhou, China, 1870–90. Watercolour and ink on paper
V&A D.917-1901

31
Spooling by Wu Jun, Guangzhou,
China, 1870–90. Watercolour and
ink on paper

V&A D.919-1901

32
Preparing warp yarns by Wu
Jun, Guangzhou, China, 1870–90.
Watercolour and ink on paper

V&A D.920-1901

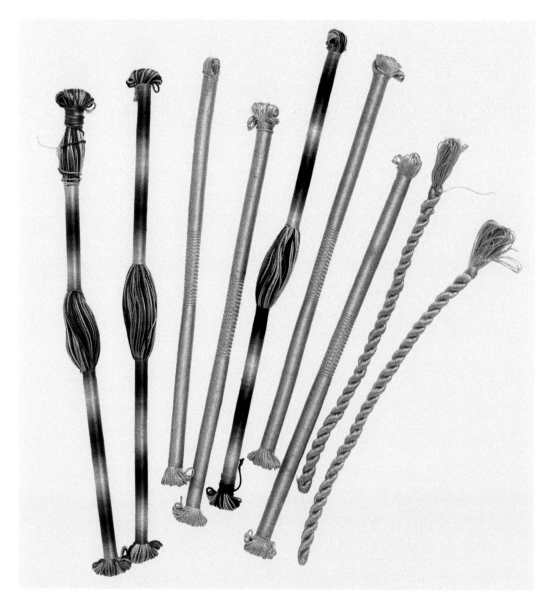

33 (ABOVE)
Skeins of naturally dyed silk floss for embroidery, China, 1840–50

Given by Janet, Annie and Colin Simpson in honour of their great-great-grandfather, Dr Lawrence Holker Potts.
V&A FE.67:2 to 102-2009

34 (LEFT)
Skeins of embroidery silks, Britain, 1800–50

Given by Mrs M.G. Graham.
V&A T.436-1966

35 (BELOW LEFT)
Silver-gilt wrapped silk thread from Hyderabad, Telangana, India, about 1855–79

V&A 6354(IS)

36 (OPPOSITE)
Wooden bobbins with sewing silk, various manufacturers, England, 1910–20

Given by Miss Jane Gregory.
V&A T.4 to K-1986

Threads of different twists and different colours may be combined with each other, or with other materials (33–6). Floss threads are lightly twisted while fine silk cord (*cordonnet*) is twisted tightly, and soft velvety chenille is a yarn made by weaving a narrow fabric, cutting it up into strips and twisting it to give it a fluffy texture. The yarns from eri silks and waste from *Bombyx mori* cocoons are slubbed yarns because short staples are being spun together into a thread suitable for plying. In some countries, the amount of raw silk produced only lent itself to local consumption, so it was reeled and spun there and used as thread for sewing rather than for weaving, having been dyed. This is probably how sericulture survived in Mexico after the Spanish crown withdrew its support: the indigenous population made enough yarn to embroider or to make fringes for their shawls into the twenty-first century.

Precious metal was combined with silk to make particularly ostentatious threads. The methods and materials differed from place to place: in China, Japan and Korea, paper coated with gold leaf was wrapped round a silk core; in the Near East, Egypt, Iran, Iberia and Italy, leather, parchment or gut was coated with gold and gilded silver before about 1100; in India, Iran, the Middle East and much of Europe, metal wire was used thereafter, wire-drawing being an independent trade usually practised by men.

At the height of silk manufacturing in eighteenth-century England and France, there were five different types of metal thread – four metal wrapped silk threads, one a simple wire. Within each category there were variations. A plain metal thread comprised a strip of metal wound round a silk core; frost was a strip round a silk core, one end of which was wound tighter than the other so the thread crinkled; flat was as its name suggests, while tinsel or clincon was a strip of flat wound round a thread of frost.[38] Gold (strictly speaking, gilded silver or what is most often – rather confusingly – called silver-gilt) was usually wound round a yellow silk core, silver round a white silk core, the metal and the silk colour harmonizing. In contrast, *sorbec* was a coloured silk with a narrow flat wire added to provide a subtle visual effect. Combining a variety of different thread types in the same woven or embroidered silk created a particularly rich effect which must have sparkled in flickering candlelight.

Not all threads were suitable for weaving in or sewing through silks, some being laid on the surface of the fabric and stitched or couched in place.[39] Similarly, in India, flexible metal wrapped thread was used in the Mughal workshop at Ahmedabad in the seventeenth century, in Varanasi from the late eighteenth into the nineteenth centuries, and right across the country in the nineteenth century (35).[40]

37
Sampler of plain weave linen
with embroidery in silk threads,
embroidered by Encarnación
Castellanos, Mexico, June 1850

The vivid colours in both a nineteenth-century Mexican embroidered sampler (37) and an eighteenth-century British court dress (38) reveal how impressively silk took colour. So important was the dyeing stage that the Chinese established a treasury department as early as the late sixth century that included a state-controlled silk dyeing workshop.[41] From the thirteenth century, in some European cities, professional trade bodies or guilds controlled the quality of dyeing and trained apprentices. In France, Louis XIV's minister of finances Jean-Baptiste Colbert championed their cause, adjusting the regulations of France's two dyers' guilds in 1669, and rewarding dyers who discovered new techniques. He explained in 1671:

> If the manufacture of silk, wool, and thread is that which serves to sustain and make commerce pay, dyeing ... is the soul without which the body would have but little life ... Not only is it necessary that colours be beautiful to increase the commerce of cloth, but they must be of good quality so that they may last as long as the fabrics to which they are applied.[42]

A late nineteenth-century Chinese watercolour reveals the first stage in the marriage of silk and colour (39). Skeins

38 (OPPOSITE)
Detail of silk brocaded with metal, floss and *cordonnet*, probably France, about 1765

V&A T.252-1959

39 (ABOVE)
Silk dyeing by Wu Jun, Guangzhou, China, about 1870–90. Ink and colour on paper

V&A D.922-1901

40 (RIGHT)
La Teinture de rivière (river dyeing), published in Denis Diderot and Jean Le Rond d'Alembert, *L'Encyclopédie, ou Dictionnaire raisonné des Sciences, des Arts et des Métiers* (Diderot et d'Alembert hereafter), vol. 27 (Paris 1772), pl. I. Engraving

National Art Library, V&A 38041800786212

Teinturier de Rivière, Atelier et différentes Opérations pour la Teinture des Soies.

41 (ABOVE)
Day dress of plain weave silk
dyed with aniline dyes of
the triphenylamine class
(probably methyl violet),
Britain or France, 1873

Given by the Marchioness of Bristol.
V&A T.51&A-1922.

42 (OPPOSITE)
Samples of silk dyed with mauve,
published in *A Record of the Great
International Exhibition held in
London in the Year 1862 ... Class
20, Silk & Velvet*, compiled by
J.C. Robinson (London 1862)

Given in memory of Joseph Barlow
Robinson Eaton and his wife Ellen
by their six grandsons.

V&A T.258-2009

of pristine reeled *Bombyx mori* threads hang from bars, having had all impurities removed to enable the subsequent easy absorption of both the dyestuff and the fixing agent, or mordant. Craftsmen in protective aprons concentrate on their duties, as they had done 100 years earlier in the steamier plate (40) in Denis Diderot and Jean Le Rond d'Alembert's *Encyclopédie* (1765), one of the most significant and widely disseminated printed descriptions demystifying the trade. A wood-fired furnace heats the water in vats which belch out vapour as a dyer removes the lid to dip or retrieve skeins. The dyers control the water temperature and monitor the chemical composition of its contents to ensure the quality, consistency and adherence of the colour. Here, colour is being applied directly to the yarn before it is made into fabric, but a plain fabric might be dyed 'in the piece' once woven.

The colouring agents available changed over time. The options expanded through scientific experimentation and spread through global trade.[43] Until the nineteenth century all dyes were natural, extracted from the leaves, flowers, fruit, rind and roots of plants, and from fungi and lichen, as well as from animals. What was available differed from region to region and different sources might yield similar colours. Purple, one of the costliest dyes, came from a mollusc of which there were three types – Japanese, Pacific and Mediterranean.[44] Reds came from the madder plant, which originated in temperate Mediterranean climes, from the kermes beetle of Iberia or lac insect from India, from the cochineal beetle from Western Asia, the eastern Mediterranean or Central America, and from safflower and sappanwood in China, Japan and Korea. Blue came from two plants: indigo in India and Japan, woad in China, Europe and the Mediterranean basin.[45] From the sixteenth century, extended commerce in dyestuffs challenged this local specificity, the best-known Spanish 'discoveries' being cochineal and logwood in Mexico, dyestuffs that provided reds/purples and black respectively. These had long been expensive colours because they were time-consuming to produce – according to the *Encyclopédie* (1765), dyeing a true black took over four days.[46] Unsurprisingly, the Spanish were keen to retain a monopoly on the distribution of such Central American treasures and did so fairly successfully until the nineteenth century.[47]

The secrets of dyestuffs and recipes for colours were jealously guarded by governments and dyers. By the middle of the nineteenth century, patents protected the inventors

43 (LEFT)

Plain weave silk with magenta and blue checks, Thanjavur, Tamil Nadu, India, about 1867

V&A 4923(IS)

44 (BELOW)

Dye book of aniline colours by BASF, Ludwigshafen, Germany, 1901

Given by Dr Stanley D. Chapman.
V&A T.180-1985

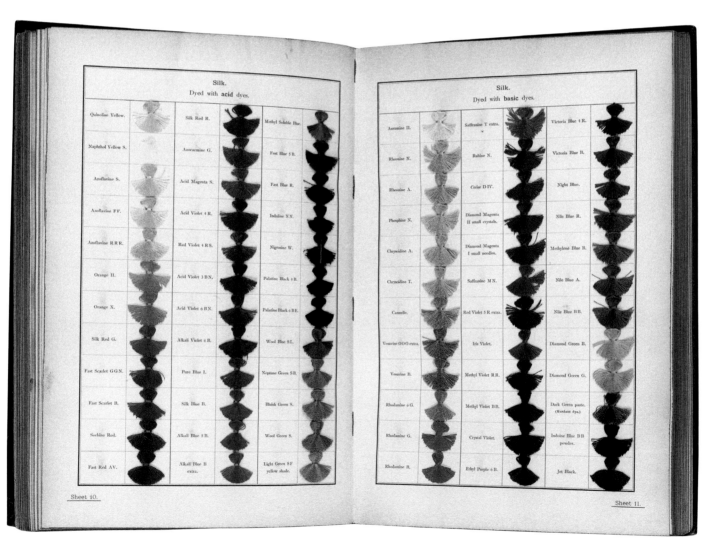

45

Silk sample, 'Silor' World Colour
Cable Card, distributed by Studio
Color, Zurich, Switzerland,
about 1950–70

Given by Elizabeth Howard.
V&A T.52-2016

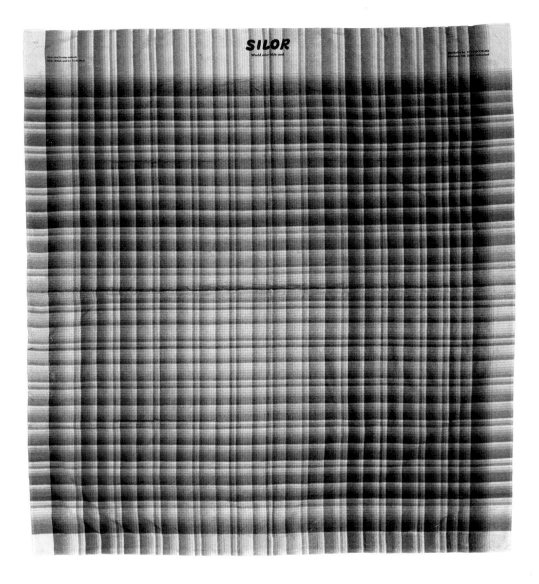

of aniline or synthetic dyes and poor harvests of plants and insects no longer unexpectedly deprived dyers in industrialized countries of raw materials.[48]

In 1863 the British illustrated magazine *Leisure Hour* noted these developments and new evocative names: 'The chemist has given [consumers] mauve, magenta, azuline, emeraldine, and a hundred other delicate colours with names as pretty as their hues. Let them use them with taste and judgement, and Regent Street [London's major shopping street] will once more be a flowerbed – the concert-room a rainbow' (41–3).[49] Some proved dangerous, however, for dyers' and wearers' health, as well as for the environment. Their synthetic successors are at the heart of twenty-first-century debates about sustainable textile production.[50] In the case of silk production, they are probably the single most toxic ingredient, after the fossil fuel used for transportation.

By the twentieth century, company colour books and cards reveal a dazzling abundance of dye options (44 and 45). Then, as now, natural and synthetic dyes, hand and machine colouring existed in different workshop and factory environments across the globe. Common to all forms of production is the premise that generally the number of colours and processes applied bears a direct relationship to the economic value of the silk textile. While colours still have culturally specific symbolic associations, they have also become fashion commodities. Silk manufacturers have played their part in this development, with the Lyonnais establishing the influential trade fair Première Vision in the mid-1970s, which continues to promote certain colours to the trade through seasonal trend cards.[51]

With threads twisted and dyed, the loom or knitting frame warped up, construction could begin. Like dyeing, silk weaving was a highly skilled craft, protected in state workshops and by urban guilds until well into the nineteenth century. The earliest silks were plain silks, like taffeta and twill, followed by gauzes or weaves with supplementary wefts, while tapestry-woven silks probably developed from as early as the third to the thirteenth and fourteenth centuries. The first complex textiles that needed a more sophisticated loom developed in China in the second century CE, arriving between the fourth and tenth centuries in Egypt, Persia and Syria and subsequently adapted by the Sassanians, Byzantines and Islamic caliphates. From the twelfth century the number of textile types rose dramatically, and virtually all the weave structures shown in this book already existed – including satin, lampas and velvet. From China to Iberia and beyond weavers used the drawloom, and then from the early nineteenth century the jacquard loom, to make these more elaborate silks.

Different methods of production and intended use determined the different branches of weaving, which coexisted in major manufacturing centres. Smaller centres often specialized in one particular product or type, usually the simpler types. The Three Textile Manufactories of Jiangnan were large-scale, capital-intensive organizations employing 2,602 weavers in 1685 and operating 800 looms, mainly making robes for the imperial household. A supervisor or chief expert managed them and the rest of the workforce, including craftsmen making warps, twisting threads, making designs, etc.[52] Each of the three factories had its own speciality products: Nanjing's were brocaded silk, Suzhou's tapestry weave and brocaded silks, and Hangzhou's plain fabrics and damasks. Similarly in France at around the same time, in many small domestic workshops, Lyonnais weavers wove wide and narrow, plain and patterned silks of all types for ecclesiastical and secular furnishings and dress, trimmings and stockings. In contrast, Nîmes in the Languedoc only made knitted silk goods and simple silks, often from silk waste, while by the mid-eighteenth century, Saint-Étienne had gradually developed a specialism in narrow wares, or ribbons.

Like dyeing, silk weaving was governed by guild regulations in many places before 1800. These rules focused on weavers' conduct and on fabrics while elected officials policed who entered the trade, their training and workshop management. In general, weaving was men's work, though women laboured in the same workshops, spinning and warping – and probably wove, too, though illegally.[53] The contents (quantity and weight of raw materials) of each

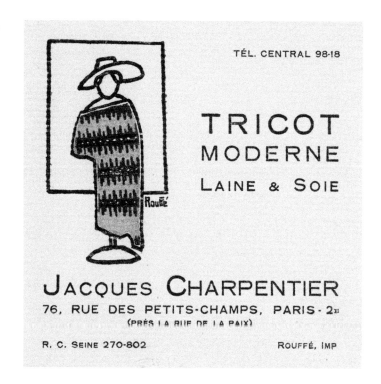

named silk, its composition (number of warp and weft threads to the centimetre) and the widths of the fabrics to be woven mostly had to conform to rules, including, in some cases, how selvedges were to be woven. Long-established local practices often determined fabric widths, largely based on what was possible on a handloom. These silks tend to be narrow in comparison with today's power-loom woven fabrics – in Europe, between 48 and 58 cm wide until the late eighteenth century when 76 cm wide furnishings began to be made, and in China usually between 55 and 78 cm wide. On the latter, inscriptions on the end of the fabric indicated provenance and official approval.[54] In France, a lead seal attached to the end of the silk carried the stamp of the approving guild until the end of the eighteenth century. Labelling, or branding, became more evident in the twentieth century, woven into or printed on selvedges.

Knitting in silk coexisted with weaving from early on in European urban centres, the silk stocking-makers being major players in France and Italy. By the end of the nineteenth century knitted silk fabrics, such as jersey, had entered fashion as smart outdoor garments. The charming trade card of Charpentier of Paris from the 1920s focused on the modernity of its wool and silk knitted goods (46). Couturier Gabrielle 'Coco' Chanel had just earned the title of 'The Jersey House' from *Vogue* (1917) because she had used unsold stock of jersey from the firm of Jean Rodier for one of her collections. She was poised to set up her own knitting

46 (OPPOSITE)
Trade card for Jacques Charpentier
knitwear in wool and silk by Rouffé,
Paris, France, 1920–6. Colour
lithography

Given by C.G. Holme, Esq.
V&A E.535-1927

47 (LEFT)
Detail of man's jacket of gauze
weave silk with mud coating,
Guangdong, China, 1920–50

Supported by Friends of the
V&A. V&A FE.78-1995

48 (FOLLOWING PAGES)
Silk wall hangings, curtains and
upholstery woven to recreate the
1823 decorative scheme for
the Saloon, Brighton Pavilion,
Brighton, England, by Humphries
Weaving, Essex, England, 2018

factory outside Paris.[55] Silk had fortuitously tumbled in price just as women's hemlines rose in the 1920s, offering manufacturers opportunities to meet new demand for luxury fully fashioned hosiery. After the Second World War, Italy received accolades for innovation, while between 1955 and 1965, the market share of warp knitting (double jersey) in Britain rose from 28 to 42 per cent.[56] By 1980 in the West, half of all textiles for clothing were knitted. Not all were in silk, but these figures are indicative of a change in preferences in construction that provided elasticity and comfort.

Various finishing processes completed the cloth to enhance its handle, appearance and durability. They included dyeing, glazing to increase lustre, and weighting to improve drape, patterning and protecting. Sometimes more than one process was applied. A man's mud silk jacket from Guangdong province in China exemplifies the complexity of some silks that look deceptively simple (47). Made of two-coloured gauze weave silk, 'fragrance cloud gauze' in Chinese, its colour was obtained by soaking the woven silk in juice extracted from a tannin-rich native yam

(*Dioscorea cirrhosa*) and then coating it with iron-rich river mud sourced from the Pearl River Delta which fixed the colour. Black disguises the transparent quality of the weave, maintaining the wearer's modesty when clothed in the jacket without an undergarment in summer. After weaving, the silk was calendered (passed under pressure between two rollers) to achieve the glazed water-resistant finish, which added further to the opacity. In contrast, in the early 1990s sand-washing became popular. Described as 'weakened silk' or 'sloppy silk' because of its wrinkled texture and softness, it is washed with sand or stones, a process that the *New York Times* claimed was 'sandblasting … with the same guns they clean buildings with'.[57] These relatively cheap silks caused consternation in professional circles, the outgoing president of the International Silk Association lamenting that they were 'banalising our noble fibre' which needed to retain its aura of luxury and inaccessibility to survive.[58]

This fear has not been borne out in the twenty-first century: silk accounts for 0.2 per cent of fibre production worldwide, with most of the raw silk coming from Asia and the vast majority of manufactured goods consumed in China, Europe and the USA.[59] Heritage organizations patronize long-established silk manufacturers by refurbishing grand apartments (48). Concurrently fashion designers and retailers continue to sell its luxurious qualities while increasingly reflecting on the ethical and environmental impact of its consumption (49 and 50).[60] The distinction between mulberry silk and Peace silk is sometimes announced on labels: the former is the traditionally produced *Bombyx mori* silk described above, while the latter refers to silkworms that are allowed to turn into moths when they emerge from their cocoons. Their farming is not always cruelty-free. Some designers seek new solutions in working towards greener ethical substitutes, a new generation of synthetic silks.[61] In the meantime, the Silk Centre in the Zoology Department at the University of Oxford has discovered that silk adapts like no other fibre to outer space temperatures. In the future, although silkworms may not travel to other planets, the properties of their filaments are set to improve the lives of those who do.[62] ACL/LEM

49 (ABOVE)
Blouse labelled mulberry silk, by Cos, Winter 2019

50 (OPPOSITE)
Shirt of silk crêpe woven in Italy, inkjet-printed with George Stubbs's *Horse Frightened by a Lion*, by Stella McCartney, Britain, 2017
V&A T.27:1 to 4-2019

The Silks in This Book

This book looks at silks through the lens of the world-renowned textile collections of the Victoria and Albert Museum, whose director considered silk production important enough to the history of art and design to plan a mosaic to enhance the newly built galleries in its North Court in 1874 (52). This drawing gives a rare, highly selective and Eurocentric view of silk production. Nonetheless, since its founding in the mid-nineteenth century, the museum had avidly acquired fine examples of the aesthetic and technical achievements of artisans, designers, manufacturers and skilled amateur needleworkers (51) from sources as disparate as a cemetery in Egypt, church treasuries and sacristies in continental Europe and South America, displays at nineteenth-century international exhibitions of art and industry, and individual owners or collectors. More recently, the museum has continued to expand its range with silks from designers' catwalk collections from the fashion capitals of North America, Asia and Europe, from auctions of textiles and fashion, as well as directly from artists, artisans and wearers.

Some silks are fragments, others are samples in manufacturers' production or sales ledgers or attached to designers' sketches; yet others are lengths freshly cut from the loom or made into full garments or furnishings. Some were created as artworks. Various acquisitions are pristine because scarcely used, while others bear the patina of light wear, or testify to the ravages of a long, hard existence. The photographs deliberately reveal how the brilliance and lustre of silk fluctuates, while also capturing creases, stains and unravelling threads.

Overall these pieces richly represent a cross-section of transnational decorative techniques and motifs, in which the exchange of ideas between cultures is clear. They are therefore a valuable physical manifestation of the journey of their raw material along Silk Roads from ancient China through the Roman empire to the Atlantic world, and an important source of knowledge about the technologies of silk cultivation and manufacturing over many centuries.

This cultural heritage has inspired many generations of artists, designers, makers and historians, who have studied silk in their quest for inspiration and knowledge – just as the founding fathers of the museum anticipated and as their successors, the curator-conservator authors of this current book, hope to encourage further.

This book has a vast historical, geographical and linguistic scope, so some notes on the conventions used may be helpful.

Language: Arabic, Chinese, Hebrew, Japanese and Korean terms have been transliterated using standard romanization.

Names: all names are expressed as given name followed by family name, except for Chinese, Japanese and Korean names which are expressed as family name followed by given name, unless the individual uses the western convention professionally.

Place names: state boundaries have shifted across the period covered, as have the names of particular cities or areas. Here place names familiar to us now are used.

Further information: more photographs and data on the dimensions and historical context of each of the silks in this book are available on the Victoria and Albert Museum website at https://collections.vam.ac.uk/, where you can search the collection using the museum number that appears at the end of each identification caption.

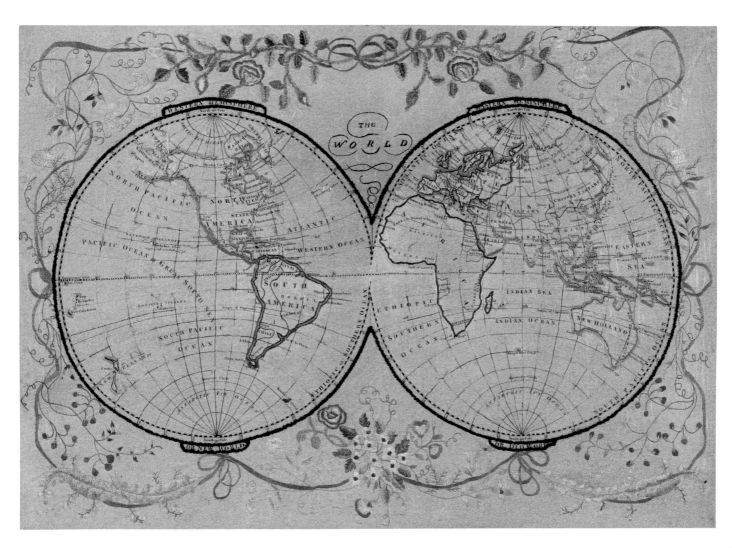

51 (ABOVE)
Sampler of silk depicting a world
map in silk embroidery, England,
late 18th century

Bequeathed by Mrs I.M.C. Robinson.
V&A T.44-1951

52 (FOLLOWING PAGES)
Sketch for decoration of upper part
of wall of the North Court, South
Kensington Museum (later the
Victoria and Albert Museum)
by Francis Wollaston Moody,
London, England, 1874. Pen and
ink and watercolour on paper

V&A 8060

FEEDING SILKWORMS.

UNWIN

8060

OCOONS. SPINNING AND EMBROIDERY.

Plain and Simple

1

Plain and Simple

53
Salome with the Head of John the Baptist by Carlo Dolci, Italy, about 1665–70. Oil on canvas

Bequeathed by Burton Vivian.
V&A P.143-1929

The play of light on a variety of monochrome silk fabrics has long fascinated European painters, many capturing their sheen, texture and drape realistically. Consider the blue gowns rendered with brio by Carlo Dolci in late seventeenth-century Italy (53) and by François-Hubert Drouais 100 years later in France (54). Salome's gown, instantly recognizable as satin, epitomizes the baroque taste of its time – soft and boldly lustrous, suited to dramatic *chiaroscuro* compositions. In contrast, Mademoiselle Doré's taffeta gown has a more modest gloss in keeping with surviving silk samples from the same date (55). It complements the lustre of her hat's black satin. The pictorial traditions of other parts of the world do not seem to capture the reflective qualities of silk in quite this way, although such silks were made and used there, too.

These two paintings reveal two of the three basic weave structures available for more than 1,000 years made by the interlacing of warp and weft threads on a loom: plain or tabby (taffeta), satin and twill, the first being relatively matte, the second resolutely glossy, and the third in between, characterized by barely perceptible diagonal lines. There were other variations in the way warp and weft threads could be disposed but the principles were the same. Silks without complex patterning were often the mainstay of major weaving centres in which patterned silks were also made, because they were less sensitive to shifts in taste, more economical in material and labour and suitable as the base for different decorative finishes. They do not demand the time-consuming and highly skilled preparatory stages typical for silks with woven patterns with more than one warp and/or weft.

54 (LEFT)
Mademoiselle Doré by François-Hubert Drouais, probably Paris, France, about 1758. Oil on canvas

Bequeathed by John Jones.
V&A 600-1882

55 (BELOW)
Plain silks from a merchant's sample book, probably Lyon, France, 1764, f.4v

Acquired with the help of Marks and Spencer Ltd and the Worshipful Company of Weavers.
V&A T.373-1972

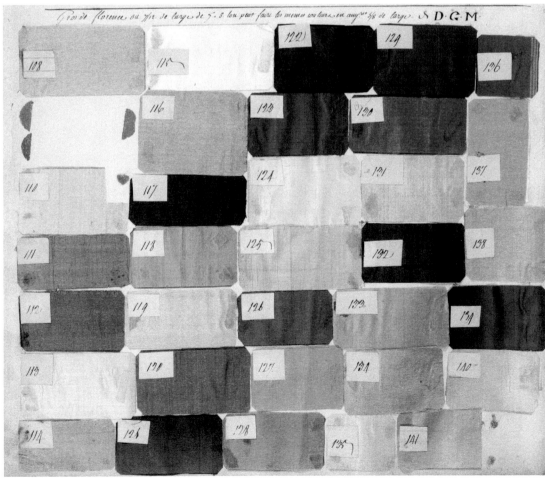

56 (OPPOSITE)
Weaver working on simple loom
by Wu Jun, Guangzhou, China,
1870–90. Watercolour and ink
on paper

V&A D.921-1901

57 (ABOVE)
Weaver in his workshop in
Spitalfields, London, England,
1820–50. Engraving

58 (TOP)
Man weaving silk on a pit loom
by John Lockwood Kipling, Agra,
Rajasthan, India, 1870.
Pen, pencil and wash on paper

V&A 0929:40/(IS)

59 (ABOVE)
Powerloom shed in Macclesfield,
Cheshire, England, 1933, showing
the belt mechanism that powered
the looms prior to the installation
of individual electric motors.
Photograph

Until the nineteenth century, these simple structures were all woven on handlooms of different types, usually in domestic workshops (56, 57 and 58). The warps running the length of the piece of fabric are held taut and attached to a harness, which the weaver operates with foot treadles to lift the warps singly or in groups in order to send the weft through from side to side. The same principle applies to the power looms that functioned in factories or sheds from the nineteenth century (59). The shuttle carrying the weft was propelled between the warps by the hand of the weaver in the former, and by steam, water or electricity in the latter. Introduced from the 1820s onwards, power looms never entirely replaced handlooms and initially they were rougher and more wasteful of the expensive raw material. In their early years they achieved some success in producing cheaper ribbons, lining materials, mourning gauze and half silks (silk mixed with wool or cotton).[1] Today, handloom weaving continues in many parts of the world, often used by craftspeople or designers interested in experimenting with unusual or irregular effects.

Variables other than the disposition of warp and weft affect the lustre, texture, opacity and drape of plain silks: the treatment of the warp and weft threads before weaving; the number and density of each per centimetre; and the finishing of the woven product. The threads may comprise different quantities of silk filaments twisted tightly or loosely in different directions. In the case of short lengths or staples of silk spun into a yarn, there is always a slubbed effect and matte appearance. Threads may also retain some of the raw silk's natural gum or be deliberately weighted. Combining different thicknesses of warp and weft creates ribs on the surface, subtle or overt, while using S- and Z-twisted yarns together can create a crinkle effect

that makes the material less shiny, as in chiffon or crêpe. In general, the finer the threads are, the more lightweight the fabric is; the thicker, the more body or substance it will have. The more closely packed the warp and weft are, the more opaque the fabric; the wider apart, the more transparent and lightweight. In gauze, for example, the warp and weft threads are spaced apart to create an open mesh. In one variation, some warp ends are crossed over others trapping the weft in between to prevent them from slipping, thus making the fabric more stable.

Many plain silks are dyed in the piece, that is, after weaving. Hank-dyed silk or pre-dyed warp and weft threads may also be used in simple structures, creating subdued or bold effects and geometric patterns when combined. Shot silks, for example, change colour depending on how the light falls on them because the warp is different from the weft. Striped and checked patterns result from the grouping of warp and weft threads of different colours and are common across cultures.

The different qualities of plain silks lend themselves to the creative juxtaposition of one texture or weight with another: in fashionable garments, satin may be set off by faille of the same colour, georgette juxtaposed with satin; in patchwork, contrasting plain silks stitched together create exciting effects.

A multitude of names are attached to the same weaves, indicative of differentiation and innovation in weight or texture. They suggest the advantages of inventing new names to sell similar goods. Often the precise technical characteristics associated with such terms change over time, as is the case with gazar, developed in the late 1950s (60). LEM

Flamenco-style evening dress by
Balenciaga in silk gazar by Abraham
of Switzerland, Paris, France,
February 1961

Given by Stavros Niarchos.
V&A T.26-1974

MONOCHROME

Lengths of silk like these – whether monochrome, two-tone, checked, striped or shot – were categorized as 'piece goods' and made speculatively to standard dimensions, usually 450 cm in length and between 30 and 80 cm in width. They were produced and exported for use in furnishings and garments. Several cities in north India, including Agra and Lahore, specialized in weaving robust silk piece goods made for washing. The raw silk was both cultivated locally and imported from Uzbekistan and Afghanistan in the west and Bengal and China in the east. The thread was dyed before weaving AF

61
Page from *The Textile Manufactures of India*, compiled by John Forbes-Watson for the India Office (1st series, London, about 1866), vol. XIV, no. 521, plain red silk from Lahore, Punjab, India (now Pakistan)

University of Huddersfield, Yorkshire, England

Prov. No. 535.   No. *521*

INDIA FABRICS.

SILK PIECE GOODS.
Plain red silk.

Extensively used in the Punjab for making up, and also as lining of various kinds of garments.

Length 17 yards 15 inches; width 21½ inches.   Weight 2 lbs. 9¾ oz.   Price 3*l.*

From LAHORE.

62 (ABOVE) & 63 & 64 (RIGHT)
Lengths of monochrome
plain weave silk
Agra, Uttar Pradesh, India,
about 1855

V&A 7192(IS), 7123(IS) & 7167(IS)

European women's ensembles of the eighteenth and nineteenth centuries often comprised an outer gown or bodice worn over a matching or contrasting visible petticoat. The silk was sewn with small running or back stitches to a backing of a less showy fabric, such as coarse linen, sometimes with a layer of wool wadding in between. The design might be simple diamond or lozenge shapes or more decorative patterns extending upwards from the hemline. Such quilted skirts provided warmth, while the silk revealed status. LEM

65 (RIGHT)
March, Robert Dighton the elder, England, about 1785. Pen and ink and watercolour on paper

V&A E.35-1947

66 (RIGHT) & 67 (OPPOSITE)
Details of petticoats of satin weave silk with quilting
Probably Britain, 1700–50

V&A 8-1897 & T.367-1910

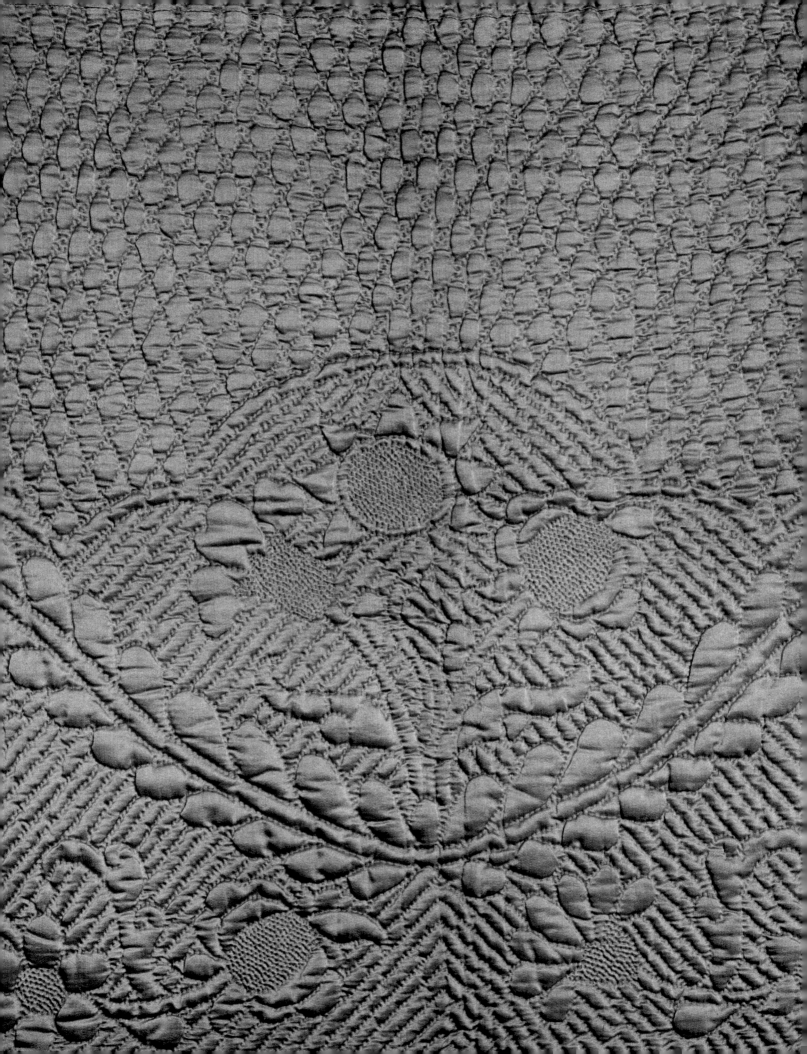

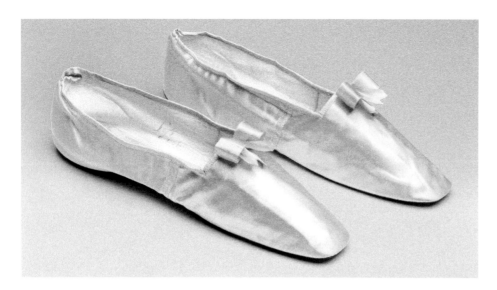

Satin-covered shoes have
contrasted or harmonized with
other elements of women's
attire over the last 200 years.
In the early nineteenth century,
they often matched sashes and
bonnet ribbons. In 1951 *The
Silk Book* stated that 'Satins
have the stiffness and "live"
characteristics of yarn-dyed
articles. In Victorian days their
special virtue was … that they
could stand up by themselves,
but nowadays they are usually
given a slightly softer finish.
Their very rich appearance
makes them a favourite
material for wedding gowns;
they are also used for evening
dresses, cloaks, for linings and
in combination with velvets.
Mention should also be made of
Shoe Satin, used for the uppers
of evening shoes.' LEM

68 (TOP)
Probably Britain, 1830–5

Given by C.M. Buckney.
V&A T.178&A-1962

69 (ABOVE)
**S. and J. Slater, New York, USA,
about 1900**

Given by Lady Hoyer Millar.
V&A T.38C&D-1961

70 (LEFT)
Rayne for Delman, Britain, 1930–40

Given by the Bata Shoe Museum
Foundation.
V&A T.76:1&2-2017

71
Retailed at Fortnum and Mason
London, England, 1950–60

Given by Coral Browne.
V&A T.330&A-1987

This wrap dress is a modern interpretation of the Korean *cheollik*, a man's military overcoat which was pleated from the waist to allow a wide range of movements during battle. It is complemented by a short vest and a voluminous tulle petticoat that enhance the wearer's silhouette. RK

72 (OPPOSITE) & 73 (RIGHT)
Contemporary dress, dress and vest of satin weave silk
By Kim Young Jin, Seoul, South Korea, 2014

Purchase funded by Samsung.
V&A FE.15-2015

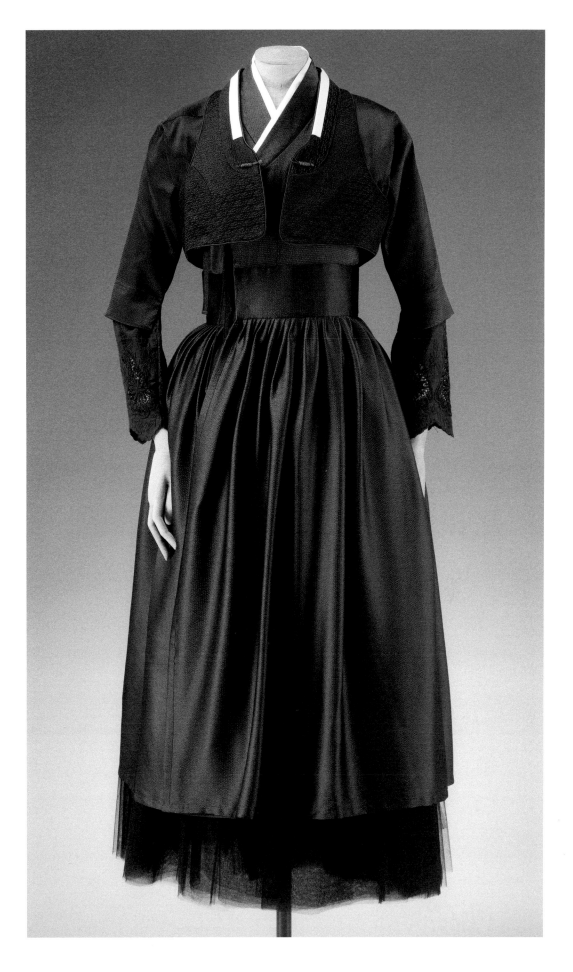

This nightgown (74) was probably made for a bride's trousseau, that is the clothes for the first stage in a woman's married life. Fashion writer Mrs Eric Pritchard would have approved. Her love of lightweight silk was demonstrated in the title and contents of her book *The Cult of Chiffon* (1902), which promoted silk nightdresses, preferably in white or pink. CAJ

74 (RIGHT)
Nightdress of silk chiffon with silk georgette and satin weave silk bows
Possibly by Lucile, London, England, 1913

Given by Mrs Wormald.
V&A T.1-1973

Lightweight and sheer, silk chiffon is graceful in motion and therefore aesthetically appealing for use in fashionable evening gowns. This example (75) demonstrates Greek couturier Jean Dessès's fascination with draping and classical form; the multiple, expertly stitched gathers epitomize the technical complexity of Dessès's garments. SS

75 (OPPOSITE)
Evening dress of silk chiffon
By Jean Dessès, Paris, France, about 1953
Worn by Opal Holt

Given by Mrs D.M. Haynes and Mrs M. Clark.
V&A T.105-1982

The convention for monochrome wedding outfits prompts designers to create interest through embellishment or texture. Two dozen flowers cascade over the shoulder of the silk wedding coat (76 and 77) by John Galliano. Some are formed from the pattern pieces of the coat itself. Others of chiffon and organza are stitched into the crevices to create an abundant bouquet of roses differentiated by texture alone. Similarly, Ossie Clark's design (78 and 79) uses carefully pleated, monochrome satin decorated with channel stitching and a monochrome cut pile chiffon. CKB

76 (OPPOSITE) & 77 (ABOVE)
Wedding outfit of silk chiffon, silk organza and satin weave silk
By John Galliano, London, England, 1987
Worn by Francesca Oddi

Given by the wearer.
V&A T.41-1988

78 (ABOVE)
Detail of wedding dress and coat of plain weave silk and cut pile silk chiffon
By Ossie Clark, probably London, England, 1971
Worn by Diane Boucher (née Radley)

Given by the wearer.
V&A T.21-2019

79 (LEFT)
Diane Boucher on her wedding day, 1971

The donning of unembellished black clothes signified mourning for families, friends or public figures in Victorian Britain, a practice encouraged by Queen Victoria's example after her husband's death in 1861. The textile manufacturer Sydney Courtauld made his fortune from mourning fabrics such as silk crêpe, which was in fact a gauze with a crimped, matte surface, widely used for trimming hats, bonnets and dresses. Peter Robinson's Mourning Warehouse specialized in supplying mourning wear, which followed strict rules about when to wear matte or more more lustrous fabrics. JL

80 (RIGHT)
Length of plain weave silk
Retailed by Peter Robinson's Mourning Warehouse, London, England, about 1890

Given by Mrs J.M. Beard.
V&A T.115-1998

81 (LEFT)
Queen Victoria, the Princess Royal, the Prince of Wales and Princess Alice with a bust of Prince Albert
Photograph by William Bambridge, London, England, 1862

V&A 3517-1953

82 (OPPOSITE)
Sample of silk crêpe
By S. Courtauld & Co., Essex, England, 1862. Published in *A Record of the Great International Exhibition ... Class 20, Silk & Velvet*, compiled by J.C. Robinson (London 1862)

V&A T.258-2009

As clothing styles became more figure-hugging towards the end of the 1920s, the weight and draping capabilities of crêpe made it an increasingly popular choice for both day and evening wear. For loyal clients unable to visit their court dressmaker (London fashion house), their personal saleswoman from the fashion house chose a selection of design sketches with attached swatches to send to them for approval. For this evening dress (83 and 84), Eva Lutyens used a contrasting plain weave silk for the ribbon bows that secure the sleeves and shoulders, offering tantalizing glimpses of the bare arms beneath. OC

83 (OPPOSITE) & 84 (LEFT)
Evening dress of silk crêpe with plain weave silk ribbons
By Eva Lutyens, London, England, 1935–40
Given by Martin Kamer.
V&A T.105-1988

85 (BELOW)
Fashion design for *La Conquête* with silk crêpe sample for evening ensemble for Mary, Princess Royal and Countess of Harewood
By Elizabeth Handley-Seymour after Jeanne Lafaurie, London, England, 1938
Given by Mrs Joyce Whitehouse.
V&A E.4438-1958

These pieces draw inspiration from the *jogakbo*, a Korean wrapping cloth traditionally made by sewing together left-over scraps of fabrics from clothing and bedding. This type of cloth is characterized by the colourful window-pane appearance achieved by triple-stitched seaming, or *kkaekki*. Here the patchwork mosaic is combined with a modern interpretation of traditional Korean dress. The sleeveless jumpsuit replaces the traditional full-length skirt, giving a fresh and modern edge. RK

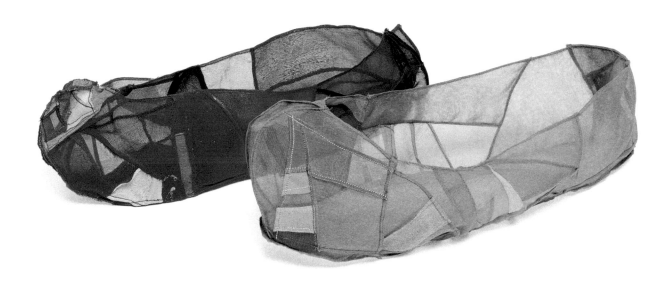

86 (ABOVE)
Shoes of silk gauze with small areas of patchwork and triple-stitched seaming technique
By Lee Chunghie, South Korea, 1992

V&A FE:280:1&2-1995

87 (OPPOSITE)
Woman's jumpsuit of silk gauze, the right sleeve of patchwork and the left sleeve partly of patchwork, with turquoise figured gauze
By Lee Chunghie, South Korea, 1992

V&A FE.281:1-1995

STRIPES
AND CHECKS

Travelling salesmen have long carried samples to show prospective clients the range of silks available and thus elicit orders. Seized by British customs in 1764 because it was illegally imported, this book contains not only the simple and relatively cheap staples shown here but also other rather more sophisticated patterned fabrics. The name of the fabric relates to certain types of patterning with a particular weave structure and weight. Here taffeta is a lightweight plain weave with or without stripes or checks, while *batavia* is a twill weave in stripes or checks. LEM

88
Pages from a French merchant's sample book showing plain and twill weave silks, ff.3v, 10r
Probably Lyon, France, 1764

V&A T.373-1972

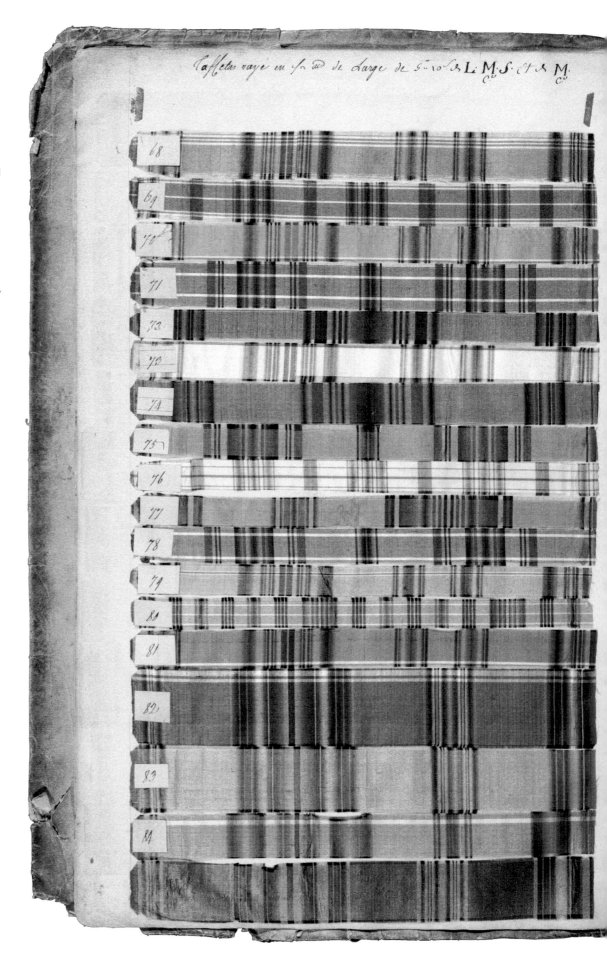

Men in Laos wore a plaid silk sarong to attend their Buddhist ordinations or weddings. The checked pattern is an indicator of manhood. Tai weavers cleverly used two-coloured twisted yarns (here, red-yellow, green-yellow) as weft threads to create a shimmering effect, adding interest to the simple plain weave. SFC

89 (OPPOSITE) & 90 (RIGHT)
Details of man's sarong of plain weave silk
Laos, 1960–70

Bequeathed by Sir John Addis.
V&A IS.73-1984

91 (BELOW)
Adjustable portions of a low-warp handloom of teak and cane, set with silk warps for a sarong and a short length of the finished fabric, Terengganu, Malaysia. Exhibited in the Malaya Pavillion at the British Empire Exhibition in Wembley in 1924

V&A IM.303-1924

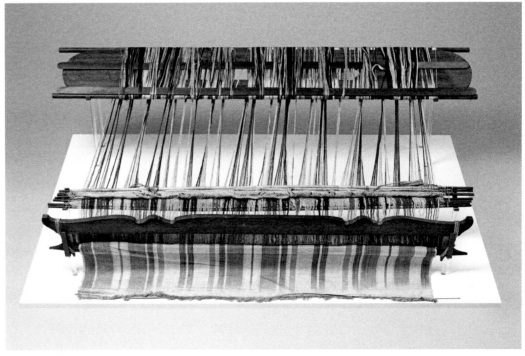

SHOT

A shot effect can be achieved in any weight of silk, with more or less subtlety according to the difference in the colours of warp and weft. Textile converter Ascher's organza (92) was launched in 1956, and was instantly in demand for couture evening and cocktail wear. He made 34 colourways, each with a different warp and weft, so that from a distance the fabric looked like a single colour, but in motion it shimmered with a second colour. In contrast, the silk of Vivienne Westwood's innovative eighteenth-century-inspired evening gown (93) is dense, the contrasting purple ribbon drawing attention to the purple yarn that is subservient to the green of the actual gown in this photograph because of the angle at which it has been taken. LEM

92
Samples of plain weave shot silk organza
Retailed by Ascher Ltd, London, England, 1956

Given by Zika Ascher.
V&A T.194-1988

93 (OPPOSITE)
Watteau, evening gown of shot plain weave silk, from 'Les Femmes ne Connaissent pas toute leur Coquetterie' collection
By Vivienne Westwood, London, England, 1996

Given by the designer.
V&A T.438:1 to 3-1996

In the mid-1970s, after nearly four decades of designing repeating patterns for commercial textiles, Lucienne Day started making one-off artworks. She chose silk as her medium, and the works were named 'Silk Mosaics' because of the tiny squares she used. This example includes different types and weaves of silk to provide a variety of surface effects, some shot, others solid colour. VB

94 (OPPOSITE) & 95 (RIGHT)
Flying in Blue, wall hanging of plain and satin weave silks
By Lucienne Day, Britain, 1985
V&A T.229-1985

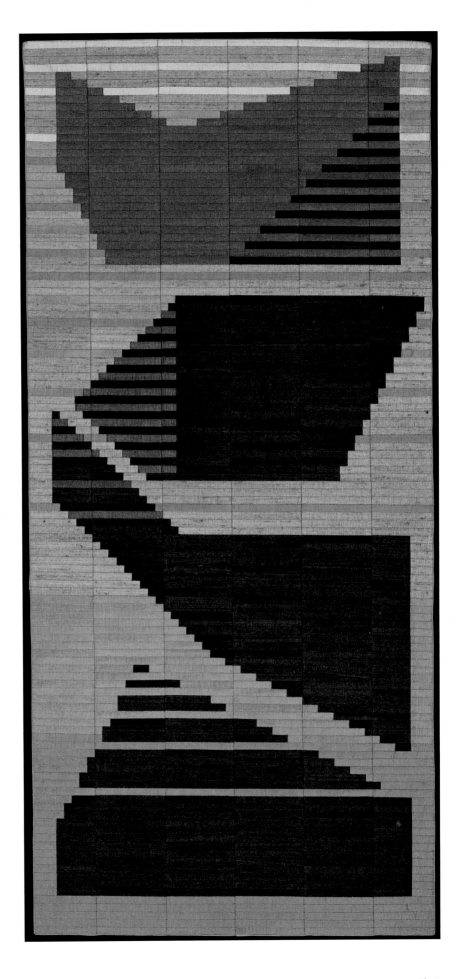

CARING FOR SILK

Plain silks – like their more decorative siblings – degrade as they age, despite the inherent resilience of the fibre. Environmental factors such as light, heat, humidity and pollution play their part. Light is particularly damaging, most noticeably when dyes fade but also when white and pale colours yellow. Light damage is cumulative and as exposure continues the fibre starts to weaken and becomes brittle, eventually breaking. The silk dress worn by 'The Old Pretender Doll' has faded spectacularly on the front and split (96). When the doll is lifted from her chair, the area that was protected from light is still bright pink and is in much better condition (97). To limit such damage, silks must be exposed for limited periods of time and, in a museum setting, are exhibited in low light levels of 50 lux.

Silks are not, however, entirely safe if hidden from light, as the linings of fashionable suits reveal. The lining of the finely tailored late eighteenth-century red wool coat (98) has suffered the impact of abrasion from two sources. The main body of the coat is lined with a vividly contrasting blue silk, flashes of which would have been seen on the coat tails as the wearer moved. The silk has split around the collar and underarm, areas that receive most stress during wear.

The tailor had used a succession of padded layers to shape the coat, including coarse linen canvas topped with hemp fibre. The silk sits on top of these rough layers with a running stitch to keep them in close contact. It is likely that this abrasive surface contributed to the damage (99), particularly because it was a form-fitting garment. During conservation in 2014, the damaged areas were supported by inserting new silk dyed to match under the splits and securing it with laid thread couching (100). EAH

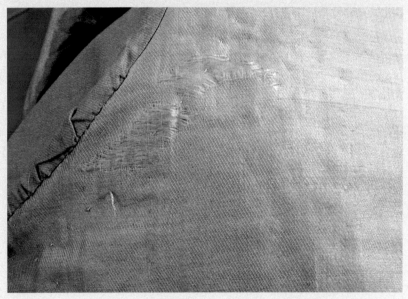

96 & 97 (OPPOSITE)
Front and back of 'The Old
Pretender Doll', wearing satin weave
silk gown with metal trimmings,
probably England, about 1680

Given by Major Vivian Nickalls
on behalf of Clare Style.
V&A W.18-1945

98 (ABOVE)
Suit of woollen broadcloth lined
in twill weave silk, France or the
Netherlands, about 1770

V&A T.214-1992

99 (TOP)
Detail of lining before
conservation in 2014

100 (ABOVE)
Detail of lining after
conservation in 2014

FASHIONING DIOR'S COUTURE

Christian Dior knew how to manipulate textiles to complement his designs, as the subtle beauty of this monochrome ball gown reveals. He often added visual interest to his dresses by juxtaposing textures rather than colours or patterns. In this model, *Cygne Noir* (Black Swan; 103), reflective high-sheen silk satin contrasts starkly with a dense pile of velvet that consumes light. The first is a simple weave, while the second is much more complex in structure and costly in its use of silk yarn.

At the beginning of each season, Dior met with textile suppliers to identify the fabrics for his forthcoming collection. He built close relationships with certain manufacturers including the Lyon-based silk firm Bianchini-Férier (101). In conversation, Dior underlined the importance of finding the right textile, declaring 'fabric not only expresses a designer's dreams but also stimulates his own ideas. It can be the beginning of an inspiration', adding 'many a dress of mine is born of the fabric alone'.[2]

We see this process at play in the original design sketch for *Cygne Noir* (102), where the areas intended as velvet are denoted by careful shading. Combining a simple satin with the more complex structure of velvet, Dior brought together the fabric he asserted was the 'most glamorous' with that which he described in his *Little Dictionary of Fashion* (1954) as the most flattering.[3] CKB

101 (ABOVE)
Advertisement for Bianchini-Férier featuring a velvet evening coat by Christian Dior, *Album de la Mode du Figaro*, October 1951

102 (ABOVE)
Sketch for *Cygne Noir* (Black Swan) dress, 1949. Dior Héritage collection, Paris. Pencil on paper

103 (OPPOSITE)
Detail of evening dress of satin weave silk and silk velvet, entitled *Cygne Noir* (Black Swan) from '*La Ligne Milieu du Siècle*', by Christian Dior, Paris, 1949–50

Worn and given by Baroness Antoinette de Ginsbourg.
V&A T.117&A-1974

Warps and Wefts

2

Warps and Wefts

Many apparently simple silk textiles have patterns created during weaving, not only by blocks of colour but also by contrasting structures. An enormous variety and combination of structures can be exploited fully with silk because the extreme fineness of threads makes a close juxtaposition of various textures possible.[1] Take the likely composition of the silk worn by the modish young man in the late eighteenth-century fashion plate (104) which is comparable to a surviving striped coat (105). Yellow and blue threads alternate in satin and plain weave structures to create not only a visual but also a textural effect, disrupting and enhancing the light-reflective surface.

This is also the principle behind damasks, ubiquitous as dress and furnishing fabrics for many centuries. Damask is a self-patterned textile with only one warp and one weft and the design is formed by contrasting two different weave structures. In its classic form damask is produced by reversing the two faces of a satin weave. A brief eighteenth-century essay on designing for silks instructs the reader that 'damask patterns require the boldest stroke of any; the flowers and leaves should always be large, and the small work omitted as much as possible, except it be in the middle of a leaf or a flower'.[2] This description is an admirable fit for a damask woven after a drawing by English designer Anna Maria Garthwaite in which a classic, monochrome example

104 (LEFT)
Fashion plate, probably Paris, France, 1780–90. Hand-coloured engraving on paper
Given by James Laver CBE.
V&A E.979-1959

105 (ABOVE)
Detail of coat pocket flap, plain weave ground with satin stripes, Britain, 1785–90
Given by Mrs N.J. Batten.
V&A T.92-1962

relies solely on how two different textures respond to light (107). In contrast, small-scale patterns of a more detailed design might suit two-colour damasks, as the upholstery of the chair in a Gilbert Jackson portrait reveals (106). Its warp is blue, its weft white, and the result is a two-tone stylized floral pattern in which the ground is glossy and the motif matte.

These examples demonstrate different means of achieving pattern in silks woven with only one warp and one weft. They are simple weave silks. In contrast, compound weaves use additional threads, either in the warp or weft, to achieve more elaborate effects and patterns. Treadle looms are adequate for basic weaves and textiles with small geometrical patterns, but a complex pattern with a repeat

106 (ABOVE LEFT)
Portrait of an Unknown Lady
by Gilbert Jackson, England,
late 1620s. Oil on canvas

Bequeathed by John Jones.
V&A 565-1882

107 (ABOVE)
Panel of a damask after a design by
Anna Maria Garthwaite, London,
England, 1752

V&A T.346A-1975

攀
華
時
態
尚
新
巧
女
工
慕
精
勤
心
手
暗
相
應
照
眼
華
紛
綜
殷
勤
抛
錦
字
曲
折
續
回
文
更
將
無
限
思
織
作
雁
背
雲

108 (ABOVE)
Drawloom weaving, from a series
of drawings 'Silk Culture and
Manufacture', China, 1662–1722, no.
23. Ink and colour on silk

V&A D.1656-1904

109 (OPPOSITE)
Drawloom, published in Diderot
and d'Alembert, vol. 27 (Paris 1772),
pl. LXII. Engraving

National Art Library, V&A 38041800774804

of over about 2 cm requires a loom on which the weaver can lift individual warp threads or small groups of them. The drawloom resolved that technicality, initially in China in the second century CE.[3] Introduced to Europe by the ninth or tenth century CE, it had two sets of harnesses through which the warp threads were passed to allow the creation of two sheds – that is the space between the warp threads that have been raised and those that have not. One set – operated by the weaver via foot treadles – provided the shed formation necessary for the weaver to pass the ground wefts through and so create the ground weave. The other set of harnesses programmed the lifting of warps for the pattern and was attached to the cords fastened above the loom.

The weaver controlled the treadles, inserted the weft threads and beat them in, while an assistant sat on a platform with the cords hanging in front (108). One or sometimes more drawboys or drawgirls – as the assistants were called – worked in tandem with the weaver to make sure that the correct warp threads were lifted at the right moment. This version of the loom was used up to the seventeenth century, when the invention of a lever permitted the assistant to work the cords from the side of the loom instead of the top (109). This improved drawloom continued in use until the early nineteenth century. Regardless of the modification, weaving remained a slow process making patterned woven silk fabrics costly.

Before the pattern was programmed on the loom, a preparatory freehand sketch was made. Once approved, the pattern was squared up and transferred to rule or point paper to create the draft on which each little square painted indicated the movement of certain warp threads (109). 'Translating' the sketch might take as long as a fortnight,

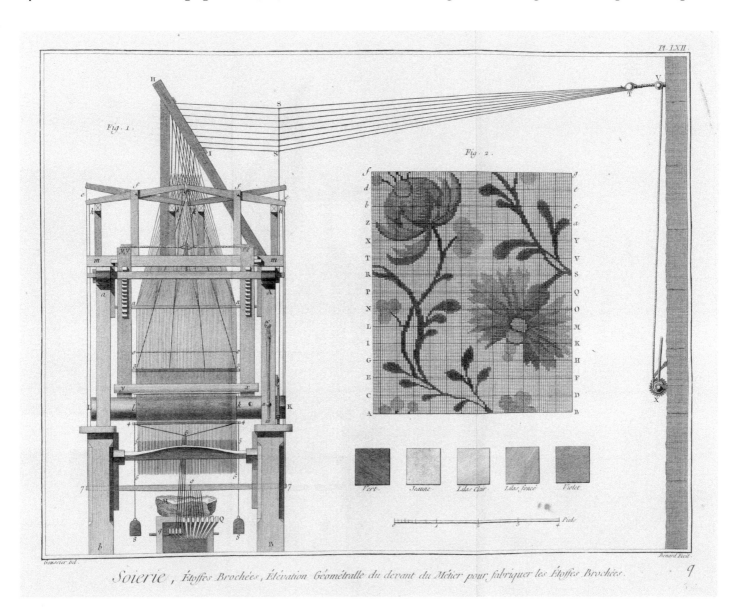

Soierie, Étoffes Brochées, Élévation Géométralle du devant du Métier pour fabriquer les Étoffes Brochées.

but it was indispensable since it informed the weaver how to thread up the loom.[4] This process was expensive and lengthy – and it grew longer and slower the more complex the pattern was. It could take three to six weeks.[5] Consequently, weaving silks with the same pattern was the most economical way of using a loom. The technical drawing remained essential even after the Jacquard mechanism revolutionized the drawloom, as a Bianchini-Férier design from the 1920s reveals (110 and 111).

The Jacquard mechanism was the result of incremental adjustments to the drawloom in France during the eighteenth century. It was brought to fruition by Joseph-Marie Jacquard at the Conservatoire des Arts et Métiers in Paris from 1801 and was in operation beyond France by the 1820s. It was an automatic shedding system that could be mounted on top of any hand- or power-operated loom with the frame to support it. A series of punched cards, perforated according to the desired pattern, was connected in the form of an endless chain, each card representing one throw of the shuttle (112). These cards were fed one at a time into the selection mechanism that 'read' them. Depending on the position of the perforations in each card, a selection of warp threads was raised to form the corresponding shed. Essentially, this mechanism was the predecessor of nineteenth- and twentieth-century punch card computers. It was groundbreaking because it enabled the mounting of a loom to be done within hours, and it allowed the weaver to operate all the functions of the loom unassisted. It also permitted the lifting of individual warp threads, so that patterns with fully rounded motifs could be created, whereas drawloom motifs have obvious stepped outlines, because the threads were lifted in groups.

Although the Jacquard mechanism significantly eased the programming of the loom, certain weaving techniques remained demanding and time-consuming, in particular brocading, a weave-patterning technique in which a supplementary or additional weft travels through the ground weave only in the area required for the motif.[6] Each brocading weft is wound on a small shuttle and

110 (OPPOSITE)
Draft for *Cortège d'Orphée* to design by Raoul Dufy for Bianchini-Férier, Lyon, France, about 1920. Pencil and body colour on point paper

V&A E.1401-2001

111 (ABOVE)
Textile sample of *Cortège d'Orphée*, satin weave with two continuous pattern wefts by Bianchini-Férier, Lyon, France, about 1920

V&A T.219-1992

112 (TOP)
Loom mounted with the Jacquard mechanism, probably Connecticut, USA, 1880s. Engraving

113 (LEFT) & BELOW (114 & 115)
Details of sari of plain weave silk
with brocading in metal thread and
with patterning by a continuous
supplementary warp, Kanchipuram,
Tamil Nadu, India, about 1935

V&A IS.42-1988

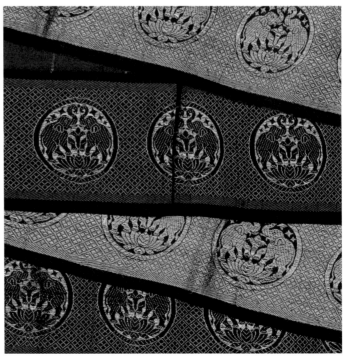

each shuttle is inserted manually, one at a time, once the appropriate ground warp threads are lifted – the greater the number of brocading wefts, the slower and more intricate the weaving. The technique is so laborious that even an expert weaver progresses only about 3 to 5 cm per working day.[7] Nonetheless, the brocading technique has two crucial advantages. The first one is economic: the use of small quantities of valuable threads significantly reduces the amount of precious material unseen on the reverse of the fabric. The other advantage is qualitative: no matter how many supplementary wefts there are, they do not significantly increase the weight of the textile as they would if carried through the fabric's full width. In the sari opposite, the elephants at the end (114), and the clover-like motifs are made with brocading wefts. As a result, the sari remains airy and semi-transparent.

Creating patterns by inserting many different discontinuous wefts is a characteristic shared by brocaded textiles (woven on drawlooms) and tapestries produced on *kesi* looms, or the local equivalents in Japan and India.[8] *Kesi* is a Chinese pictorial silk tapestry with roots in the seventh century. It is woven with undyed silk warp and multicoloured silk wefts that create both the ground weave and the pattern (116 and 117).[9] The weft does not pass from selvedge to selvedge but is instead carried back and forth, interwoven only in the part of the warp required for the pattern. Unlike treadle looms or drawlooms, *kesi* looms do not have a shed opening system or a frame to beat in the weft. Each coloured weft is wound on a separate bobbin and the weaver

handpicks the desired number of warp threads, raises them and passes the shuttle or bobbin underneath, thus inserting the weft so that it follows the shape of a particular motif naturally. The cartoon or finished design sits under the warp threads to guide the weaver. Today many weavers also draw the design's outline on the warp with ink or black markers.

In some textiles, where the designs are too detailed or minute to be brocaded, the weaver will introduce continuous supplementary threads either as warps or wefts. For example, the elephants on the border decoration of the sari (113 and 115) are achieved by an additional metal wrapped warp, stretching continuously along its length. It emerges on the surface only when required for the design (115). When not producing the pattern on the front, the threads lie along the back. This technique is more frequently applied with wefts than warps and is especially advantageous for weaving motifs over larger surfaces.

Early eighteenth-century lampas (118) is an example of a particularly complex textile woven with an abundance of supplementary wefts, predominantly brocading ones. However, the silk thread densely wrapped with a fine silver-gilt strip extends through the entire width of the fabric, appearing on the right side only when needed to create the gleaming ground. In this case, the substantial number of patterning wefts called for a means of holding them in place without weakening the ground weave or spoiling the lavish appearance. The ingenious solution was the introduction of an additional silk warp, not as dense as the ground one. It is of a very light colour, its only role being to hold

116 (ABOVE LEFT) & 117 (RIGHT)
Weaver at Fan Yuming's *kesi*
workshop in Suzhou, China

118 (ABOVE)
Part of the canopy used at the
coronation of King George I (r.
1714–27), lampas weave silk with a
satin weave ground and multiple
supplementary wefts (continuous
and brocading), Venice, Italy or
Lyon, France, 1712–13

V&A T.448-1977

119 (ABOVE RIGHT)
Portrait of a Man (detail),
attributed to Alexis-Simon Belle,
France, about 1712, illustrating
lampas weave silk. Oil on canvas

V&A P.12-1978

the numerous silk and metal wrapped wefts in place. It is
called a binding warp and is one of the features that defines
lampas. It is so fine that it is only visible when magnified.

The most lavish lampas was rich in precious metal
threads. The only silk fabric to rival it in cost was velvet,
with its distinctive, soft and lustrous surface formed by a
supplementary warp, the pile warp. The loom for weaving
velvets needs to incorporate two warp beams – one for the
ground warp, the other for the pile and two shaft harnesses.
The main warp is wrapped round a beam, while the pile warp
comes from a rack carrying hundreds of aligned bobbins
(120). As the pile threads are lifted, the weaver inserts a rod
underneath them (121). A round rod is used to create a velvet
made up of innumerable tiny loops. A grooved rod is used to
form small tufts obtained by cutting the pile warp threads
by hand with a small blade that the weaver runs down the
groove in the rod.

The cutting process is risky. If the blade slips, it will
cut the warps and the piece will be ruined. Consequently,
weaving velvets called for meticulous attention and great
skill and a highly specialist weaver could not produce more
than 20 to 25 cm of fabric per day.[10] Even monochrome cut
velvets commanded high prices because the quantity of silk
used in their weaving was six times greater than that for a

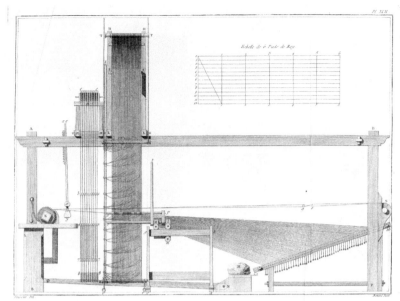

Soterie, Velours Élévation Latéralle du Métier pour fabriquer le Velours Ciselé. Vu dans l'instant qui précede celui de la Tire

plain weave silk.[11] Their cost increased with the complexity of the pattern. Polychrome velvets woven in seventeenth-century Genoa had as many as three piles, which required three bobbin racks on the loom and used an enormous quantity of silk (122).

This overview touches on the most widespread of the great variety of compound weaves that exist worldwide and some of the loom types that made them possible. By the twentieth century, the looms for some of these techniques could be operated by power, and later still electronically. The tradition of handloom weaving has, nonetheless, survived, providing patterned silks for discerning and wealthy consumers and for the renovation of palatial interiors in heritage sites across the globe. SB

120 (TOP LEFT)
Drawloom for weaving figured velvets, published in Diderot and d'Alembert, vol. 27 (Paris 1772), pl. XCII. Engraving

National Art Library, V&A 38041800774804

121 (ABOVE LEFT)
Weaving of a polychrome *ciselé* velvet (with cut and uncut pile), Italy, 2019

122 (ABOVE)
Ciselé velvet; three pile warps and the ground covered with silver-gilt continuous weft, probably Genoa, from the archives of Tessiture Cordani in Zoagli, Liguria, Italy, 1650–1700

V&A 339-1891

SIMPLE WEAVES

This Chinese silk fragment, once part of a garment, was allegedly discovered in the necropolis of El-Azam, near Asyut in Upper Egypt. The maker of the garment probably could not read Chinese as the stylized woven characters have been incorporated upside down. Regardless, the quality of the silk would have communicated the wearer's social status and wealth. HP

123
Fragment of damask weave silk
China, 1300–1400

V&A 1108-1900

A large repeating design of a Chinese incense burner among acanthus-like foliage adorns the damask of this European-made gown. The garment's simple kimono-like construction with no fastenings or shoulder seams allows for the correct orientation on the back, but the pattern appears upside down as it comes over the shoulders and down the front. LEM

124
Back of man's gown of damask weave silk
China (silk woven for export to Europe) and Britain or the Netherlands (garment made up), 1720–50

V&A T.31-2012

These two examples of damask may have been used for either dress or furnishings. The pattern of the two-colour damask opposite (127) incorporates a diamond, one of the Medici family's symbols, while the monochrome fabric above (125 and 126) features a bee, a dove with an olive twig and three mounds, emblems of the Barberini, Pamphili and Chigi families respectively, who produced three consecutive popes in the seventeenth century. SB

125 (ABOVE LEFT) & 126 (RIGHT)
Front and back of fragment of damask weave silk
Florence, Italy, about 1660

V&A 1053-1888

127 (OPPOSITE)
Detail of a fragment of damask weave silk
Florence, Italy, 1525–50

V&A 8679-1863

W.55-1914

Elaborate textiles were used to cover upholstered furniture, often harmonizing with the wall hangings in grand rooms. The back was usually covered in a less expensive material so this cover (128) was probably reupholstered later, though the fabric is roughly contemporary with the chair frame. VB

128 (OPPOSITE)
Chair back upholstered in damask weave silk
Probably Lyon or Tours, France, after 1735

V&A W.55-1914

Weaver Giovanni Panichi's mark is incorporated into the design of the Six of Hearts in this pack of 48 playing cards with silk fronts (129). The court cards – King, Queen and Knave – are based on a French design and colours are introduced to the simple satin weave ground with supplementary wefts, making this a compound weave rather than a simple weave like damask. SB

129 (ABOVE)
Pack of playing cards (incomplete) of satin weave silk with supplementary wefts
By Giovanni Panichi, Florence, Italy, 1730–40

V&A 271-1866

Rinzu, a patterned satin similar to damask, was introduced into Japan from China in the sixteenth century. The soft, fluid fabric (130) was a popular choice for kimono, replacing the stiffer silks used previously. This nineteenth-century example was part of a gift of objects given to Queen Victoria by the last-but-one military ruler (*shōgun*) in 1860. AJ

This black damask (131) has a design of horizontal zigzag bands filled with Arabic inscriptions. It once draped the outer walls of the Ka'bah, the cubic stone building in Mecca, Saudi Arabia, which is the holiest site in the Islamic world. The set of silk covers (*kiswah*) is changed every year. Once removed, these textiles are valued as holy relics. TS

130 (OPPOSITE)
Detail of damask weave silk for a kimono
Probably Kyoto, Japan, 1850–60

Given by HM Queen Victoria.
V&A 330:1-1865

131 (ABOVE)
Part of the cover for the Ka'bah of damask weave silk
Probably Cairo, Egypt, 1917–18

Given by Mr W. Hastings.
V&A T.439-1966

From a distance, this waistcoat (132) looks like embroidery, so cleverly does the woven-to-shape floral design imitate hand stitching. Its design is found in two colourways in a book of silk samples (133) from the firm of Maze and Steer for 'Fancy Vestings and Handkerchief Goods'. SN

132 (BELOW RIGHT)
Man's waistcoat of figured satin weave silk
By Maze and Steer, London, England, 1789–92

Given by Mrs Edmund de Rothschild.
V&A T.371-1972

133 (BELOW LEFT)
Page from book of samples of 'Fancy Vestings and Handkerchief Goods'
By Maze and Steer, London, England, 1786–91, p. 177
V&A T.384-1972

Mashru is a specialty fabric used for many purposes in India. Woven with a silk satin face and cotton back, the fabric has the outward shine of pure silk with the added coolness and moisture-absorbing properties of cotton. This length (134) is patterned with damasked paisley motifs (*butis*) worked with a supplementary silk weft. AF

134 (OPPOSITE)
Detail of satin weave silk and cotton
Hyderabad, Telangana, India, about 1880

V&A IS.2137-1883

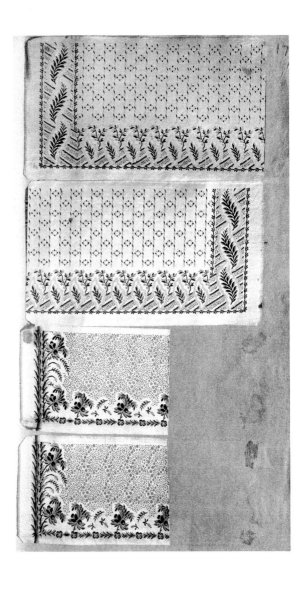

Sheer fabrics, including simple striped silk gauze, were fashionable for western womenswear around the time that this wedding dress was made. The gown (135) was worn by a Quaker bride and likely satisfied a desire to look unobtrusive but well-dressed. CAJ

135 (LEFT)
Detail of wedding dress of silk gauze with satin weave stripes, trimmed with satin weave silk and silk lace
Probably Britain or France, about 1872–4
Worn by Lucretia Crouch

Given by Miss Felicity Ashbee.
V&A T.68 to B-1962

Tsuchiya is inspired by the beauty of the landscape, in this case (136) the brisk air and clear waters of Mount Qingcheng in Sichuan Province, China. The delicate gauze (*monsha*) is woven with naturally dyed threads, in a sophisticated pattern that produces squares within squares decreasing in size from the lower left to the upper right. This creates the impression of cascading water. AJ

136 (OPPOSITE)
Detail of *Blue Mountains and Green Rivers*, kimono of silk gauze
By Tsuchiya Yoshinori, Seki, Japan, 2004, made into garment 2006

V&A FE.144-2006

COMPOUND WEAVES

Gauze weaving is one of the oldest textile techniques in China. In the Han dynasty (206 BCE–220 CE) weavers were already producing plain gauze with geometric patterns. The pattern of peonies and butterflies woven in plain weave with floating warps used for this woman's robe (138) is typically Chinese, whereas the floral motifs on the sleeveless jacket (137) are not. It may be that this later gauze was imported from Europe or made in China in imitation of European textiles, as, by the turn of the twentieth century, it was fashionable there to use foreign materials. SFC

137 (RIGHT)
Sleeveless jacket of figured silk gauze with supplementary weft
China, 1900–10

Given by M. Laurent Long.
V&A FE.405-2007

138 (OPPOSITE)
Woman's summer robe of figured silk gauze with supplementary patterning
China, 1800–1900

V&A 1609-1901

The style of this Korean hat originates in the form worn by a high-ranking official of the Joseon dynasty (1392–1910), and its name *samo* derives from the fine silk gauze or *sa* that covers it. This silk is woven with the cloud pattern that symbolizes longevity and rising in the world through self-cultivation and study. RK/EL

139 (ABOVE)
Bridegroom's hat of silk gauze with supplementary weft, over bamboo frame
Korea, 1800–1900

V&A T.516-1919

This *cheongchoui* is part of the *jobok* ceremonial robe worn at the Joseon royal court (1392–1910), its dragon motifs symbolizing authority and protection. Historically, such robes were made of fine plain weave silk, handwoven at the official workshop. After the Japanese invasion of the Korean peninsula (1592–8), court attire was reformed and court officials gradually adopted the colour blue. RK/EL

140 (OPPOSITE)
Inner robe of silk gauze with supplementary weft
Probably Seoul, Korea, 1880–1910

V&A T.196-1920

Silks made in China, Central and Western Asia were traded on the Silk Road. Best known are silks with animals in pearled roundels and delicate patterns such as this heart-shaped petal design (141). The weave, a weft-faced compound twill made with Z-twist threads, confirms the origins of the fragments. HP

141 (RIGHT)
Fragment of compound weave silk
Central/Western Asia, 750–900 CE

Stein Textile Loan Collection, on loan from the Government of India and the Archaeological Survey of India.
V&A LOAN:STEIN.338:1

Excavated in Loulan, a town located in the middle of the Silk Road, this small fragment (142) combines Chinese technique with western-influenced design. It is of warp-faced compound plain weave with a continuous silk filament with little or no twist, which is typically Chinese. The two confronting rams with twisted bodies within lozenge compartments are typical of Sassanian or West Asian design, reinterpreted into Chinese ornament. HP

142 (FAR RIGHT)
Fragment of compound plain weave silk
China, 200–400 CE

Stein Textile Loan Collection, on loan from the Government of India and the Archaeological Survey of India.
V&A LOAN:STEIN.214

143 (BELOW)
Fragment of lampas weave silk with gilt membrane threads
Almeria, Spain, 1100–50

V&A 275&A-1894

The workshops of Islamic Spain in the south of Iberia, most importantly in Almería and Granada, wove sophisticated silks with complex patterns in rich materials between the twelfth and fifteenth centuries (143–5). These silks were traded in Europe and the Mediterranean. Their designs incorporated animals (143), geometric patterns evoking the architecture of the Alhambra Palace, Granada (144), and Arabic inscriptions (143 and 145). The example below reads 'Glory to our Lord the Sultan'. ACL

144 (RIGHT) & 145 (BELOW)
Fragments of lampas weave silk
Granada, Spain, 1330–1450,
1300–1400

V&A 1312-1864 & 1105-1900

Lampas weave combines two or more structures. Comparison of the front (147) and back (146) of this piece reveals how it works. The wefts run from left to right, interlinking with the warps to change the colour of the pattern as required. The design of Chinese phoenixes with pseudo Arabic inscriptions suggests that the meeting of these two cultures influenced the development of Italian silk weaving. ACL

146 (BELOW) & 147 (OPPOSITE)
Back and front of fragment of lampas weave silk with gilt-metal thread
Italy, 1300–1400

V&A 765-1893

765-1893

Europeans called this rich silk (148) *panni tartarici* (Tartar cloths). It embodies an international repertory of design: its woven structure is sufficiently distinctive to allow attribution to Mongol-ruled Iran while the garment itself is a Roman Catholic dalmatic, a church vestment worn by deacons. The flower scrolls are reminiscent of Chinese motifs, while for Christians the pelicans symbolized Christ's self-sacrifice. TS

148 (LEFT)
Detail of dalmatic of lampas weave silk with gilt-metal threads
Iran, 1300–1400

V&A 8361-1863

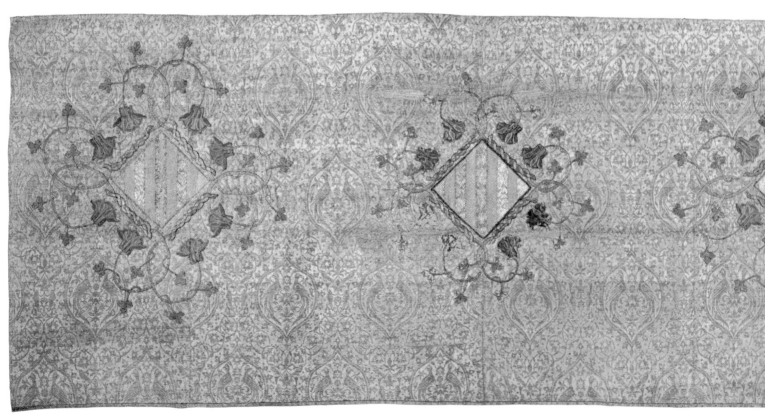

These two fabrics are made with similar designs, materials and techniques, and served as ornaments for church, court and other ceremonies in Europe. The frontal (150) was probably made in one of the major cities in Aragon (Spain) as the coat of arms of the Aragonese crown has been applied to the ogival-medallion patterned silk, probably from the Near East or Iran. The chasuble's pattern (149) is typical of silks woven in Egypt or Syria during the Mamluk Sultanate (1250–1517), and widely exported to Europe. ACL

149 (RIGHT)
Chasuble of lampas weave silk with gilt-metal threads
Near East or Egypt, about 1400–25

V&A 664-1896

150 (OPPOSITE BELOW)
Lampas weave silk and gilt-metal threads with appliqué embroidery in silk and gilt-metal threads
Probably Near East or Iran (silk woven) and Valencia or Barcelona (embroidered), Spain, about 1375–1450

V&A 792-1893

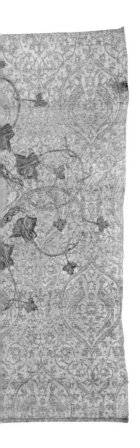

Like other holy sites in Islam, the mausoleum of the Prophet Muhammad in Medina, Saudi Arabia, is dressed with silk textiles that are renewed every year. Those made for this building always have a green ground and a zigzag pattern filled with religious inscriptions in Arabic. TS

151 (ABOVE)
Part of a hanging of lampas weave silk
Probably Bursa, Turkey, 1517–1600

V&A 779-1892

This fragment is from a very grand garment whose pattern indicated its wearer's high status, both through its figurative content and technical complexity. A youthful attendant stands ready to serve wine, just as a page probably waited on the wearer in real life. The boy's courtly dress and bland good looks match the idealized nature of the setting, a springtime landscape. TS

152 (ABOVE)
Piece of lampas weave silk
Iran, 1500–1600

V&A 282-1906

In the Islamic world, rich textiles transformed walls into plant-filled arcades. Here the arch contains a tree-like arrangement that was already a design motif in pre-Islamic Iran (before 651 CE). In contrast, the leaf and flower forms are based on Chinese models introduced in the thirteenth century and the more realistic flowers in the spandrels of the arch recall the designs on sixteenth-century Ottoman tiles. TS

153
Part of a hanging of lampas weave silk and metal wrapped thread
Iran, 1600–1700

V&A T.9-1915

The conventional depiction of
tiger stripes in much of Asia
consists of pairs of wavy lines.
In this version, the 'stripes' – in
white outlined in blue – define
the wider, wavy gold band
between them. This textile
was used for a child's kaftan
that almost certainly belonged
to a member of the Ottoman
dynasty. TS

154
Child's kaftan of lampas weave silk
with brocading in silk and metal
wrapped threads
Probably Bursa, Turkey, about 1590

V&A 753-1884

Iranian rulers awarded 'robes of honour' of the highest quality silk to their leading subjects. The distinctive patterns marked the wearers' allegiance to the monarch. Few robes of honour made before 1800 survive in their original form. Most of this *sakkos* – the main vestment of a Christian Orthodox bishop – was made by cutting up such a robe. TS

155
Liturgical garment of lampas weave silk with gilt and silver wrapped threads (excluding yoke)
Iran, 1650–1700

V&A 576-1907

In the mid-sixteenth century an Assamese prince commissioned a saint to supervise the weaving of a great silk scroll depicting the early life of the god Krishna. The original scroll was lost. This fragment (156) is one of the oldest and finest of known examples of Assamese lampas weave silk, with patterns portraying events in Krishna's life, and may come from the original scroll. AF

156 (LEFT)
Fragment of lampas weave silk
Assam, India, about 1560–70

V&A IS.365-1992

This textile (157) was acquired at the Great Exhibition in London in 1851. It is a type of veil worn by wealthy Tunisian women outside the home. The black unwoven bands of warp (at the bottom of the photograph) covered the face, yet allowed the wearer to see out, while the decorative weaving covered the head and body. ACL

157 (OPPOSITE)
Detail of veil of lampas weave silk with gilt-metal thread
Tunisia, before 1850

V&A 830-1852

The technique of weaving *tanchoi* (158), a satin-faced silk made up of two warps and multiple continuous wefts in each pass, is believed to have arrived in India from China in the mid-nineteenth century. India's Parsi communities, many of whom were active in Indo-Chinese trade, drove demand for *tanchoi* fabrics and garments fusing Chinese and Indian styles. AF

In Punjab and Sindh silk weavers used double-faced weaving techniques to create soft and luxurious reversible silk garments called *lungis* (159). These were made to wear as shawls over the shoulders, sashes around the waist or as turban cloths. The finest and most expensive had side borders and end bands of silver-gilt wrapped thread. AF

158 (OPPOSITE)
Detail of sari of *tanchoi* weave silk
Probably Surat, Gujarat, India, about 1875–1925

Given by Lady Ratan Tata.
V&A T.247-1920

159 (ABOVE)
Detail of wrapped garment of double-faced silk with cotton and silver wrapped thread
Bahawalpur, Punjab, India (now Pakistan), about 1855

V&A 0556(IS)

Fifteenth-century inventories reveal European aristocrats' preference for Italian silks, especially those from Lucca and Venice. The patterns on such silks took inspiration from a variety of sources. Pomegranates, flowers and leaves have a Near East aesthetic, while the bird of prey plummeting towards a startled partridge in the right-hand example refers to the elite activity of hunting. SB/ACL

160 (RIGHT) & 161 (OPPOSITE)
Details of lampas weave silks with brocading in gilt-metal thread
Italy, 1400–50

V&A T.27-1922 & 713-1907

These two fragments (162 and 163) are typical of the patterned silks woven extensively in Italy during the second quarter of the seventeenth century for men's and women's dress. Their golden, brocaded motifs echoed the decorative motifs on Persian silks, which were objects of desire and inspiration for many Europeans. SB

(162 & 163) OPPOSITE ABOVE
Fragments of plain weave silk with brocading in silver-gilt threads
Italy, 1625–50

V&A 1114-1899 & T.196-1910

Striped silks were highly fashionable in late seventeenth-century Europe. The wide blue and thin gold stripes of this pattern (164) are achieved using three alternating warp threads, while a brocading weft is used for the two differently decorated broad bands. SB

164 (OPPOSITE BELOW)
Detail of satin weave silk with brocading in metal threads
France, 1685–1700

V&A T.427-1976

This fragment (165) may have been a panel from a woman's skirt or petticoat, similar in shape to those in a tailoring book published in Spain in 1720. The silk was probably woven in Spain, though the design is in the dominant French taste of its time. Its texture is enhanced by both chenille and highly twisted *cordonnet* thread. ACL

165 (RIGHT)
Fragment of plain weave silk with brocading in silk
Probably Valencia, Spain, 1700–20

V&A T.276-1910

Satin with brocaded patterns was the most desirable and highly valued of all silks in China during the Ming dynasty (1368–1644), used for luxury garments and upholstery. This fragment (168) is delicately made with an extremely fine ground weave while flat gold threads outline the clouds and flowerheads. HP

168 (ABOVE)
Fragment of satin weave silk with brocading in silk and gold strip
Probably Suzhou or Hangzhou, China, 1500–1650

Purchased with Art Fund support.
V&A T.81-1948

These fashionable women's shoes (166 and 167) are a typical style of eighteenth-century European footwear. They are made of a silk woven in Iran during the Safavid dynasty (1501–1722), patterned with stars and ogees (S-shaped curves). They were probably made from scraps left over from a much larger garment. SN

166 (OPPOSITE) & 167 (ABOVE)
Pair of women's shoes of silk with brocading and metal thread
Britain, about 1720–30 and Iran, 1600–1700

Given by Messrs Harrods.
V&A T.444&A-1913

New textiles from France, Italy
and Asia inspired the exotic
designs in English silks between
about 1680 and 1710. This
example, woven after a design
by the talented designer and
weaver James Leman, reveals a
clear understanding of how to
convert a freehand drawing (169)
into a woven fabric with a repeat
pattern (170), using the intricate
mechanism of the drawloom.
Many of Leman's other 103
surviving designs in the Victoria
and Albert Museum carry
manufacturing instructions
as well as the names of the
customers for whom they were
commissioned. LEM

169 (RIGHT)
Design commissioned by Isaac
Tullie, a leading Covent Garden
mercer, London, 15 July 1709
Watercolour and bodycolour
on paper

V&A E.1861:98-1991

170 (LEFT)
**Length of dress fabric of lampas
weave silk with brocading**
By James Leman, London, 1709
V&A T.156-2016

France dominated the manufacture of fashionable dress and furnishing silks in eighteenth-century Europe. These two silks were probably made into a woman's gown; from the 1720s to 1770s, the fashion for wide petticoats and flowing backs displayed such patterns perfectly. The earlier example (172) has a bold naturalistic pattern with a long repeat typical of the 1730s, while the other (171) has more refined sprays of stylized bouquets tucked in undulating scalloped ribbons typical of the later date. The famed Lyonnais silk designer Jean Revel introduced the dovetailing of colours around 1733, which made it easier to achieve naturalistic motifs. SB/LEM

171 (RIGHT) & 172 (OPPOSITE)
Lengths of plain weave silk with brocading in silk and silver threads
Probably Lyon, France, about 1765–70 and 1735–40

V&A 108-1880 & T.170-1965

According to the author of the first manual on silk design published in Paris in 1765, every designer had to understand the full range of materials used in weaving as well as the weaving process in order to make aesthetically pleasing silks that used expensive yarns economically. The back of this silk (173) reveals just how little metal thread was wasted, while the front (174) displays the richness that would have made this silk suitable for wearing to the court, theatre or opera. LEM

173 (OPPOSITE) & 174 (RIGHT)
Back and front of length of silk with brocading in silk and metal and a foot-figured ground
Probably Lyon, France, 1745–60
V&A T.115-1912

By the seventeenth century, the Dutch Republic had a significant silk-weaving industry that supplied both domestic and export markets with fashionable silks. The Dutch East India Company was established in 1602 and traded with Japan until its dissolution in 1799, making the Dutch the only European nation allowed to do so during the 'Isolation of Japan' (1639–1853). As a result, Dutch weavers developed a style inspired by Chinese and Japanese taste. Striking and playful designs catered for the European appetite for chinoiserie, incorporating exotic flowers, fishing boats, pagodas, parasols, Chinese-looking figures and the rather large, stylized winged insect visible in all three of these examples. SB

175 (RIGHT)
Detail of back of chasuble of satin weave silk with brocading in silk threads
Netherlands, 1733–40

V&A 611-1896

176 (BELOW)
Detail of dalmatic of satin weave silk with brocading in metal threads
Probably Netherlands, 1720–30

V&A CIRC.466-1919

177 (OPPOSITE)
Detail of furnishing fabric of satin weave silk with brocading and weft patterning
Netherlands, 1735–45

Given by HM Queen Mary.
V&A T.73-1936

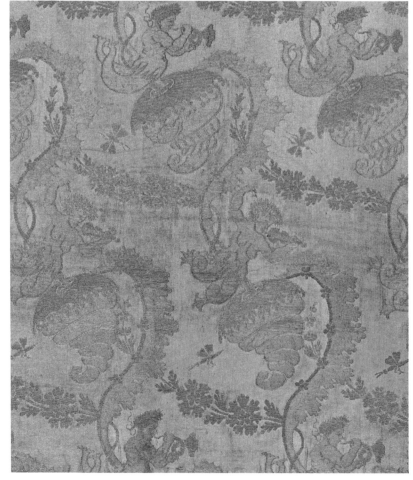

In eighteenth-century Europe many of the most elaborate patterned silks were for furnishings. This example (178 and 179) was probably to adorn a palace interior for King Charles IV of Spain. It was made by a Lyonnais manufacturer, formerly an official supplier of the French royal household whose family business continued to weave luxury furnishing textiles into the twenty-first century. LEM

178 (ABOVE) & 179 (RIGHT)
Length of furnishing silk with brocading in silk and silver threads
Designed by Jean-Démosthène Dugourc for the manufacturer Camille Pernon et cie., Lyon, France, about 1797–8

V&A T.69-1951

The French emperor Napoleon I favoured classical emblems, such as the urn and incense burner, which he used to proclaim the legitimacy of his rule. The Swedish weaver of this textile (180) probably imitated such designs to provide the francophile Swedish royal family and nobility with similar luxury fabrics. The woven inscription 'IPM41' reveals his identity. JL

180 (OPPOSITE)
Detail of furnishing fabric of satin and twill weave silk
By Jean Pierre Mazer, Stockholm, Sweden, 1813

V&A T.32-1988

Nō is a form of classical
Japanese theatre. *Karaori*
are robes worn by male
actors playing female roles,
the predominant red colour
of this example indicating
the character of a young
woman. It has three layers of
simultaneously woven pattern:
the red ground, the gold
geometric design and
the surface floral roundels
of glossy silk. AJ

181 (OPPOSITE) & 182 (ABOVE)
Robe for the *Nō* theatre of figured
compound weave silk with gilt-
paper strips and brocading in silk
Kyoto, Japan, 1780–1820

V&A T.194-1959

Indian silks inspired nineteenth-century British designers. This sari (183) was displayed at the Great Exhibition held in London in 1851 where the designer Owen Jones saw it. Jones later included its pattern in his book *The Grammar of Ornament* (London 1856), which became a foundational text in modern British design (184). AF

183 (ABOVE)
Detail of sari of plain weave silk with brocading in silver-gilt wrapped thread
Varanasi, Uttar Pradesh, India, about 1850

V&A 767-1852

184 (RIGHT)
Detail of preparatory drawing of plate for *The Grammar of Ornament*
By Owen Jones, Britain, 1856
Pen, bodycolour and gilding on paper

V&A 1624

Brocaded silks of this kind (185) were used to mount covers for Buddhist religious texts in China. The gold-faced supplementary wefts form an overall pattern of lotus flowers against a red satin ground. They are made of flat paper strips with gold leaf applied only on one side as the reverse would not be seen after mounting. SFC

185 (OPPOSITE)
Front (faded) and back of detail of satin weave silk with brocading in flat gilt-paper strips
China, 1825–75

V&A 6559(IS)

The Gujarati cities of Ahmedabad and Surat were leading exporters of this type of silk, which was categorized according to the quantity of precious metal used in the pattern and ground. Although its cut and embellishments suggest this man's robe (186), or *angarkha*, may have been worn in Sindh, the rich red silk was probably woven in Gujarat. AF

186 (LEFT)
Man's garment of plain weave silk with brocading in silver-gilt wrapped thread
Probably Gujarat, India (tailored in Sindh), about 1867

V&A 05648(IS)

Silks woven with silver and silver-gilt were abundant in India's royal courts. This woman's blouse (187) from the princely state of Nawanagar is made up of two brocaded silks trimmed with two styles of silk ribbon. The material may have been imported from nearby Ahmedabad, which specialized in costly silks of this type. AF

187 (ABOVE)
Blouse of plain weave silk with brocading in silver and silver-gilt wrapped thread
Probably Ahmedabad, Gujarat, India (tailored in Nawanagar, now Jamnagar, Gujarat), about 1867

V&A 05499:2/(IS)

Japanese Buddhist priests wear a *kesa*, a rectangular garment draped over the left shoulder and under the right arm. These are normally made of cloth cut up and rearranged in symbolic representation of the Buddhist cosmos. This example (188), however, is a pictorial *kesa* in which lengths of elaborately woven silk were sewn side by side and silk cord then couched onto the surface to evoke the usual patchwork divisions. AJ

188 (FOLLOWING PAGES)
Detail of Buddhist priest's mantle of figured silk with resist-dyed warp threads, gilt-paper strips and silk cord
Kyoto, Japan, 1800–50

Given by T.B. Clarke-Thornhill.
V&A T.80-1927

Warm and colourful shawls imported from Kashmir were draped over white muslin dresses in late eighteenth-century Europe. Weavers in London, Norwich, Edinburgh and later Paisley adapted their production to provide these luxurious accessories in different qualities and designs, using silk, wool and cotton. From the 1820s, the Jacquard loom attachment facilitated the production of ever more complex designs, often elaborations on the classic Indian *buta* motif, which came to be known in Britain as the paisley pattern. JL

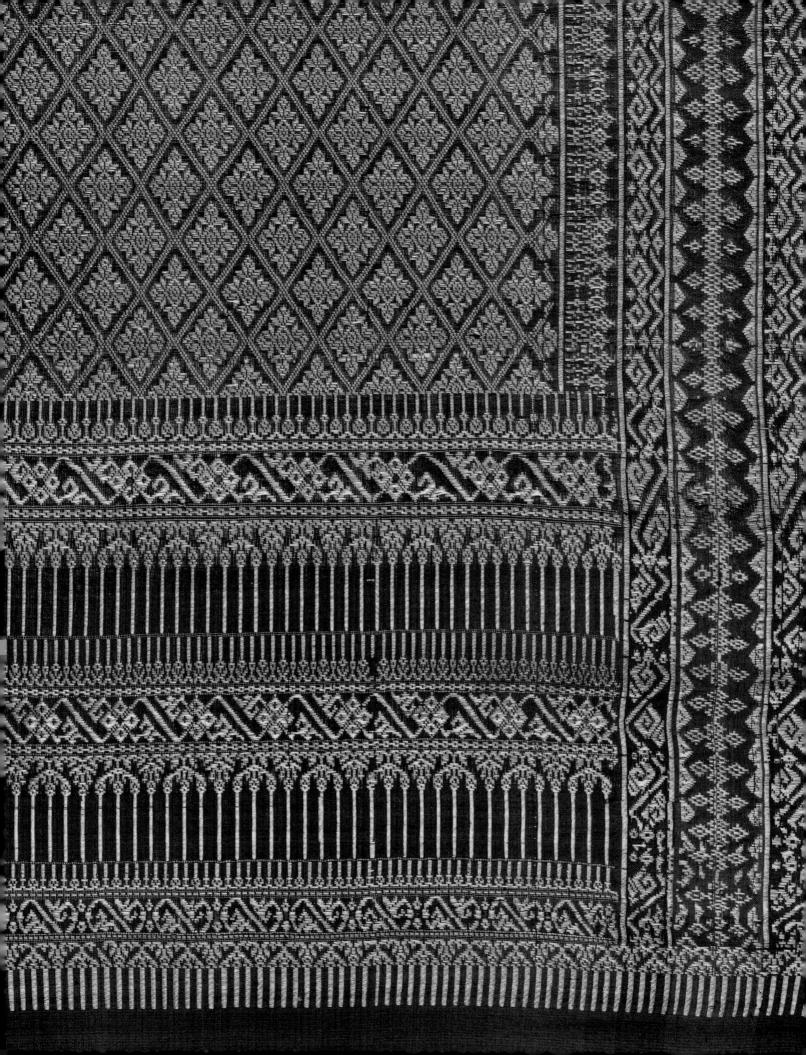

The Thai (then known as Siamese) court traditionally preferred using imported silk textiles from India and Cambodia for ceremonial dress and as royal gifts. Thai brocades were only developed under royal patronage at the turn of the twentieth century, their designs reminiscent of early Indian brocades produced for the Thai court. SFC

192 (OPPOSITE)
Detail of skirt-cloth of plain weave silk with brocading in silver wrapped yellow silk thread
Thailand, 1900–35
Given by HM Queen Mary.
V&A IM.9-1936

This *kor* (193) exemplifies the intricate weaving techniques practised by Chin women using back-strap looms. The main diamond-shaped *tial* motifs formed by a discontinuous supplementary weft are symbols of high social status. The warp-faced weave is found on the vertical stripes of the upper body but disappears in the lower section where the weft-faced weave dominates. Dividing them are bands of twill weave herringbone pattern. SFC

193 (ABOVE RIGHT)
Woman's blouse of plain and twill weave silk with brocading
Chin state, Myanmar, 1900–50
V&A IS.42-1997

Royalty or high-ranking nobles wear this type of ceremonial sarong in Malaysia (194). The brocaded silk textile is called *songket* in Malay, referring to the supplementary weft-patterning technique with metal threads. It is densely decorated with stylized motifs of local plants, such as mangosteen and bamboo shoots. SFC

194 (RIGHT)
Detail of man's ceremonial skirt-cloth of plain weave silk with brocading in gilt-metal threads
Terengganu, Malaysia, 1924
V&A IM.269-1924

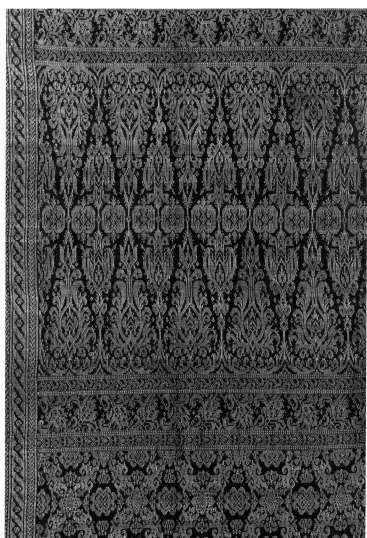

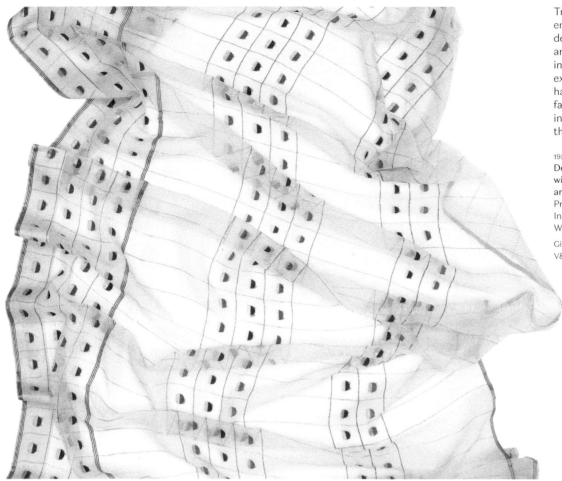

Transparent silk saris, often embellished with modern designs, became fashionable among high society women in India from the 1930s. This example (195) was probably handwoven in Varanasi, a city famous for weaving, and, in this instance, the pattern is in both the warp and the weft. DP

195 (LEFT)
Detail of sari of plain weave silk with brocading in silk, gold wire and gold-coloured thread
Probably Varanasi, Uttar Pradesh, India, 1930–50
Worn by Mrs Mayura Brown

Given by the wearer.
V&A IS.51-1998

The *jamdani* technique – a form of brocading – is particular to Bengal: an extra weft thread is introduced during the handloom-weaving process to create a pattern. In this silk sari (196), the decorative end, thrown over the shoulder when worn, has a cycle rickshaw woven into it in this way. DP

196 (RIGHT)
Detail of sari of plain weave silk with weft-inlay *jamdani* technique for the rickshaw motif
Designed by Abraham & Thakore, woven in the Nutan Falia Tantubay Samabay Samity Ltd Cooperative, Nadia District, West Bengal, India, 2010

Given by Abraham & Thakore.
V&A IS.30:1-2012

Yamaguchi Genbei is the tenth-generation head of Kondaya Genbei, a family textile business in Kyoto. He also devotes his time to the creation of extraordinary works that push his artisans to the limits of their technical skills. The stylized hemp-leaf design of this sash is a classic one, but the way in which it has been woven, with supplementary wefts of shell, is extremely unusual. Thin sheets of shell were adhered to Japanese paper with lacquer and then cut into narrow strips for weaving into the fabric. AJ

197
Detail of *obi* (waist sash) of silk woven with shell
By Yamaguchi Genbei, Kyoto, Japan, 2015

Given by the designer.
V&A FE.82-2016

TAPESTRY WEAVE

In the medieval Islamic world, linen fabrics with tapestry-woven silk bands were highly regarded and presented as gifts by the caliph. Such silks with inscriptions are known as *tiraz*, and sometimes mention the caliph's name. In this case, the inscription wishes its owner 'success and prosperity'. This fragment (198) was found in a burial site. ACL

198 (BELOW)
Fragment of plain weave linen with tapestry weave in silk
Egypt, 1050–1150

V&A 755-1898

This robe (199) is the earliest datable whole garment in the Victoria and Albert Museum's collection of Chinese textiles. Its brightly coloured and boldly patterned fabric was woven to shape and would have been very costly, as at least 22 different colours of silk, as well as gold, were used. The various symbols suggest it was associated with a birthday: the peony motif signifies wealth and distinction, while the crane and the longevity characters represent good wishes for a long life. HP

199
Robe of tapestry weave silk
with gold thread
China, about 1600

Purchased with a grant donated
by Lady Garner.
V&A FE.41:1-1985

Kesi translates literally as 'weft-woven silk' in modern Chinese. It is used to describe pictorial silk tapestries produced in China from the Tang dynasty (618–907 CE) onwards. Multiple colours of discontinuous weft threads pass through undyed warp threads, enabling the weaving of highly intricate and reversible designs. Early *kesi* from the Song dynasty (960–1279) imitated and at times reproduced famous scrolls and album paintings, bestowing on textiles the status of collectable paintings. In the later Ming and Qing dynasties (1368–1911), fine details such as people's faces were often painted on the woven *kesi* surface using a brush, as in the tapestry panel from the dragon boat festival scene (203). The discontinuous weft technique of tapestry weave allowed garments such as the woman's robe opposite (200) to be woven to shape directly on the loom. YC

200 (OPPOSITE)
Detail of woman's tapestry weave silk robe with metal threads
China, 1800–1900

Purchased with Art Fund support.
V&A T.223-1948

201 (LEFT)
Tapestry weave silk panel
China, about 1900–40

V&A T.180-1948

202 (ABOVE)
Central panel of tapestry weave silk picture
China, 1600–1800

Purchased with Art Fund support.
V&A T.232-1948

203 (FOLLOWING PAGES)
Tapestry weave silk picture showing a dragon boat festival scene
China, 1750–1800

V&A 1647-1900

Since the eighteenth century, Burmese weavers have produced luxurious wave-patterned silks known as *luntaya acheik*, woven by a highly skilled weaver manipulating 100 to 200 weft threads to create the warp patterns. Usually a striking feature of Burmese dress, this example is, in contrast, a magnificent hanging, decorated with Buddhist motifs. FHP

204 (ABOVE)
Young woman wearing a *luntaya acheik* **patterned** *hta-mein* **(woman's skirt)**
Photograph by Philip Klier, 7 August 1906

205 (RIGHT)
Hanging of tapestry weave silk with metal wrapped threads
Burma, about 1850

V&A 9753(IS)

Silk tapestry weaves were used to pattern side and end borders on wrapped garments in several centres in central India, where this sari was made. The structure includes supplementary warp patterning in the border and tapestry weaving in the decorative end, which makes it appear double-sided. AF

206 (RIGHT)
Fragment of a sari of tapestry weave silk with metal wrapped thread
Medak, Telangana, India, about 1867

V&A 4388B/(IS)

This two-tone tubular skirt (*malong landap*) would have been worn by a woman of the Maranao people of Mindanao. The main features are the tapestry-woven strips that hold the tubular garment together. Woven by Muslim weavers, the curvilinear designs on these strips reflect the Islamic love of geometric and stylized patterns. SFC

207 (RIGHT)
Detail of woman's skirt of plain weave silk with tapestry weave silk strips
Mindanao, Philippines, 1900–95

V&A IS.40-1997

Tai weavers often use a multitude of weaving techniques to create a single textile. This densely woven example (208) demonstrates the weaver's mastery of dovetail tapestry and supplementary weft techniques. Some weavers occasionally incorporated tapestry into narrow bands on skirts. Its use as the central portion of this large hanging is a contemporary development. FHP

208 (ABOVE)
Detail of hanging of tapestry weave silk
By Mrs Sasem Khakamphan, Sam Tai district, Hua Phan province, Laos, 2015

V&A IS.14-2017

This Japanese textile cover (209) is called a *fukusa* and would have been draped over a gift. It is woven using the complex, time-consuming technique of tapestry weave velvet in which extra, different coloured pile warps create the pattern. Such velvets are rare as they were only produced for a few years. The motif of a cock, hen and three chicks symbolizes a family living in harmony and may derive from the work of the famous eighteenth-century painter Maruyama Ōkyo. AJ

209 (OPPOSITE)
Detail of gift cover of tapestry weave silk velvet
Probably Kyoto, Japan, about 1860

V&A 361-1880

PILE FABRICS

Velvet is distinguished by the softness and three-dimensionality of its pile, which may be woven in up to three different heights. These examples reveal how the pile can form a pattern by employing threads of different colours, by combining cut and uncut loops, and by leaving the ground weave partially visible. The price of velvet grew with the complexity of its pattern. The most luxurious examples had multiple and polychrome piles and supplementary wefts in precious metal. SB

210 (RIGHT)
Detail of panel of a two-colour voided silk velvet with brocading in silver-gilt thread
Italy, 1425–50

V&A 859-1894

211 (BELOW)
Panel of figured uncut and cut silk velvet, probably intended for the back of a settee
Italy, about 1700

V&A T.80-1958

212 (OPPOSITE)
Detail of dalmatic of voided silk velvet
Venice, Italy, 1400–25

V&A T.87-1912

This jewel-toned velvet fragment (213) evokes the opulence of what was once a Mughal Indian floor spread. The colour of the lac-dyed silk shifts subtly with the direction of the pile, while in the void areas of the flowerheads traces of metal wrapped thread remain. AF

213 (LEFT)
Detail of cut silk velvet
India, possibly Gujarat, about 1700

V&A 281-1893

This velvet (214) was used as a hanging or cover. Elegant male figures, each holding a narcissus flower to his nose, stand on either side of a cypress beside a fish pond. In Persian poetry, handsome youths are conventionally 'as erect as a cypress'. TS

214 (OPPOSITE)
Hanging of cut silk velvet with voided satin ground and metal wrapped threads
Iran, 1550–1620

Purchased with Art Fund support, and the assistance of Mr I. Schwaiger, Selfridge & Co. Ltd, Mr A.F. Kendrick, Mr O.S. Berberyan, G.P. and J. Baker Ltd and Mr A. Benardout.
V&A T.226-1923

In seventeenth-century Iran new designs incorporating recognizable garden flowers challenged an older tradition of conventionalized floral patterns. Here the two traditions are combined, with roses, irises, carnations and lilies arranged in a formal pattern of stylized scrolling tendrils (215). TS

215 (RIGHT)
Length of cut silk velvet
Possibly Isfahan, Iran, 1600–1700

V&A 733-1892

The design of the flowers on this border (216) dates to about the 1640s, when the Mughal floral style first began appearing on textiles. Single, naturalistic, whole flowers are arranged in characteristically ordered rows, the lilies formed of silk pile against a ground of silver wrapped thread. The weavers used pile warp substitution, a technique borrowed from Iran, to add extra colours of silk. AF

216 (BELOW)
Border of floor spread of cut silk velvet with silver wrapped thread
Possibly Ahmedabad, Gujarat, India, about 1640–50

V&A 320-1898

This floor spread's pattern incorporates three popular motifs of the seventeenth century: cypress trees, naturalistic whole flowers and a scrolling border of flowerheads (217). Silk velvets were among the most expensive and highly prized textiles ever made in India. They were used on floors and walls and as door hangings, balustrade covers, tent panels and canopies, furnishing fabric and animal trappings. AF

217
Floor spread of cut silk velvet
Possibly Ahmedabad, Gujarat, India, 1650–1700

V&A IS.16-1947

The close stylistic and structural similarities between Mughal (Indian) and Safavid (Iranian) velvets of the seventeenth and eighteenth centuries often make differentiating between the two challenging. The colours of this velvet fragment (218) come from the domestic Indian dyes lac and indigo, and the latticed design of naturalistic leaves and flowerheads reflects the Mughal style. AF

218 (ABOVE)
Fragment of cut silk velvet
Possibly Gujarat, India, 1650–1700

V&A 664A-1883

Large-scale floral patterns were characteristic of Ottoman silks in the mid- to late sixteenth century. Here flattened tulip shapes rise from a complex 'stem' and end in a tiny pomegranate finial (219). A large gilt rosette lies towards the base of each flower. Arrangements of floral forms in red complete the pattern. TS

219 (ABOVE RIGHT)
Strip of cut silk velvet with metal wrapped threads
Probably Bursa, Turkey, 1550–1600

V&A 1061-1900

Cushions played an important role in furnishing Ottoman houses. After 1600 the velvet weavers of Bursa in north-west Turkey turned to the production of cushion covers with a standard form – rectangular, with a row of woven-in lappets at either end. The main field was filled with a wide variety of inventive patterns, usually based on earlier Ottoman textile designs. Large numbers were exported to Europe. TS

220 (OPPOSITE)
Cushion cover of cut silk velvet with metal wrapped threads
Possibly Bursa, Turkey, 1650–1700

V&A 4061-1856

In Europe men's waistcoats might be cut from a length of velvet or woven to shape, like the eighteenth-century example below (222). Three different weave effects create a variety of tonal effects, throwing the monochrome design into relief – a trail of roses climbs along the hems and front edges and across the pocket flaps against a lozenge-patterned background. In the nineteenth-century waistcoat (221), cut and uncut velvet are complemented by horizontal and vertical stripes in two ribbed effects. By this date, waistcoats offered an opportunity for men to brighten their otherwise relatively sombre attire. SN/CKB

221 (RIGHT)
Waistcoat of cut and uncut silk velvet with vertical stripes of *cannelé* and horizontal stripes of weft-faced ribbing
Britain, 1840–50

Given by Mary Gifford.
V&A T.150-1996

222 (BELOW)
Detail of man's waistcoat of cut and uncut silk velvet with voided satin ground
France or Britain, 1750–60

V&A 664-1898

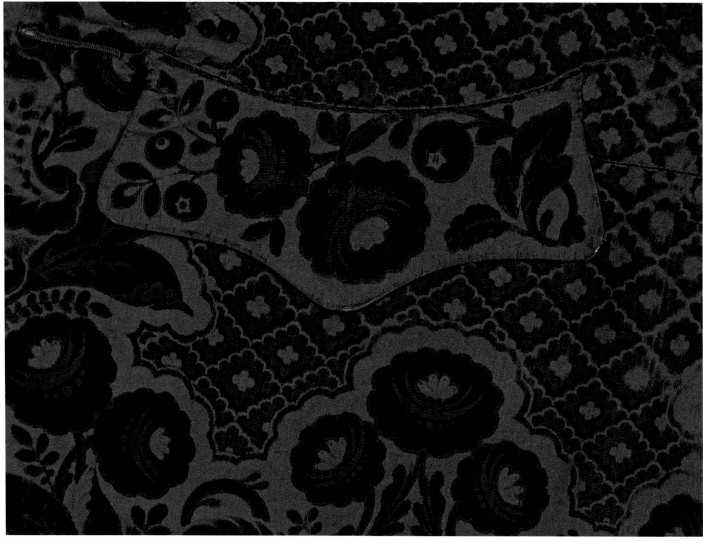

Velvet became fashionable for garments and furnishings during the Ming and Qing dynasties (1368–1911), the cities of Zhangzhou and Nanjing in the Fujian and Jiangsu provinces being the centres of production. So great was the production in Zhangzhou that the colloquial term for velvet was '*Zhang Rong*'. This length was probably intended for a Chinese woman's robe. YC

223
Detail of cut and uncut silk velvet with voided satin ground
China, 1850–80

V&A 435-1882

Carpets with a silk pile and extensive areas brocaded with metal wrapped thread began to be produced in substantial numbers in seventeenth-century Iran. Many were exported, especially to Poland, giving rise to the name 'Polonaise' for the type. Most have muted colours. The usual explanation – that silk holds dye less well than wool – is simply not true. The paler colours must have been a deliberate choice. It may be that the new type of carpet was appreciated principally for the sheen and brilliance of the expensive materials employed. TS

224 (RIGHT)
Carpet fragment of knotted silk pile on a silk foundation with brocading in metal wrapped thread
Possibly Isfahan, Iran, 1600–25

V&A T.36-1954

225 (OPPOSITE)
Carpet of knotted silk pile on cotton warp and wool and silk weft, with brocading in metal wrapped thread
Possibly Isfahan, Iran, 1600–50

Bequest of George Salting.
V&A T.404-1910

JACQUARD-WOVEN FABRICS

The pair of portraits of Queen Victoria and Prince Albert may have been made to showcase the remarkable detail that could be achieved on jacquard looms, which had been patented less than 60 years before in France. A century later similar portraits of rulers were still being woven, such as this example of Chairman Mao, which was produced in China in hundreds of thousands for propaganda purposes. Much larger than the portraits of Victoria and Albert, these souvenirs of events in Mao Zedong's life were hung in homes and offices and received as rewards for personal and political achievements. RH/SFC

BELOW (226 & 227)
Portraits of Queen Victoria and Prince Albert of jacquard-woven silk
After engravings by F. Bacon, based on a painting by William Charles Ross
By Barrallon et Brossard, Saint-Étienne, France, about 1861
V&A AP.119-1862 & AP.120-1862

228 (OPPOSITE)
Portrait of Chairman Mao Zedong of jacquard-woven silk
Based on the 1964 official portrait by an unidentified photographer, retouched by Chen Shilin
Hangzhou Brocade Factory, Hangzhou, China, 1972–6
Given by Andrew Bolton.
V&A FE.8-2001

毛泽东同志

中国杭州织锦厂制　27×40公分

The manufacturer Daniel Walters & Son was a family firm that relocated to Essex from London. Descendants still weave silk in East Anglia today. This silk (229), with its design of roses, shamrocks and thistles representing England, Ireland and Scotland, was well suited to cover the walls of the ballroom at Buckingham Palace where foreign dignitaries were received. It was taken down in 1902, a year after Queen Victoria's death. JL

229 (OPPOSITE)
Furnishing fabric of jacquard-woven silk
Designed by Prince Albert, woven by Daniel Walters & Son, Braintree, Essex, England, 1856

Given by the manufacturer.
V&A 4759A-1859

This silk (230) was possibly designed by Owen Jones, or inspired by his preparations for his publication *The Grammar of Ornament*. Subtle depth is created by contrasting a satin weave for the blue elements with a twill weave in the other colours. Despite the title of this design, it was not in fact inspired by the Alhambra, but by ornaments in the late fifteenth-century New Mosque in Constantinople (now Istanbul), illustrated in Jones's volume (231). CKB

230 (RIGHT)
Alhambresque, furnishing fabric of jacquard-woven silk
By Daniel Keith & Co., probably London, England, 1855

Given by Warner & Sons Ltd.
V&A T.132-1972

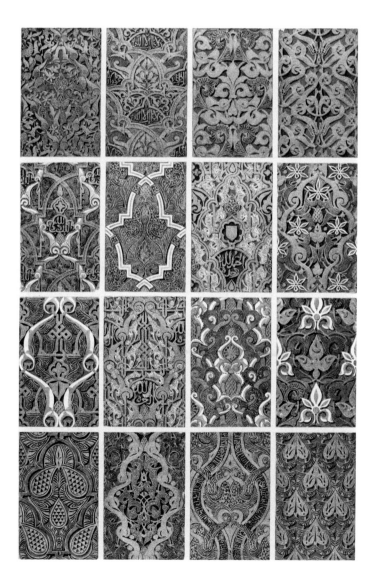

231 (LEFT)
Preparatory drawing of plate for *The Grammar of Ornament* by Owen Jones, Britain, before 1856
Pen, bodycolour and gilding on paper

V&A 1614

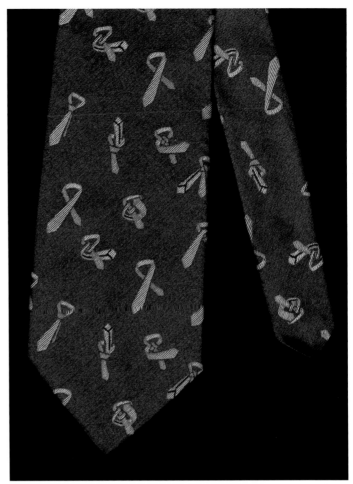

A necktie can lighten the sobriety of a traditional suit. This staple of men's wardrobes becomes a wearable artwork when featuring imagery by the artist Pablo Picasso (232). It bears the label 'SPADEM', a French organization that protects artists' intellectual property rights. In contrast, Moschino's witty diagrams (233) poke fun at a ritual of male dressing through their step-by-step instructions on how to tie a necktie. SS

232 (ABOVE LEFT)
Necktie of jacquard-woven silk with reproduction of an artwork by Pablo Picasso
France, probably 1960–70

Given by Martin Battersby.
V&A T.260-1967

233 (ABOVE)
Necktie of jacquard-woven silk
By Franco Moschino, Italy, 1991

V&A T.141-1991

This silk (234) was the vibrant star among the gowns in Lady Mary Eliza Ingram's wardrobe at the time of her death in 1925. The jacquard-woven oranges are expertly shaded to appear three-dimensional, so tactile they could almost be plucked off the silk. Yet the weaver used only two colours to achieve this effect. RH

234 (OPPOSITE)
Detail of dress of jacquard-woven silk
Britain, 1890–5

Given by the Ingram family.
V&A T.201-1927

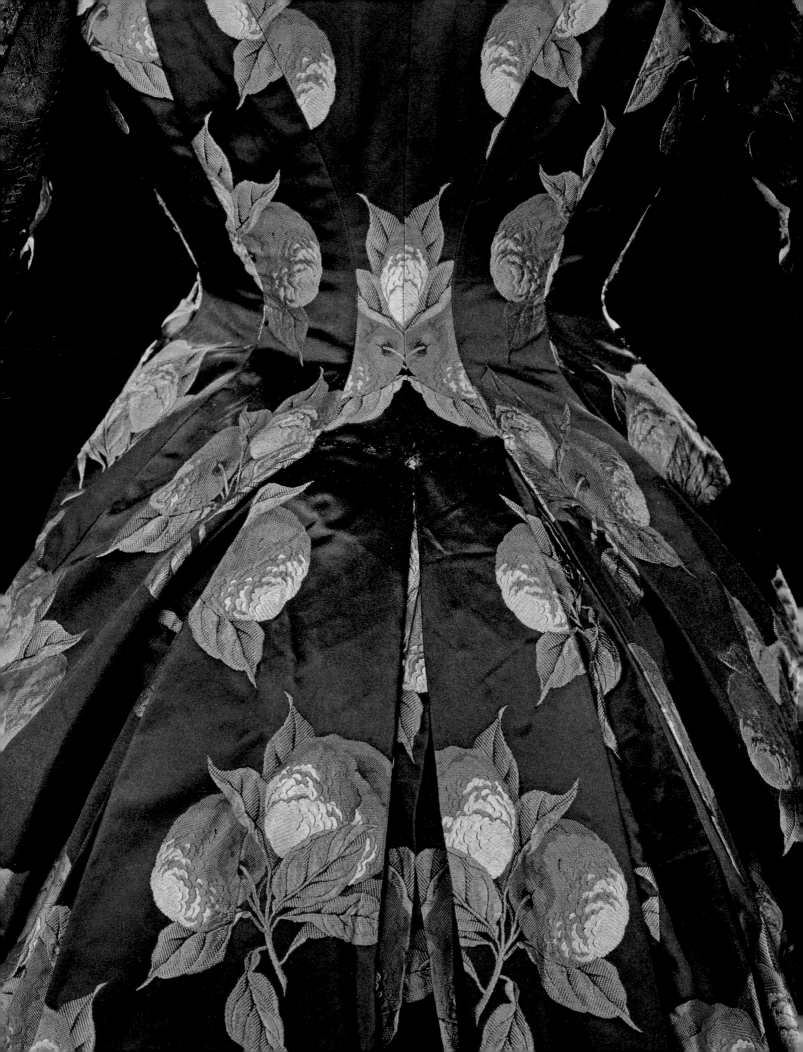

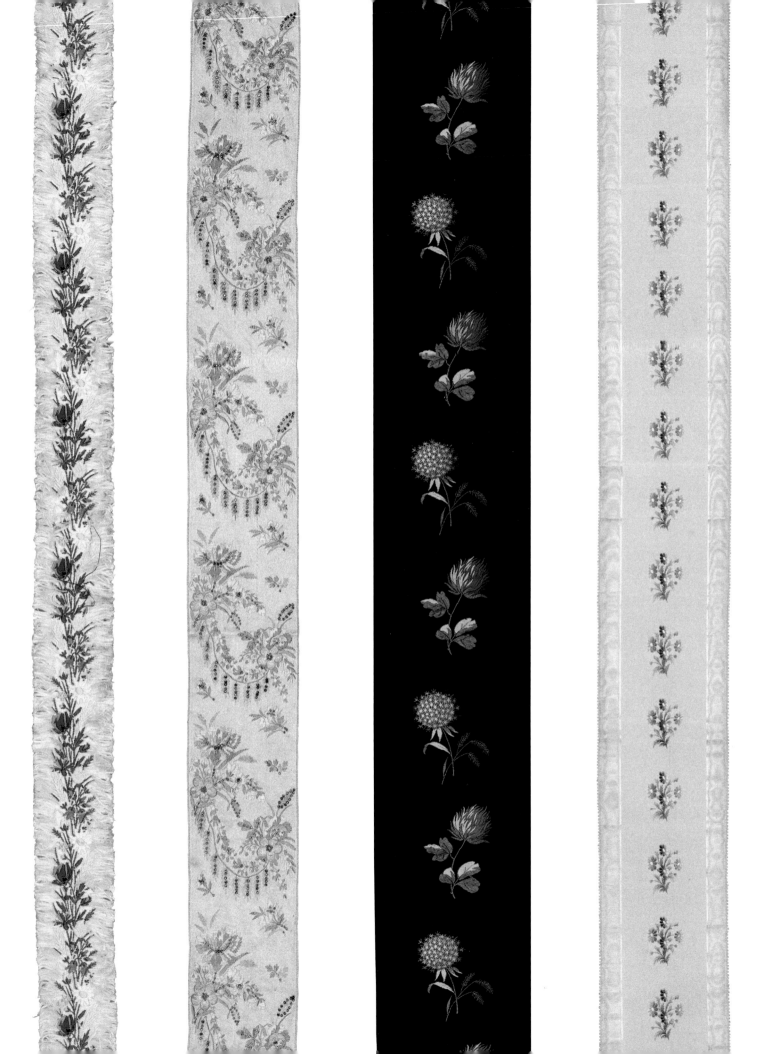

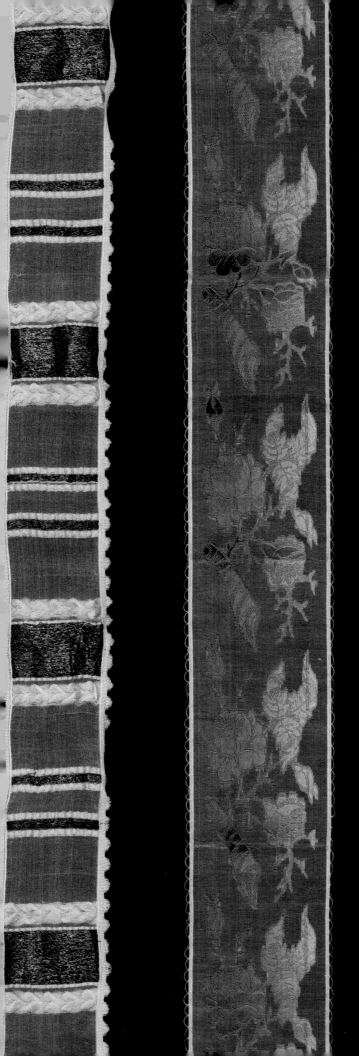

RIBBONS

Flushing, like brocading, is a technique in which supplementary threads are introduced into localized areas during weaving to create often elaborate and colourful design features. It refers to additional warp threads, whereas brocading relates to weft threads. These nineteenth-century ribbons have a variety of grounds, from dense ribbed weave such as *gros de Tours* to translucent gauze. Their motifs are formed using variations on flushing and brocading. The most complex (236) has four supplementary silk threads and one metal thread that creates small flower petals. Faceted beads were hand-sewn onto the ribbon as a final touch of embellishment. HF

235 (OPPOSITE, FAR LEFT)
Gros de Tours plain weave silk with brocading
England, 1850–60

Bequeathed by Miss M.E. Pleydell-Bouverie.
V&A T.325A&B-1965

236 (OPPOSITE, CENTRE LEFT)
Satin weave silk with brocading and beads
Possibly England or France, 1880–90

Given by Mrs James Leahy.
V&A T.364-1971

237 (OPPOSITE, CENTRE RIGHT)
Jacquard-woven silk
England or France, about 1860

Given by Miss F.M. Purnell.
V&A T.157-1965

238 (OPPOSITE, RIGHT)
Plain and satin weave silk with flushing and *gros de Tours* weave and looped-weft edge
Britain or France, 1800–50

Given by Miss B. Hinton.
V&A T.149-1971

239 (THIS PAGE, FAR LEFT)
Gauze weave silk with brocading, the borders of scalloped, looped weft threads, *gros de Tours* and satin weaves
Britain, 1825–49

Given by Miss C. Frewer.
V&A T.135A-1959

240 (LEFT)
Plain weave silk with brocading, flushing and scalloped, looped edge
Britain, 1820–40

Given by Mrs E.B. Thorn.
V&A T.116-1962

These ribbons (241–245) reveal the variety of effects achieved in the weaving of narrow wares. The first imitates the appearance of lace, woven with a black weft and black and yellow warp. A few strands of black warp threads on either side of the ribbon divide the borders from the centre design (241 and 242). This feature ingeniously makes the ribbon reversible. In contrast, the ribbon samples in two colourways (243 and 244) incorporate a range of weave techniques to create a complex texture that looks like *ciselé* velvet. The number and type of threads make a stiff, thick ribbon with areas that appear padded. The much broader ribbon (245) was a demonstration piece for display at the Great Exhibition in London in 1851 and is typical of those manufactured to trim fashionable bonnets and dresses. Coventry was the main English centre of production, which is why this style of ribbon became known as the Coventry 'Town Ribbon'. HF

LEFT (241 & 242)
Back and front of ribbons of jacquard-woven silk, Britain, 1860–80

Given by Mrs D.E. Whitcher.
V&A T.123-1972

243 (OPPOSITE ABOVE) & 244 (CENTRE)
Ribbons of jacquard-woven silk with metal thread, France, 1870–1900

Given by Jackie Unsworth.
V&A T.32&A-1990

245 (OPPOSITE)
Ribbon of jacquard-woven silk By M. Clack, Coventry, England, 1850–1

V&A AP.394:2

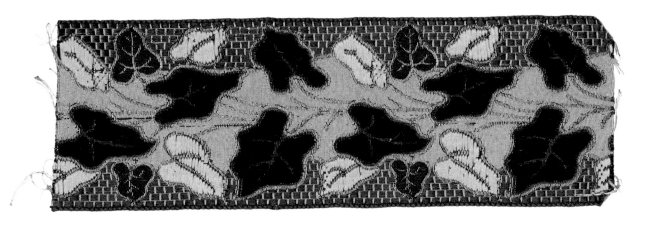

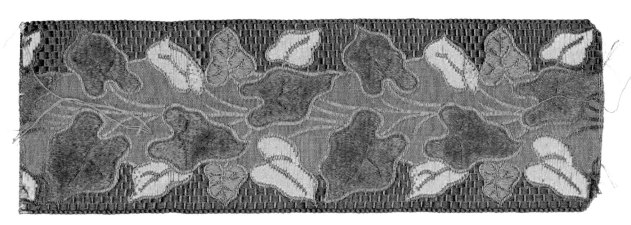

GOLD AND SILVER

This sash was one of the Tunisian textiles acquired from London's Great Exhibition in 1851 and one of the first African objects in the Victoria and Albert Museum's collection. Such textiles were praised as exhibiting 'true principles' of design and the appropriate 'fit' of ornament to form. A sash like this would have been wound several times around the waist, with the decorated ends hanging ostentatiously in front. MRO

246
Man's sash of lampas weave silk with gilt-metal thread
Probably Tunis, Tunisia, about 1850

V&A 761-1852

Between the sixteenth and nineteenth centuries, *patka* waist sashes were an essential male accessory in courtly Indian fashion. The richest examples were woven of silk with decorative ends and borders worked in silver-gilt (247 and 248). Compound structures of interlaced and brocaded layers made these sashes some of the most opulent and technically complex textiles ever produced in India. Rows of naturalistic flowers at either end became a popular design motif under the Mughal empire in the mid-seventeenth century and remained in vogue until *patkas* fell out of fashion altogether in the nineteenth century. AF

247 (OPPOSITE)
Waist sash in plain and compound weaves in silk and metal wrapped thread
Probably Gujarat, India, about 1700–30

V&A 317-1907

248 (OPPOSITE)
Waist sash in plain and compound weaves in silk and metal wrapped threads
Probably Gujarat, India, about 1700–30
V&A IM.25-1936

This silk garment (249) was probably designed to be swathed several times around the waist as a large and luxurious wrapper, a popular style of courtly accessory for men in nineteenth-century India. The contrasting colours of the double-faced silk field would be revealed as the sash was twisted around the body, culminating with the deep silver-gilt end border at the front. AF

249 (RIGHT)
Wrapped garment of double-faced silk with tapestry weave borders and end in silk and metal wrapped threads
Pune, Maharashtra, India, about 1855
V&A 0785(IS)

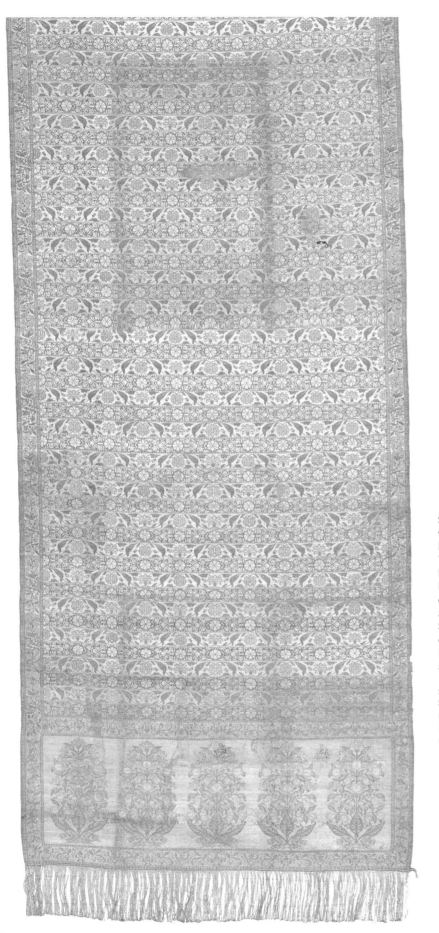

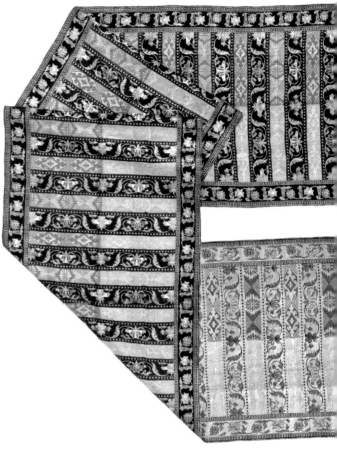

Sashes of this type (250) were worn around the waist by Iranian men of high rank. They were also exported in large numbers. This example bears a stamp with a later date of 1746, when it belonged to a local ruler in southern India. Sashes formed part of the orientalizing costume adopted by the Polish nobility in the seventeenth century. TS

250 (LEFT)
Sash of silk with brocading in silver-gilt wrapped thread
Iran, 1700–25

V&A T.49-1923

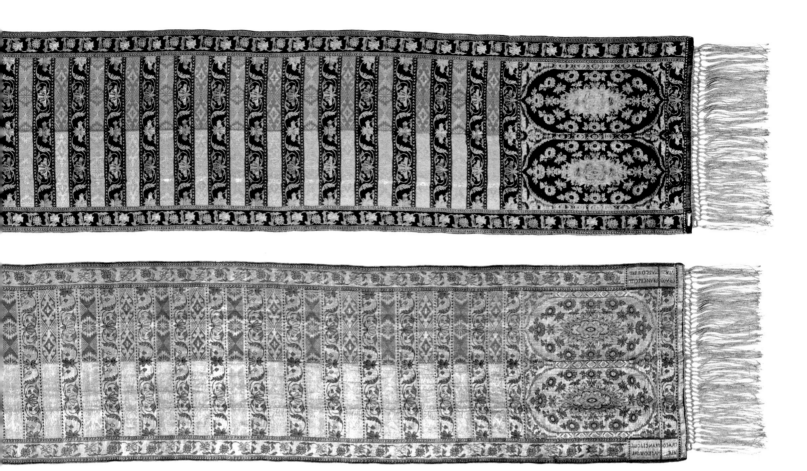

Polish noblemen adopted sashes as a prominent feature of national dress during the seventeenth and eighteenth centuries (252). From around 1740, these previously imported items began to be woven in Poland under the direction of Armenian weavers. The most beautiful and original designs, combining Iranian, Chinese and Turkish motifs, were produced in Słuck. This example (251) from Masłowski's workshop in Kraków could be folded to display any of four possible colourways, the brightest part worn for festive events, the dark background for sombre occasions. LEM

251 (ABOVE)
Sash of compound weave silk with gold, silver and silver-gilt threads
By Francis Masłowski, Kraków, Poland, 1786–1806

V&A T.98-1968

252 (RIGHT)
Portrait of Stanislaw Kulbicki
By Józef Peszka, 1791
Oil on canvas

National Museum, Warsaw

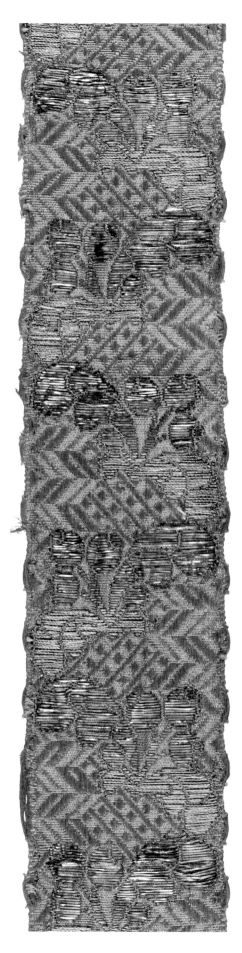

Silk ribbons were used in the eighteenth century for a multitude of utilitarian and decorative purposes, to tie, edge or ornament garments and furnishings. Simple ones could be bought at fairs or from travelling pedlars, more elaborate ones from the high-class retailers in major cities. Their weaving was carried out in a number of European centres, the most complex in Lyon, Paris and Tours and later in Saint-Chamond and Saint-Étienne in France. There, guild regulations stipulated ribbons had to be less than 40 cm in width, at least 10 cm narrower than a dress silk. LEM

(253, 254 & 255) OPPOSITE
Ribbons of silk with brocading in silk and metal threads
Probably France, 1700–20, 1720–70 and 1740–60

V&A 1354-1871, 1355-1871 & 1357-1871

Designed by Lucien Lelong for the 1925 Paris International Exhibition of Modern Decorative and Industrial Arts, this dress (256) illustrates the influence of East Asian art and culture on European fashion in the 1920s. The design is centred around two Chinese dragons woven in golden metal thread and embellished with beading (detail, 257). The design plays with weight and movement, contrasting the dark, heavy blue silk satin with the lightweight beaded pale silk chiffon. EM

256 (RIGHT) & 257 (FOLLOWING PAGES)
Dress of silk chiffon, with band of satin weave silk with metal wrapped silk warp and band of blue satin weave silk with supplementary metal wrapped silk weft
By Lucien Lelong, Paris, 1925

Given by Mrs William Gordon.
V&A T.50-1948

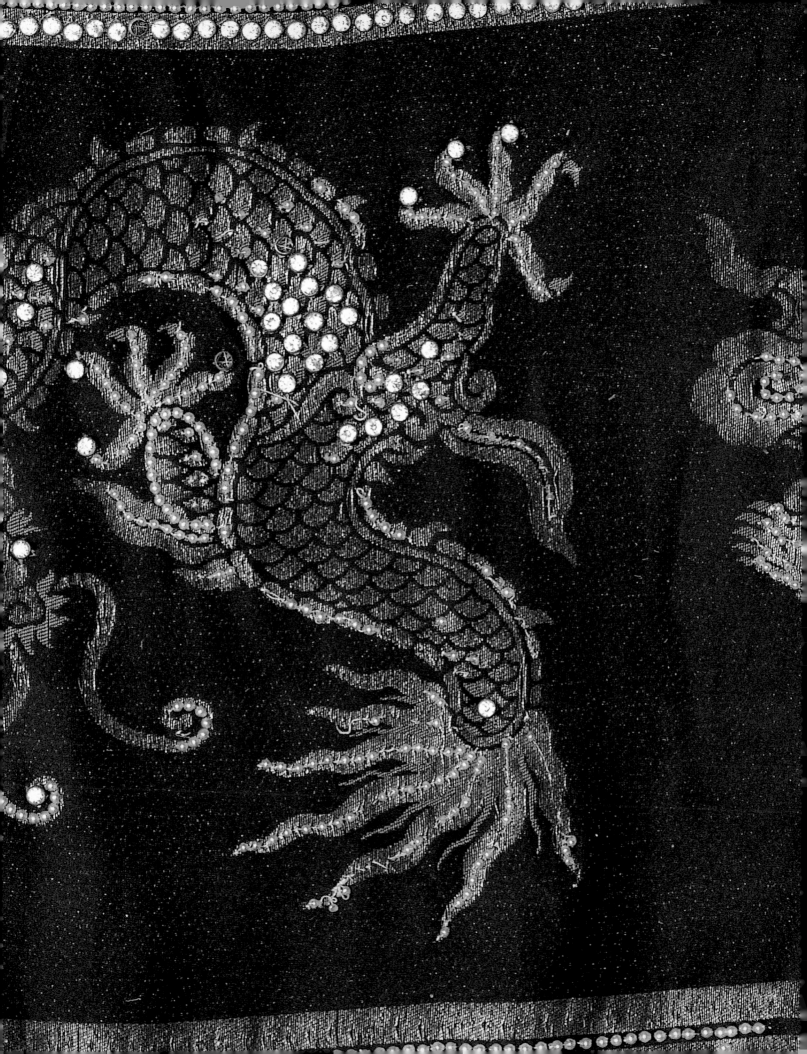

WOVEN IN CHINA, TAILORED IN ITALY

258 (BELOW)
Man's banyan made of a woven-
to-shape Chinese imperial robe
(1730–50) of satin weave silk
brocaded with gold thread and
peacock feathers, Italy, 1740–60

V&A T.77:1-2009

259 (BELOW RIGHT)
Matching waistcoat, Italy, 1740–60

V&A T.77:2-2009

260 (OPPOSITE)
Magnified view of peacock feather
yarns from waistcoat

V&A T.77:2-2009

Exchanges between China and Italy were frequent in the sixteenth century, with the imperial courts fascinated by European art and technology. Italian artists such as Giovanni Gherardini, Matteo Ripa and Giuseppe Castiglioni were working in Beijing in the early eighteenth century.[12] This Italian banyan and waistcoat (258 and 259) made of an imperial Chinese dragon robe tell a story of these two cultures united by the beauty of a brocaded silk, which a Yongzheng or Qianlong emperor probably gave to a favoured Italian at his court.

The silk was woven in a design with nine dragons to make a robe for a member of the Chinese imperial family. Imperial robes came in four colours – yellow, red, blue and 'moon white' (pale blue) – appropriate to the temples where offerings were given.[13] This one was a particularly luxurious production as the eyebrows and hair of the dragons have been woven with a silk yarn entwined with peacock feathers (260).[14]

The silk dates to before 1750, when the Emperor Qianlong changed and standardized the design of the robes. After 1750 the clouds were always shown in five colours and parallel, diagonal lines representing 'standing water' appeared at the hem, growing deeper in later decades (following pages: 261 and 262).

The shapes of a robe were worked on two lengths of silk, stitched together at centre back, with another length of silk sewn to the centre front to wrap over and fasten above the right chest (261). However, an imperial robe did not materialize from this silk. Instead it became a fashionable informal gown – in the latest style known as a banyan – with a sleeved waistcoat for an Italian gentleman. His tailor made a front opening by unpicking the centre-front seam. The under-front of the robe became the waistcoat fronts, with areas of brocaded silk at their hems (p. 221: 263 and 264). The tailor cut the plain silk around the brocaded shapes to make the sleeves and back of the waistcoat. Sleeved waistcoats were going out of fashion by the mid-eighteenth century, so this ensemble was probably made before 1760. SFC/SN

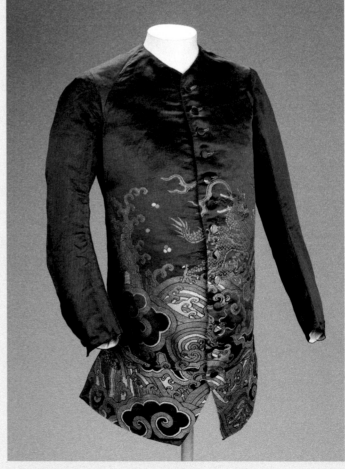

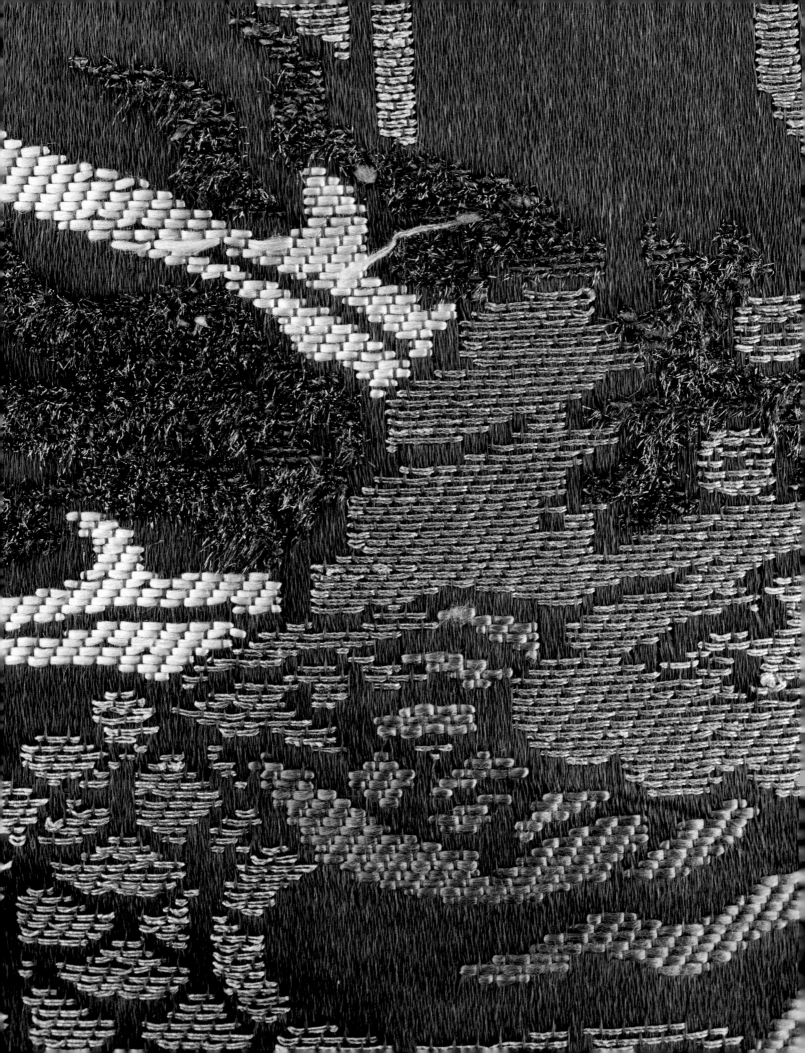

文七品蟒
袍圖

261 (ABOVE)
Dragon robe for a civil official of the
seventh rank, page from manuscript
of 'Illustrated Regulations for
Ceremonial Paraphenalia of the
Present Dynasty Qing Dynasty',
1750–9. Ink and colour on silk

V&A D.1949-1900

262 (OPPOSITE LEFT)
Embroidered imperial robe, uncut,
showing the back and front pieces
with an additional front piece to
overlap, China, about 1850

V&A CIRC.305-1935

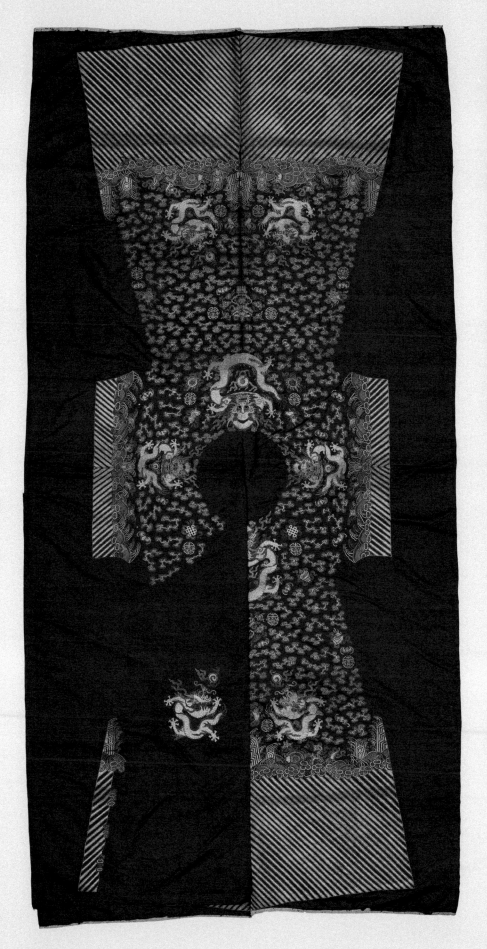

263 (TOP)
Conjectured design of the robe
as woven

264 (ABOVE)
Conjectured cut of the waistcoat
from the underside of the
robe front

WOVEN IN INDIA: RAJESH PRATAP SINGH MEETS WILLIAM MORRIS

The striking tasar silk sari (267) was designed by Rajesh Pratap Singh and handwoven by Haji Sharfuddin in Varanasi, a city in north India famous for its brocade weaving. Pratap Singh has long been fascinated by the work of William Morris, the nineteenth-century English textile designer and advocate of handmade craftsmanship (265). In this sari made for his 2018 collection entitled 'Welcome to the Jungle', Pratap Singh merges Morris's classic *Brer Rabbit* design (266) with the Indian imagery of Rudyard Kipling's *The Jungle Book* (1894).

A sari is an unstitched garment, usually five to nine metres long with a central field encompassed by borders along both lengths and a decorative end called a *pallu* that is draped over the shoulder. Pratap Singh has created a golden *pallu* in which he replaces Morris's song thrushes with parrots while rabbits make way for howling wolves and roaring tigers (268). The rhythmic pairing of birds and animals references the sixteenth-

and seventeenth-century European silks that inspired Morris in his designs.

Motifs from the *pallu* are woven throughout the sari: parrots sit gracefully on a line running along the bottom border, their chests made up of delicate flowers, and dotted across the field are the same flowers just slightly enlarged.

The use of tasar silk gives the sari an elegant muted tone and lends weight to the fabric, making it easier to drape. Red silk thread is subtly incorporated into the weave: the flowers have red centres, the eyes of the tigers and wolves glare in red, and in the left-hand corner of the *pallu* glows a fierce roaring tiger (269), burning bright, as it alone is woven entirely in red.

Morris was an admirer of Indian artisan skills and were he alive today he would most likely have appreciated the fine detailing of this sari. It represents a meeting of two cultures through high quality craftsmanship and design, across time and boundaries. DP

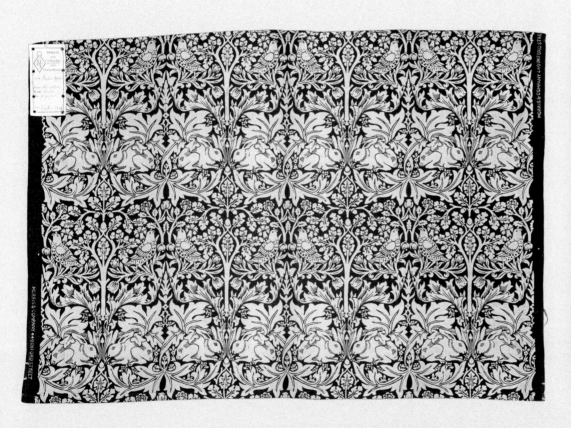

265 (ABOVE)
Sample of *Brer Rabbit* furnishing textile of indigo-discharged and block printed cotton, also sometimes known as *Brother Rabbit*, by William Morris, Merton Abbey, London, England, 1880–1

V&A T.648-1919

266 (ABOVE RIGHT)
Digital design sheet showing the *Brer Rabbit* print, by Rajesh Pratap Singh

267 (OPPOSITE RIGHT)
Silk sari with gold brocading, from the 'Welcome to the Jungle' collection, designed by Rajesh Pratap Singh, Delhi, India, 2018. Photograph

Courtesy of the designer.
V&A IS.1495:1-2019

268 (OPPOSITE, ABOVE LEFT)
Digital design sheet showing Rajesh Pratap Singh's adaptation of the Brer Rabbit print

269 (OPPOSITE, BELOW LEFT)
Close-up of the *pallu* of the sari quarter length showing red tiger.

V&A IS.1495:1-2019

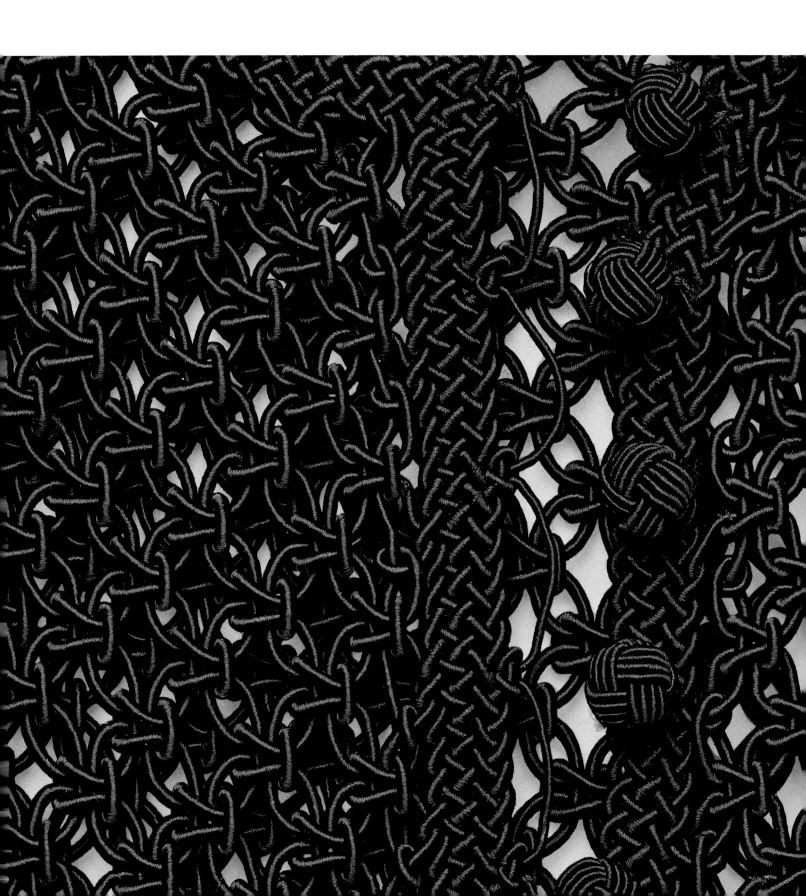

Twine and Twist, Net, Knot and Knit

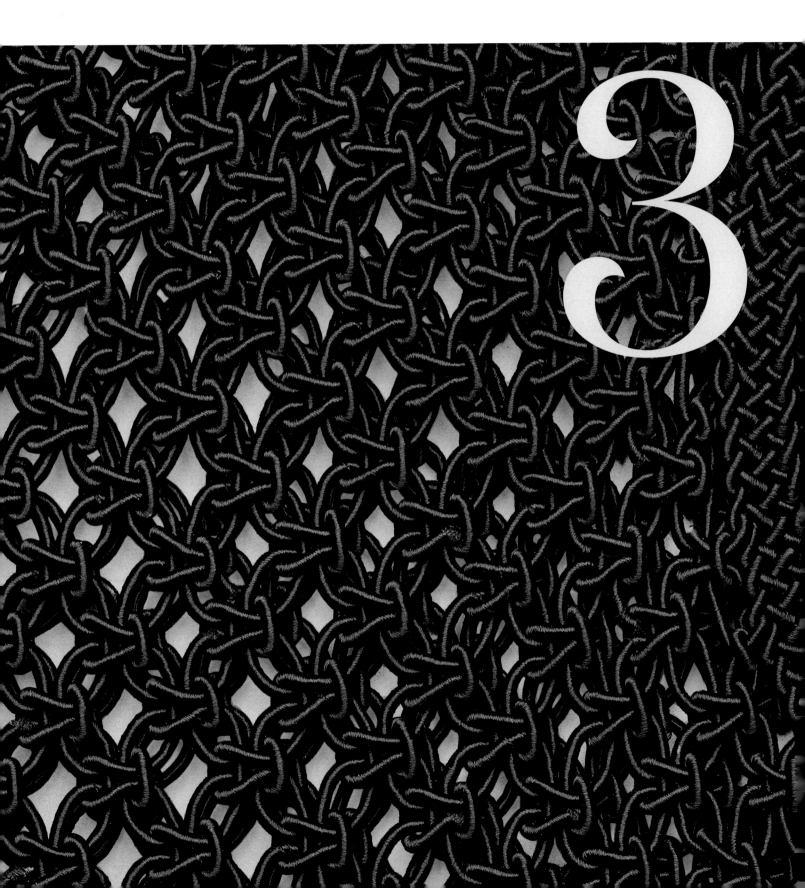

3

Twine and Twist, Net, Knot and Knit

270 (ABOVE)
Woman plaiting threads, Guangzhou, China, about 1790. Watercolour on paper

V&A D.53-1898

271 (OPPOSITE LEFT)
Maker of braided cords, from the series *Collection of Fashionable Artisans* by Utagawa Sadahide, Tokyo, Japan, about 1840. Woodblock print on paper

V&A E.14730:18-1886

272 (OPPOSITE RIGHT)
Book of patterns for purse strings, Britain, 1625–50. Vellum, paper, ink, braided silks and metal threads

Given by the National Library of Wales, from the Frank Ward Bequest.
V&A T.313-1960

The properties that make silk so desirable for weaving – its sheen, smooth texture and absorption of vivid dyes – make it equally attractive for a variety of techniques. Silk has been used around the globe to create beautiful materials and objects in lace, crochet, knitting, macramé, netting, passementerie and sprang. Their production was part of the luxury textile trades worldwide, usually fashioned by men professionally, but also created by elite women for their own use and gifts. Like weaving and embroidery, the precise origins of many of these techniques are unknown. They developed independently on various continents, required simple tools – if any – and instructions for them were passed down orally for centuries, rarely described in print before the nineteenth century. Little documentation of their use remains. Archaeological digs have revealed scant evidence of them, no doubt because of silk's relative fragility, so we have only a few surviving objects on which to build their history.

A variety of textiles and trimmings from around the world can be created by twining or twisting yarns. Netting is the simplest and oldest, twisting a single strand of yarn around itself, using a single tool with a notch at each end, to create an open-textured textile. When executed with silk yarn, it creates a very fine, almost transparent textile, which can be used for veils and is sometimes embellished with embroidery (276).

Another form of 'knotless netting', known in Europe by the Swedish word 'sprang', is made by stringing a continuous warp on a frame and then twisting the strands together to create an open mesh-like fabric. This technique is ancient and used throughout the Americas, Europe, Central and South Asia and the Middle East. By virtue of its unique method of making – both ends worked with each manoeuvre of the yarn – sprang is quick to produce. The resulting fabric has considerable stretch, a quality difficult to achieve before the invention of modern elastics. These properties made sprang particularly useful for drawstrings for trousers worn by men and women in India, as well as the sashes of army officers' uniforms in eighteenth-century

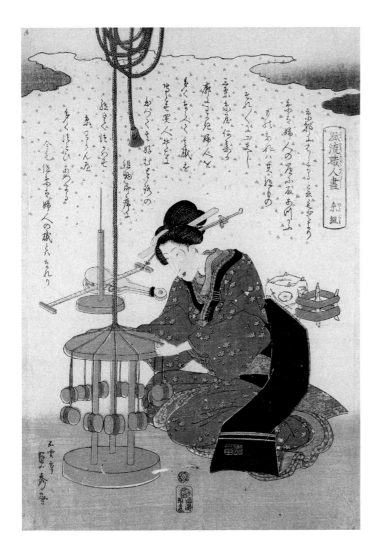

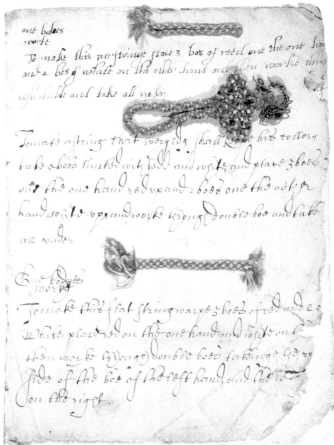

Britain. In India, these were produced domestically and also by specialist 'weavers'.[1] In Britain, they were probably made by the silk women who produced a wide range of 'narrow wares' (ribbons and laces).

A variation of twisting is braiding, where more than two threads cross over each other. Braiding is the foundation of many forms of cording with a wide range of uses around the globe (270). In Korea knotting has been an important art form for centuries. Silk was fashioned into cords of various structures made with even numbers of strands. A single cord was worked into an elaborate knot inspired by everyday things and nature, such as the dragonfly and lotus bud. Knotting adorned furnishings and musical instruments, and fastened accessories such as swords, as well as being worn as jewellery. Braided cords (*kumihimo*) were elaborately knotted for either functional or purely decorative purposes in Japan. Braiding created fine silk cords in a variety of structures (271), such as *marudai*,

tsukushi and *karakumi*.[2] These were used for many purposes including lacing together pieces of armour, threading *inrō*, *netsuke* and *ojime*,[3] securing and embellishing clothing and making belts. In Tang-dynasty China (618–907 CE), braided silk ribbons worked in a range of colours and patterns were used as wrapper ties for Buddhist scrolls. Other braids edged the borders of clothing, and in the 'braid embroidery' of the Miao in south-west China, these were couched to festive garments. Silk cord, known as frogging in Europe, was stitched to clothing in decorative loops and knots as a fastening. Finger-looped silk cords ending in intricate finials were used as purse strings in seventeenth-century England and manuscripts survive with instructions and samples of different patterns (272). The structures of these cords were similar but achieved in different ways, using tools specific to each culture and period.

Twisted and plaited threads are also the foundation of the European technique of bobbin lace, where they are

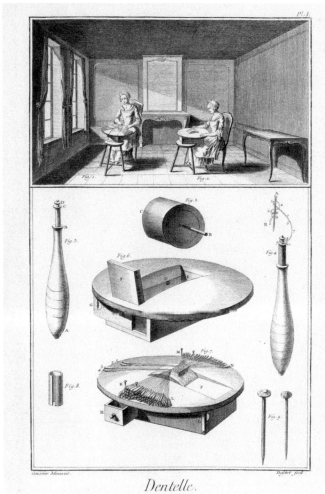

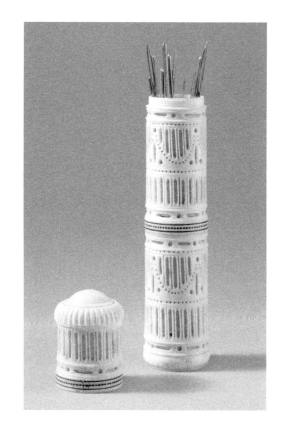

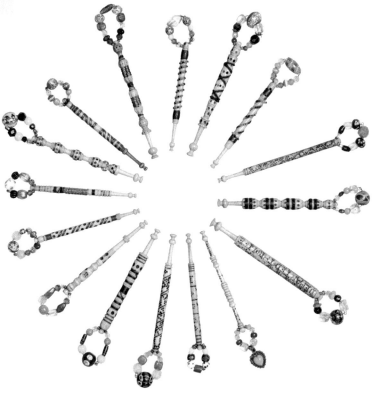

273 (ABOVE)
Lace, published in Diderot and d'Alembert, vol. 28 (Paris 1772), p. I. Engraving

274 (ABOVE RIGHT)
Netting tools, Britain, 1800–1900

Given by Mrs J. Taylor.
V&A T.287-1979

275 (RIGHT)
Bone, metal and glass-bead lace bobbins, Buckinghamshire, England, 1853

Given by Miss E.M. Turnham.
V&A T.25-1936

worked around a series of pins set in a particular pattern (273 and 275). Needle lace was buttonhole stitched over threads laid on parchment, which was then cut away. Both types used fine linen yarns, but as silk absorbs dyes more easily it can be used for coloured as well as white laces.

Knotting is another simple manipulation of thread that constructs nets and meshes from a single yarn (274). Nets of coarse fibres have been used for fishing, hunting and carrying around the globe for millennia. When fashioned from silk, nets contained and styled the hair (277), and were used for bags, gloves, veils and aprons.

Knotting with multiple yarns has been used for centuries to create yet another range of textiles and trimmings. Sailors employ a variety of knots for both practical and decorative purposes, such as lanyards. The use of knotting to make fringes appears to have developed in the Middle East and was introduced into Iberia, the rest of Europe and Asia via trade (278). In China knotted silk fringes embellish the hems of court dress. Woven and embroidered silks edged with fringing were used for the elaborate saddlery worn by camels, elephants and horses in the Middle East, India and Europe respectively. When knotting became a fashionable craft in nineteenth-century Europe, it was named 'macramé', either from the Arabic *miqramah*, Turkish *makrama* or Persian *meqrameh*, terms referring to functional textiles that often have a knotted fringe.

276 (TOP)
Cap of silk net with silk trim and embroidery in silk, about 1400. Treasury of the Cathedral of St Paul, Liège, Belgium. Inv. 462

277 (ABOVE)
Silk hairnet and curls, Britain, about 1840

V&A T.23-1936

278 (LEFT)
Man and two boys making a fringe for an elephant by John Lockwood Kipling, India, 1870. Pen, pencil and wash on paper

V&A 0929:44(IS)

279 (LEFT)
Silk fringe and tassels, Melville bed (illustrated in full on p. 22), Britain, about 1700

Given by the Rt Hon. the Earl of Melville.
V&A W.35-1949

280 (OPPOSITE)
Silk knotted fringe for a bed hanging, China, 1930–40

Supported by the Friends of the V&A.
V&A FE.75-1995

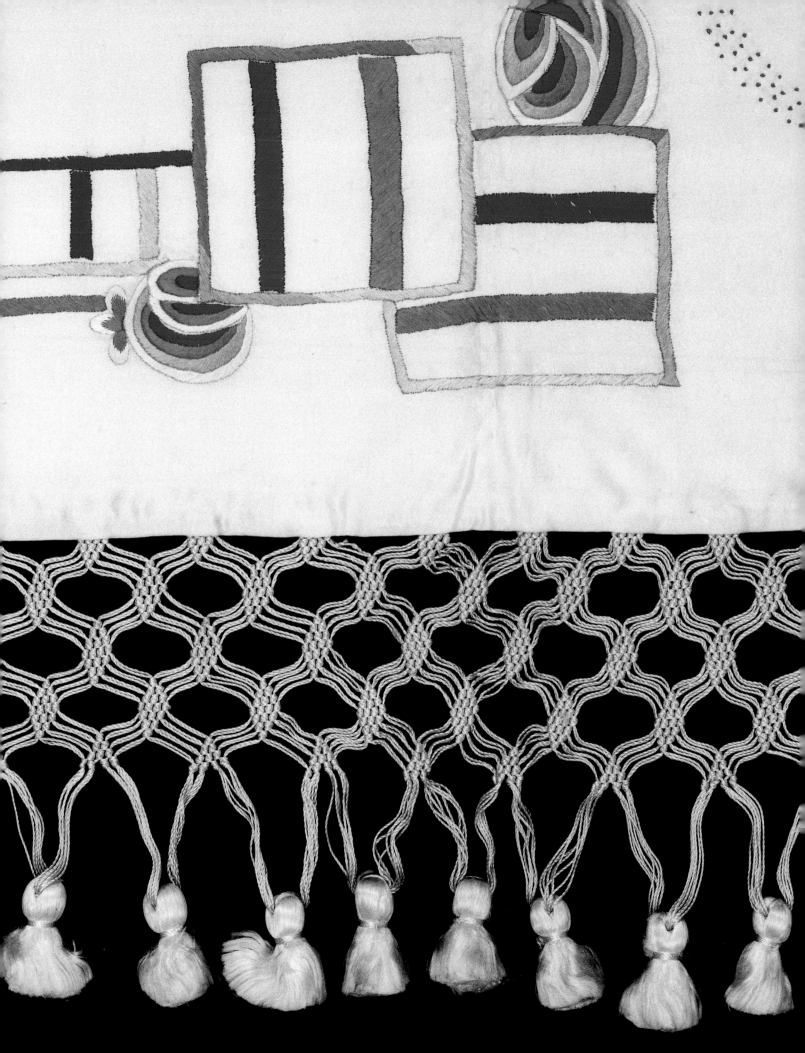

Knotting combined with braiding, weaving and other techniques such as silk wrapped wire and paper creates a variety of textures and structures, known as passementerie in Europe. Silk borders, edgings, fringes and tassels feature among its many varieties, used to adorn luxurious clothing and furnishings around the world (279 and 280).

Knitting builds a fabric using a continuous yarn manipulated by two needles to create consecutive rows of interlocking loops (281). It probably developed in the Middle East, sometime around 1000 CE, and spread to Europe through Iberia.[4] Knitting is a useful way of shaping a solid textile to fit awkward, three-dimensional shapes, such as feet, hands and heads. Silk's lustre and smooth texture made it the desired fibre for stockings worn by the nobility – both men and women – in sixteenth-century Europe, although it is less elastic than wool when knitted.

The invention of the knitting frame in England in the late sixteenth century increased the speed of production, making silk stockings and socks available to a wider public (282). Warp knitting – a cross between knitting and weaving

that does not unravel – was invented in 1775.[5] It fashioned a variety of open textures that resembled patterned hand-knitting or lace, and silk net made with the warp frame soon replaced the handmade variety. Warp frames and circular knitting machines (283) also produce the fabric now known as jersey, which drapes like knitting, but can be cut and sewn like a woven fabric.[6]

Crochet is another looped structure using a continuous yarn and a hook. Its exact origins are unknown. The technique probably developed from the chain stitching of yarn to make imitation lace and from tambour embroidery – chain stitching with a hook through fabric.[7] Crocheting with silk became a popular craft for middle-class women in nineteenth-century Europe, particularly for making bags and purses.

Today machines produce some of these non-woven structures, such as knitting and braiding, but others such as crochet, macramé and some trimmings can still only be made by hand. Highly skilled craftspeople continue to fashion these ancient structures for luxury markets as well as for pleasure. SN

281
Unfinished knitting, inscribed 'My dear sister's work, as she left it the last time she did any – she died 29 December 1825', England, 1825

Given by Miss V. Atkinson.
V&A T.126-1972

282 (ABOVE)
The Art of Stocking Frame-Work Knitting, published in *The Universal Magazine of Knowledge and Pleasure* (London 1750). Engraving

283 (RIGHT)
Circular-knitting machine, Denizli, Turkey, 2019

Twine and Twist, Net, Knot and Knit   233

TWINING AND TWISTING

Buddhist ancient texts, or sutra, were stored in wrappers while not in use. In this example, silk threads hold the bamboo splints together. Fittingly they show a seated Buddha. The warp-twining method is used in which two or more ends of the warp twist around each other as they interlace with the bamboo splints. HP

284 (RIGHT)
Wrapper of bamboo splints held together with bands of twined silk
Dunhuang, China, 800–1000 CE

Stein Textile Loan Collection, on loan from the Government of India and the Archaeological Survey of India.
V&A LOAN:STEIN.100

Drawstrings (285) are used to fasten skirts and *paijama* trousers around the waist. Indian drawstrings were often made of silk sprang. They were not solely functional, but also added flair. The sprang was worked in different patterns, the ends finished with silver and silver-gilt bindings and small fixings onto which different styles of tassel could be hooked. AF

285 (OPPOSITE)
Drawstrings of silk sprang
India, about 1855–79

V&A IPN.1491, TN.683-2019, 5903(IS), 5910(IS) & 0201A(IS)

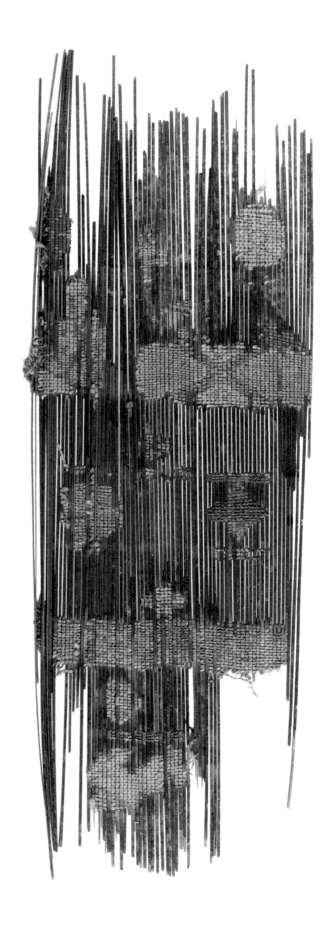

In the eighteenth century, British army officers wore crimson silk sashes around their waists, which could be used as stretchers. 'GR THE 3 / 1773' was worked into this sash, probably made with a circular warp. Britain was not at war in 1773 and no regiments were raised that year so it may record when the owner purchased his commission. SN

286 (LEFT)
Detail of officer's sash of silk sprang
Britain, 1773

V&A T.193-1957

287 (BELOW)
Lieutenant George Belson,
Corps of Marines (detail)
By Richard Livesay, about 1780
Oil on canvas

National Army Museum, London

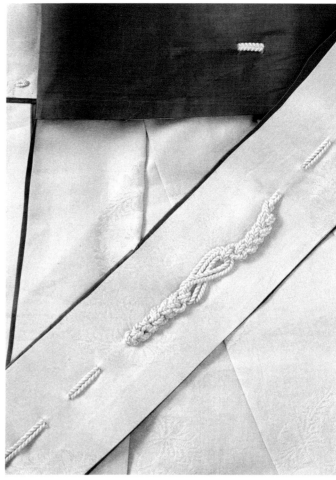

Richly woven figured silks were an important feature of Japanese armour. This archer's sleeve, one of a pair, employs such fabric at the wrist and shoulder, with monochrome figured silk in between. The curving border between the two fabrics is edged in silk cord, which has also been used around the wrist and to lace up the sleeve under the arm. AJ

288 (ABOVE)
Detail of an archer's sleeve of figured silks with embroidery in metal threads, silk crêpe, silk cords and iron mail
Kyoto, Japan, 1750–1850

V&A M.36-1932

These outer *hakama* would have been worn over another pair, and with various layers of long upper garments, by a member of the Japanese imperial court. Laced double silk cords reinforce parts of the seams, and pairs of cords, elaborately knotted at intervals, decorate the long waist bands. AJ

289 (ABOVE)
Man's pleated lower garment of figured twill weave silk with silk cord
Kyoto, Japan, 1800–80

Given by T.B. Clarke-Thornhill.
V&A T.66-1915

KNOTTING

Norigae are decorative pendants tied to the sashes on the jacket or skirt of women's traditional Korean costume (*hanbok*). They are made of three parts: a hook, a main ornament in the middle, and a set of single-cord knots and tassels. The main ornament is usually expensive hardstone, modest handmade embroidery, or a practical object such as a needle case or perfume container. These pendants (290 and 291) were often worn as lucky charms, the shape of their main ornament and knots symbolizing the wearer's desire for fertility, long life and wealth. EL/RK

290 (BELOW) & 291 (OPPOSITE)
Ornamental pendants of knotted and braided silk cord
By Kim Eun-young
Seoul, South Korea, 1991

(290) V&A FE.427:1-1992 &
(291) V&A FE.426:1-1992 (silk cord)
& FE.86-2009 (white ornament)

This tassel (292) from Tang-dynasty China possibly hung from a canopy. It is made of thick spun silk threads that comprise two filaments of silk plied together, one set with a Z-twist, the other with an S-twist. Murals in the Mogao Caves in the Gansu province of China depict such canopies with heavy tassel-like decorations. HP

292 (RIGHT)
Tassel of silk with knotting in metal holder
Dunhuang, China, 618–907 CE

Stein Textile Loan Collection, on loan from the Government of India and the Archaeological Survey of India.
V&A LOAN:STEIN.482

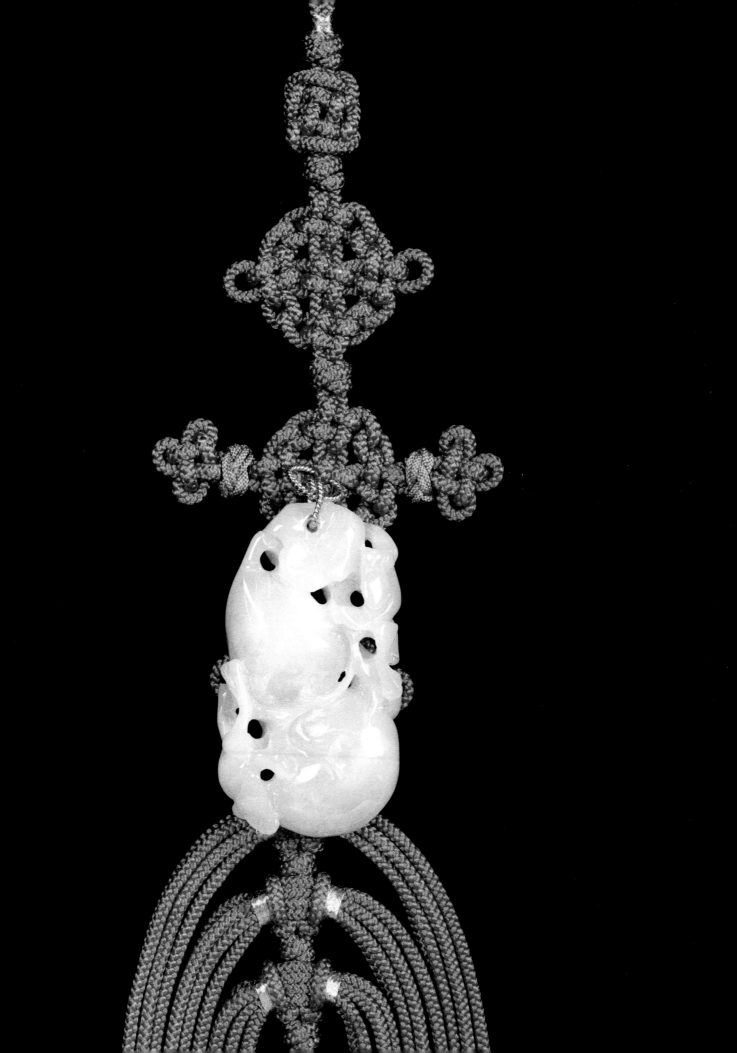

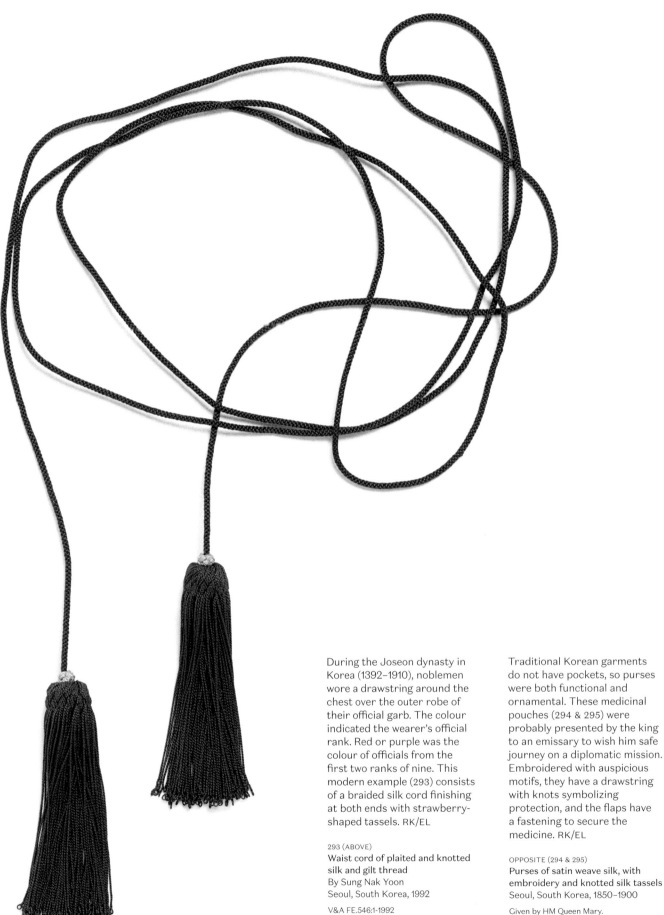

During the Joseon dynasty in Korea (1392–1910), noblemen wore a drawstring around the chest over the outer robe of their official garb. The colour indicated the wearer's official rank. Red or purple was the colour of officials from the first two ranks of nine. This modern example (293) consists of a braided silk cord finishing at both ends with strawberry-shaped tassels. RK/EL

293 (ABOVE)
Waist cord of plaited and knotted silk and gilt thread
By Sung Nak Yoon
Seoul, South Korea, 1992

V&A FE.546:1-1992

Traditional Korean garments do not have pockets, so purses were both functional and ornamental. These medicinal pouches (294 & 295) were probably presented by the king to an emissary to wish him safe journey on a diplomatic mission. Embroidered with auspicious motifs, they have a drawstring with knots symbolizing protection, and the flaps have a fastening to secure the medicine. RK/EL

OPPOSITE (294 & 295)
Purses of satin weave silk, with embroidery and knotted silk tassels
Seoul, South Korea, 1850–1900

Given by HM Queen Mary.
V&A T.102-1924 & T.103-1924

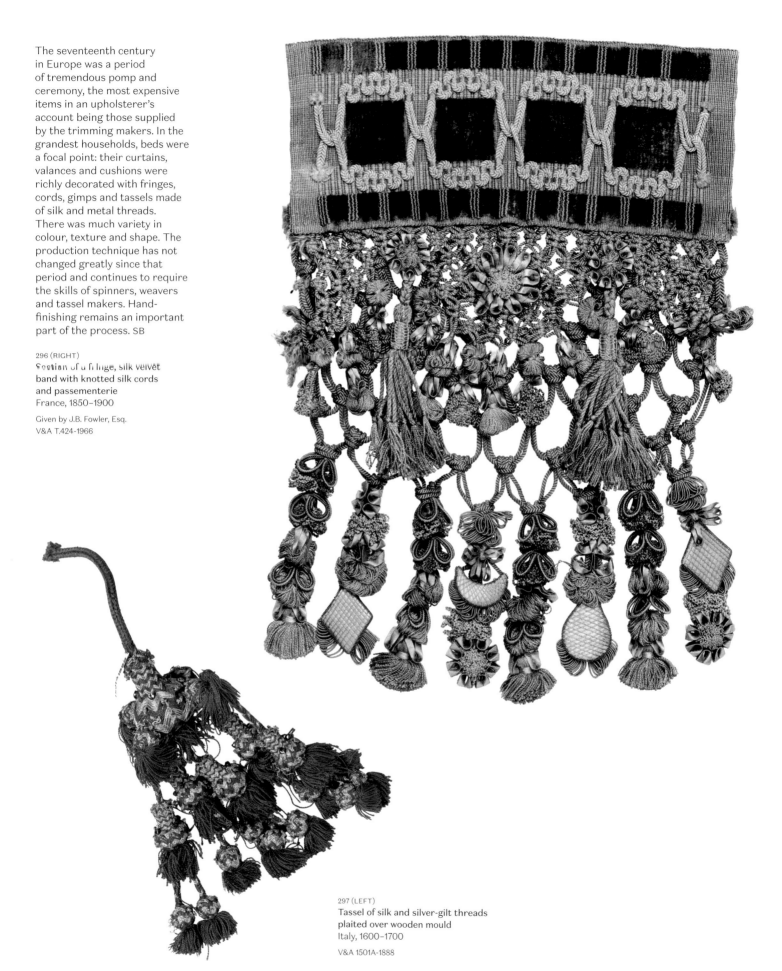

The seventeenth century in Europe was a period of tremendous pomp and ceremony, the most expensive items in an upholsterer's account being those supplied by the trimming makers. In the grandest households, beds were a focal point: their curtains, valances and cushions were richly decorated with fringes, cords, gimps and tassels made of silk and metal threads. There was much variety in colour, texture and shape. The production technique has not changed greatly since that period and continues to require the skills of spinners, weavers and tassel makers. Hand-finishing remains an important part of the process. SB

296 (RIGHT)
Section of a fringe, silk velvet band with knotted silk cords and passementerie
France, 1850–1900

Given by J.B. Fowler, Esq.
V&A T.424-1966

297 (LEFT)
Tassel of silk and silver-gilt threads plaited over wooden mould
Italy, 1600–1700

V&A 1501A-1888

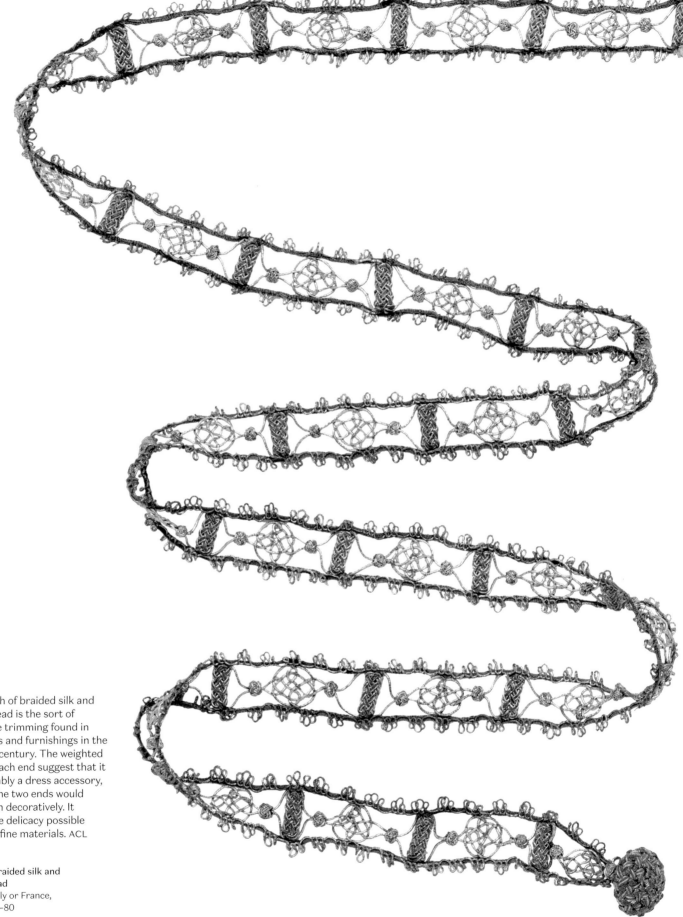

This length of braided silk and metal thread is the sort of decorative trimming found in both dress and furnishings in the sixteenth century. The weighted knots at each end suggest that it was probably a dress accessory, in which the two ends would hang down decoratively. It reveals the delicacy possible with such fine materials. ACL

298
Girdle of braided silk and metal thread
Possibly Italy or France, about 1540–80

V&A T.370-1989

This saddle cloth, along with a matching headstall and tail ornament, was designed to adorn a horse during a procession. Lavishly decorated with velvet and brass studs, it is finished round the edges with rich knotted fringes. To make it, cotton cord wrapped with red silk thread and silver-gilt strip was knotted into a latticed band, from which silk and silver wrapped thread tassels hang. AF

299
Saddle cloth of cut silk velvet, with fringe of knotted cord wrapped with silk and silver-gilt strip, and silk and silver-gilt wrapped thread tassels
Udaipur, Rajasthan, India, about 1800–50

V&A 888-1852

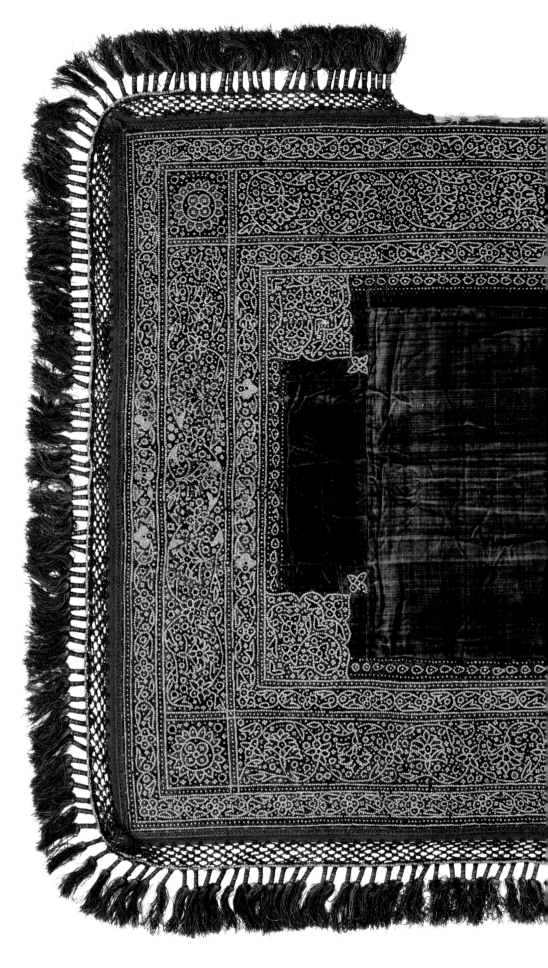

This overgarment (300) is completely open at the sides. It was worn draped over a woman's festive robes on celebratory occasions. The deep fringe ends are made of silk macramé backed with gilded paper. Chinese tassel knots lengthen the garment to the floor. The tassels would have swayed dramatically with each step made in Manchurian platform horse-hoof shoes. YC

300 (OPPOSITE)
Woman's overgarment of satin weave silk with brocading and with cut silk velvet trimming, and silk macramé fringe and tassels, lined with red silk
China, 1700–1800

Purchased with Art Fund support.
V&A T.193-1948

In western Europe in the 1960s and 1970s, macramé was strongly associated with plant hangers made from robust, usually brown or cream, materials. Around this time designer Yves Saint Laurent used the technique rather differently, to make this elegant macramé top from black silk. CAJ

301 (ABOVE)
Bolero of silk macramé with tassels
By Yves Saint Laurent,
France, 1967–8

V&A T.331:2-1997

An apron (302 and 303) was part of the *jobok* ceremonial attire worn at the Joseon royal court (1392–1910). It consisted of a *husu* (an embroidered panel with net and tassels) and a *daedae* (belt). Here (302) the net is made in the macramé technique. Its colour – blue – was worn by all court officials, high and low ranking, military and civil. In both examples, the two gold-plated rings, the number of flying cranes and the use of four colours of embroidery thread indicate the high rank of the wearer. RK/EL

302
Apron of satin weave silk with embroidery in silk and gold thread with net and tassels
Probably Seoul, South Korea, 1880–1910

V&A T.196A-1920

303
Panel of wool with embroidery
in silk with silk net and tassels
Probably Seoul, Korea, 1850–1950

V&A FE.46-1999

LACE

This impressive example of polychrome lace, called *frisado* in Spanish because of its metal loops, is worked in buttonhole stitch in coloured silks over silver-gilt thread. Such rich needle lace was used mostly for ecclesiastical textiles such as this altar frontal, which was possibly made in a convent in the north of Spain. ACL

304 (RIGHT) & 305 (OPPOSITE)
Altar frontal of needle lace of silk and silver-gilt threads
Possibly Valladolid, Spain, 1630–60

V&A 57-1869

Bobbin lace was made by twisting together threads wound on bobbins. This panel (306) is worked with a very fine cream silk thread for the ground and with thicker, coloured silks for the profile portrait of a classical warrior. His gleaming metal helmet reveals the maker's exceptional skill. SB

306 (OPPOSITE)
Panel of silk bobbin lace
Probably France, 1790–1800

V&A T.214-1985

Silk bobbin lace was a fashionable alternative to traditional linen laces in the eighteenth century. Silk's ready absorption of dyestuffs allowed for trimmings that coordinated with the colours in the woven silks fashionable in European women's gowns of the mid- to late century. In this case (307), a narrow green, pink and cream lace complements the polychrome flower brocaded into the silk. SN

307 (RIGHT)
Detail of woman's court petticoat of figured silk with silk bobbin lace edging
London, England, 1750–60

V&A T.44A-1910

Black lace accessories and trimmings were fashionable in mid-nineteenth century Europe and North America, following the taste of Eugenia de Montijo, empress of France from 1853 to 1870. Women carried parasols out of doors to protect their faces from exposure to the sun. This cover of Chantilly-type lace (308), with its typical floral design worked in silk on a light twist net ground, may have been made in the renowned lacemaking towns of Bayeux, Enghien or Turnhout. JL

308 (RIGHT)
Parasol covered with silk bobbin lace, lined with plain weave silk
Bayeux or Enghien, France or Turnhout, Belgium (lace), about 1880
V&A T.363-1980

Lacemakers in Caen specialized in distinctive handmade coloured silk lace in the face of increasing competition from machine-made laces. Decorative caps, sometimes with trailing lappets (309), were traditionally worn by married women indoors. JL

309 (BELOW)
Cap of silk bobbin lace
Possibly Caen, France, about 1860
V&A T.217-1982

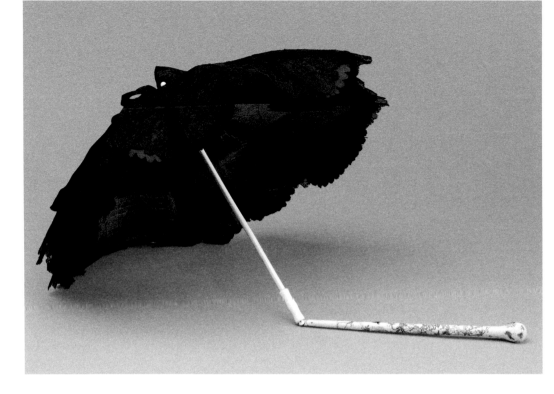

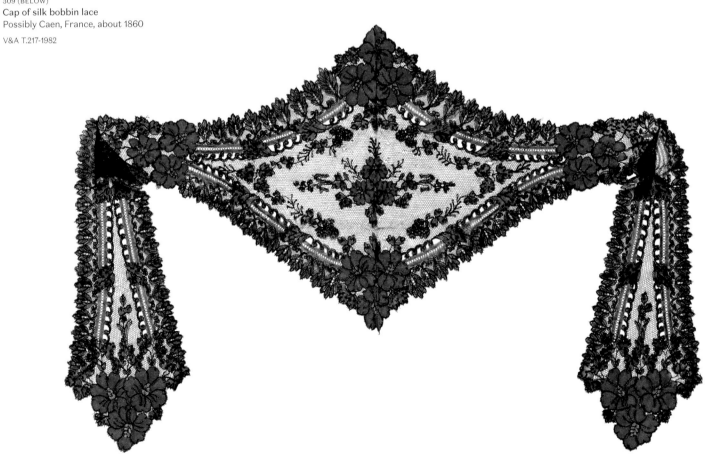

The design of this Chantilly lace fan (310) exploits the full potential of bobbin lace worked in black silk thread to delineate tiny details and differentiate shade and texture against a fine net ground. The lacemaker has depicted an entire fantasy garden scene, with a brick pavilion, a fountain, delicate trees, a peacock and pool of water, all with astonishing clarity. JL

310
Fan of silk bobbin lace with turtleshell sticks
Probably France, about 1860; retailed by Duvelleroy, London, England

V&A T.5-1916

KNITTING AND CROCHET

The knitted pattern of this glove (311) deliberately echoes the construction of a pair of leather gloves. Although the glove is knit in the round, lines of single moss stitch mark the 'seams' of the small insertions used in sewn gloves. Moss stitch outlines the reinforcement that sometimes covered the thumb seam of a sewn glove. SN

311 (RIGHT)
Bishop's glove of hand-knitted silk
Spain, 1500–1600

V&A 276-1880

Social etiquette in Europe dictated the wearing of gloves outdoors and indoors before the mid-twentieth century. Pale-coloured gloves soiled easily. In contrast, this black silk elbow-length glove (312) would not have shown the dirt so quickly, and was suitable for indoor social events, its embroidery adding visual interest. JR

312 (FAR RIGHT)
Glove of machine-knitted silk in stocking stitch with lace eyelets and hand embroidery
Britain, 1850–60

V&A 963-1898

Purses in the shape of this colourful example (313) were popular in nineteenth-century Britain. They were called 'stocking purses' because they were either hand- or warp-knitted like stockings. They are also known as 'miser's purses', because the opening for coins was narrow and removing a coin required multiple moves of the metal rings. SN

313 (ABOVE)
Stocking purse of warp-knitted silk
Britain, 1800–50

Given by Messrs Harrods.
V&A T.1293-1913

This purse (314) imitating a pineapple is a tour-de-force of circular knitting. Its textured surface has been carefully knitted and each spine topped with a glass bead; the shaded green silk suggests the stages of ripening. Knitted around the top are the coloured petals of a pineapple flower, mingled with green leaves sprouting from the fruit. SN

314 (RIGHT)
Purse of hand-knitted silk
Britain, 1800–30

Given by Messrs Harrods.
V&A T.1348-1913

This purse (315), with its colourful bands of abstract patterns, stylized birds, trees and flowers, was bought by the donor in Jolfa, the Armenian suburb of Isfahan. This type of cylindrical purse with a drawstring fastening was typically knitted, although beaded examples also survive, both part of domestic textile production during the Qajar dynasty (1789–1925). SN

315 (LEFT)
Purse of hand-knitted silk
Iran, 1850–99

Given by Mrs Waite.
V&A T.224-1923

Like knitting, crochet was a popular technique for making bags and purses in the nineteenth century. The metal-framed purse (316), worked in double [single, US] crochet with steel-cut beads, was made for a chatelaine – a decorative collection of useful implements worn by women in the Victorian era (1837–1901). Amy Boggs-Rolfe, the maker of the purse below, was a close friend of the ballerina Marie Taglioni when she lived in London and crocheted this purse for Marie's chatelaine. The base of the colourful example opposite (317) is worked in a circle of double [single, US] crochet, edged with a shell pattern, with the sides of the bag worked in a filet of two treble [double, US] crochet. SN

316 (BELOW)
Purse of crocheted silk with cut-steel beads
By Amy Boggs-Rolfe, London, England, 1871–80

Cyril W. Beaumont Bequest.
V&A S.824-2001

317 (LEFT)
Bag of crocheted silk
Britain, 1840–70
Given by Lt Col G.B. Croft Lyons, FSA.
V&A T.142-1909

These socks, as shown by the front (318) and the sole (319), are structured and patterned in a manner typical of traditional Kurdistan footwear. They are knit in the round starting at the toe, using a triangular shaping for both heel and toe. The custom of removing shoes indoors made the socks visible when the wearer was seated, so the soles were patterned. SN

(318 & 319) BELOW
Pair of hand-knitted silk socks
Sulaimaniya province, Iraqi
Kurdistan, about 1930

Given by Mr C.J. Edmonds.
V&A T.4&A-1968

By the eighteenth century, silk stockings were frame-knitted, and the vibrant colours and decoration of this one (320 and 321) are characteristic of Spanish stockings. The clock is knit in carnation pink and the birds and trees embroidered over vertical lines of stocking stitch, giving them their slightly abstract style. SN

320 (RIGHT) & 321 (OPPOSITE)
Stocking of frame-knitted silk with embroidery in silk
Probably Barcelona, Spain, about 1780

Given by Miss B. Hinton.
V&A T.156-1971

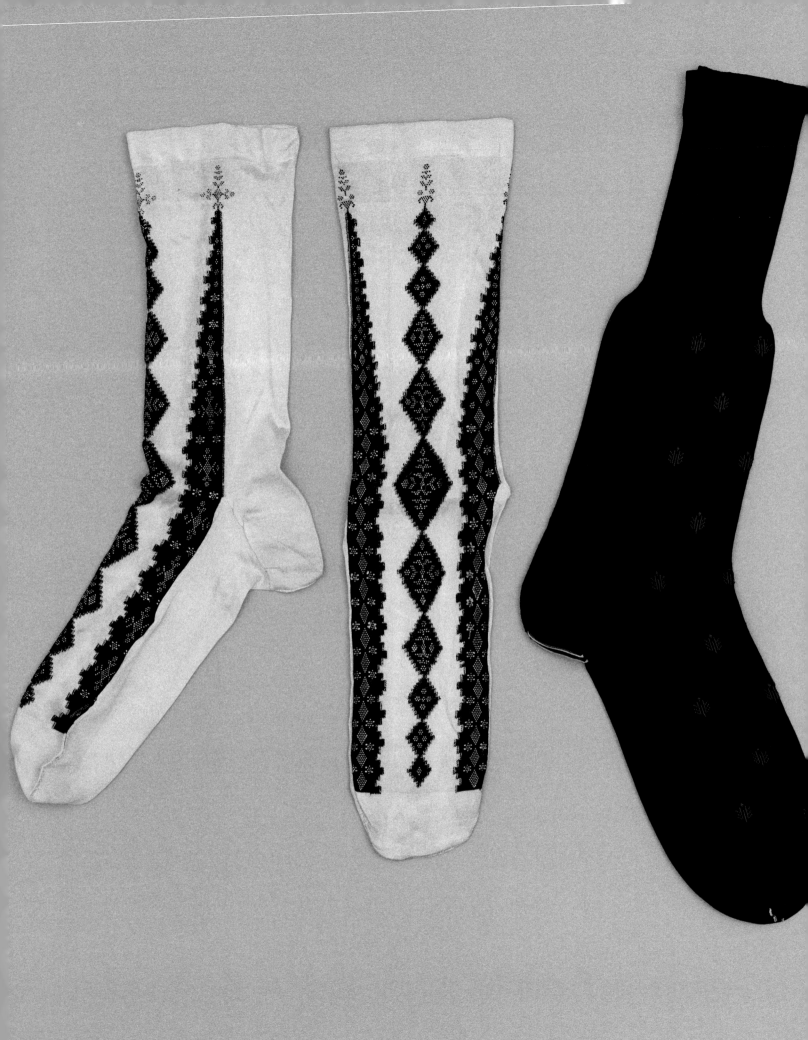

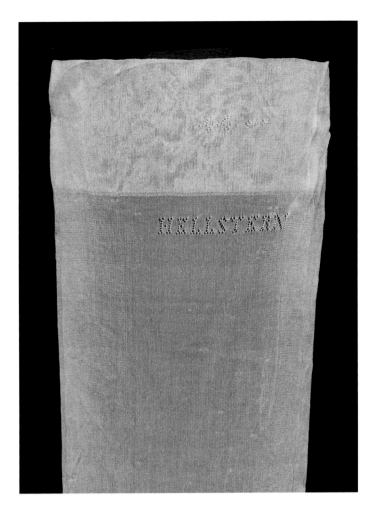

In early nineteenth-century Europe, trousers replaced the breeches men had worn since the late seventeenth century. Trousers now covered men's legs to the ankle, so their stockings shortened to mid-calf length socks. Silk remained the most luxurious material for footwear and this nineteenth-century pair (322 and 323) is decorated with stripes and diamonds in black and white, imitating black lace. The wear around the toes of these socks indicates that they were much used. The black sock with demure red sprigs (324) is typical of the 1930s. I. & R. Morley was established about 1780 and became one of Britain's largest hosiery and knitwear manufacturers. SN

322 (OPPOSITE LEFT) & 323 (CENTRE)
Men's socks of machine-knitted silk
Britain, 1850–4

Given by Miss R. Scarlett Smith.
V&A T.204&A-1962

324 (OPPOSITE RIGHT)
Man's sock of machine-knitted silk
By I. & R. Morley, Nottingham, England, 1930–40

Given by Mr F.H. Hawkins, on behalf of I. & R. Morley Ltd.
V&A T.150-1975

As the technology of knitting developed in the nineteenth century, stockings could be made of finer yarns and the shaping of toes and heels done by machine. The tradition of using open patterns to knit the manufacturer's name in the top of the stocking continued. When the hemline of women's skirts rose after the First World War (1914–18), the ability of stockings to flatter a shapely leg became increasingly important. Synthetic polymers were invented in the late 1920s and a pair of nylon stockings was displayed at the New York World's Fair in 1939, signalling the decline of the silk variety. SN

325 (ABOVE LEFT)
Detail of woman's stocking of machine-knitted silk
By Hellstern & Sons, Paris, France, 1890–1900

Given by Mrs D. Roberts.
V&A T.227A-1962

326 (ABOVE)
Detail of woman's stocking of machine-knitted silk
By I. & R. Morley, Nottingham, England, 1914

Given by Mr F.H. Hawkins, on behalf of I. & R. Morley Ltd.
V&A T.137-1975

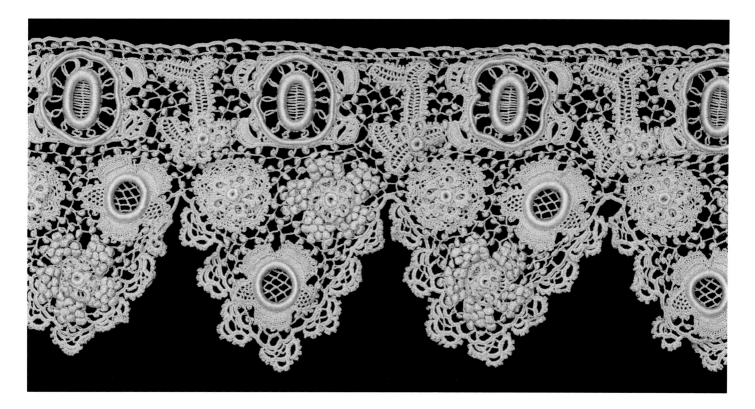

The Shetland Islands were renowned for their shawls of fine local wool, worked with thin needles in open patterns resembling lace. In this shawl (327), the use of silk and addition of a hood were exceptional, probably for the luxury fashionable market, yet the pattern fillings are typical of shawls knit on the Isle of Unst. SN

327 (OPPOSITE)
Detail of woman's hooded shawl of hand-knitted silk
Shetland Islands, Scotland, 1850–75

Given by Mrs J. Drummond.
V&A T.137-1966

Certain patterns of crochet resembled the three-dimensional texture of late seventeenth-century Venetian needle lace. In the late nineteenth century, 'Royal Irish Guipure' worked in thick cream silk was a luxurious variation of the popular, crocheted Irish linen 'laces'. The 'Vandyked' lower edge of this border (328) echoes the 'points' of early seventeenth-century needle lace. SN

328 (ABOVE)
Detail of border of crocheted silk
Ireland (now Republic of Ireland), about 1890

Given by Mrs Ethel Hill.
V&A T.69-1972

Bonnet veils were fashionable during the Victorian era (1837–1901). They were attached to the brim of the bonnet, so that they could be worn over the face or draped behind. To allow the wearer to see through them, veils were made of net or lace or, as in this example (329), an open-patterned warp knit. SN

329 (ABOVE)
Detail of woman's bonnet veil of warp-knitted silk
Britain, 1840–70

Given by Messrs Harrods.
V&A T.1787-1913

The reverse of this jacket (330) reveals the fineness of the unplied silk threads, which would have been very difficult to knit without splitting (331). The gold and silver elements of the design are very thin strands of yellow or white silk partially wrapped with silver strip. Each has been doubled, requiring careful handling by the knitter. SN

330 (ABOVE LEFT) & 331 (OPPOSITE)
Jacket of hand-knitted silk, with silver and silver-gilt thread
Italy, 1600–1700
V&A 473-1893

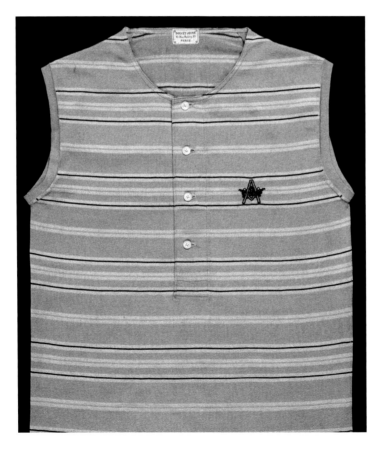

This fully fashioned, fine machine-knitted vest (332) is an example of extravagant men's underwear. Such silk underwear was warm, comfortable and fitted the body snugly. Purchased from a Parisian maker of high-end men's clothing and undergarments, it bears the monogram 'M.A.', denoting the 5th Marquis of Anglesey, Henry Cyril Paget. Paget had a reputation for sartorial flamboyance and excessive spending on clothing and jewellery. CKB

332 (LEFT)
Vest of machine-knitted silk
By Doucet Jeune, Paris, France, 1898–1904
Given by John Leathwood.
V&A T.89:1-2003

The stretch properties of jersey enable experimental approaches to emphasizing and adapting the contours of the body. Innovative designer Matilda Etches used a heavy gauge of jersey in this dress (333 and 334), wrapping the body in different ways. The skirt extends and can attach to the shoulder to be worn as a cape, a hood or a train. In contrast, Georgina Godley manipulated the silhouette with much finer jersey in this dress and matching body suit (335). The fluid fabric clings to the figure while boning in the neck, wrists and hemline dramatically flares the fabric outwards from the body. OC

333 (OPPOSITE) & 334 (ABOVE)
Evening dress of silk jersey
By Matilda Etches, London, England, about 1948

Given by Silvia Harris.
V&A T.94-2016

335 (ABOVE)
Evening dress of silk jersey
By Georgina Godley, England, 1986

Given by the designer.
V&A T.7&A-1988

DRESSING AND WEIGHTING

Silk has historically been treated or dressed with a variety of organic products to alter the handle of the fabric, ease its manufacture or ensure retention of shape during wear. Such products include starch and gum arabic. Seldom visible to the naked eye, these coatings can be destructive in the longer term. An early nineteenth-century machine-made silk net overdress trimmed with straw decoration and glass beads filled with wax (336 and 338) provides a fine example. The net is now brittle and yellowed, light damage having affected not only the fibre but also its dressing. An overall loss of flexibility, compounded by the weight of the heavy decoration, has caused the net to split in multiple places. Examination of a small sample of the net through a scanning electron microscope at very high magnification revealed the culprit: characteristically round starch granules that coat the silk filaments (337).

Other damage results from the deliberate weighting of silk with metallic salts and is often associated with silks dating from the mid-nineteenth to the early twentieth century. The metallic salts were added either to the yarn or to a woven piece, often at the time of dyeing as they also acted as a mordant to fix the colour. They increased the body of the fibre and enhanced the distinctive rustling sound of silk.

Unfortunately, this kind of treatment accelerates the natural ageing process, splitting and cracking the silk in places that bear no relationship to normal patterns of wear. The condition of the lining fabric of a walking coat worn by the English socialite Heather Firbank around 1910 is so poor that it has had to be removed from the coat and stored separately (339). Analysis of the silk using a non-destructive technique called X-ray fluorescence (XRF) confirmed the presence of tin. While a variety of metallic weighting agents was available, tin salts, patented in 1883, were the preferred option from the late nineteenth century onwards and were still being used in the 1940s.

A similar problem has caused the degradation of the black silk embroidery on a nineteenth-century *obi* (waist sash) from Japan. the silk has almost disappeared, revealing the inked template below (340). The dyestuffs used were naturally acidic tannins fixed to the fibre with iron-sulphate mordants in a process that weakens the silk and hastens natural deterioration. EAH

336 (BELOW)
Dress of silk net with embroidery in straw, probably Britain, about 1810
LOAN: AMERICANFRIENDS.732:3-2018

337 (BELOW TOP RIGHT)
Scanning electron microscope photography (SEM) of dressed silk fibre from dress

338 (BELOW BOTTOM RIGHT)
Detail of trim of dress showing straw decoration and wax-filled glass beads

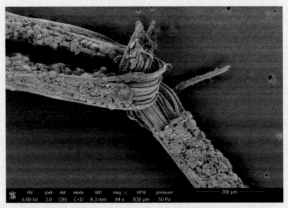

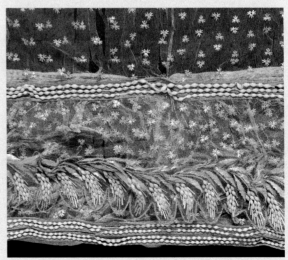

339 (RIGHT)
Detail of tin-weighted fragment
of lining of walking suit, Britain,
about 1910

Given by Lilla Pennant from the estate
of Johanna Firbank.
V&A T.3-2018

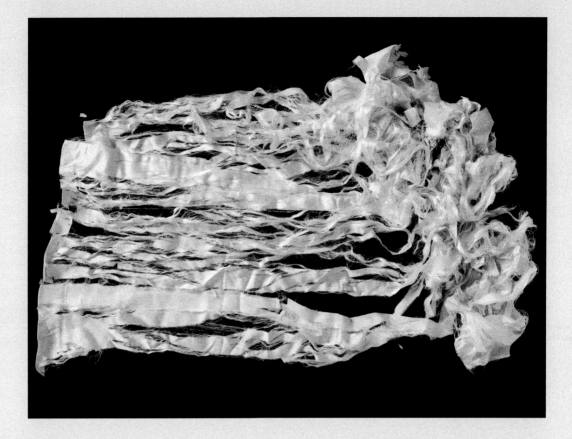

340 (RIGHT)
Degradation of silk due to weighting
(see black areas), detail of *obi*
(waist sash) of satin weave silk
with embroidery in silk and metal
threads, Japan, 1850–1900

Given by Mrs Mockett.
V&A T.270-1960

KNOTTING
AND PROPAGANDA

In China carpets were mainly produced in the north-west of the country until the late thirteenth century when the Yuan imperial court (1279–1368) established the first official carpet workshop in Beijing.[8] In the early years of the People's Republic of China (PRC; 1949–present), a state and private collective enterprise called Carpet Producers' Cooperative organized carpet workshops, which subsequently grew into factories.[9] Made in Beijing Carpet Factory Number One, this wall carpet (343) was probably destined to be a diplomatic and propaganda gift at the start of the Great Leap Forward (1958–62). This campaign aimed to turn agricultural China rapidly into an industrial nation.[10]

The main body of the rug is made of hand-knotted silk pile – a technique thought to have been introduced to China during the thirteenth century.[11] The yellow macramé fringe with knotted tassels has been attached separately to the ends of the rug,

rather than being made up of the remaining warp threads.

Under the insignia of the PRC in the centre are dancing figures representing the country's different minority ethnic groups. In each corner is a symbol that promotes the PRC as a prosperous and unified nation: a bucket of molten steel (342), a wheatsheaf, cotton balls and a coal truck (343).

These emblems and the rug's borders are woven using *panjin*, a weft-wrapping technique in gold thread. The highest density of threads is approximately 40 rows per square centimetre. Use of metal threads may allude to the importance of metal production during the Great Leap Forward campaign when there was a considerable increase in small backyard furnaces across the country (341).

The combination of techniques gives the carpet texture, with the knotted silk pile raised in relief against the flat metallic woven area. YC

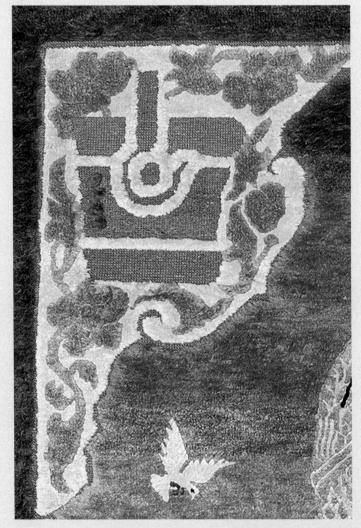

341 (OPPOSITE LEFT)
Mobilize the Whole Population, to Make Sure that Steel Is Doubled!, Shanghai, China, September 1958
Colour process printing

Private collection

342 (OPPOSITE RIGHT)
Detail of stylized bucket of molten steel from the corner of *Whole Nation All Ethnic Groups United*, wall carpet

V&A FE.15-1991

343 (RIGHT)
Whole Nation All Ethnic Groups United, wall carpet, knotted silk pile and metallic threads, Beijing Carpet Factory Number One, China, 1958

V&A FE.15-1991

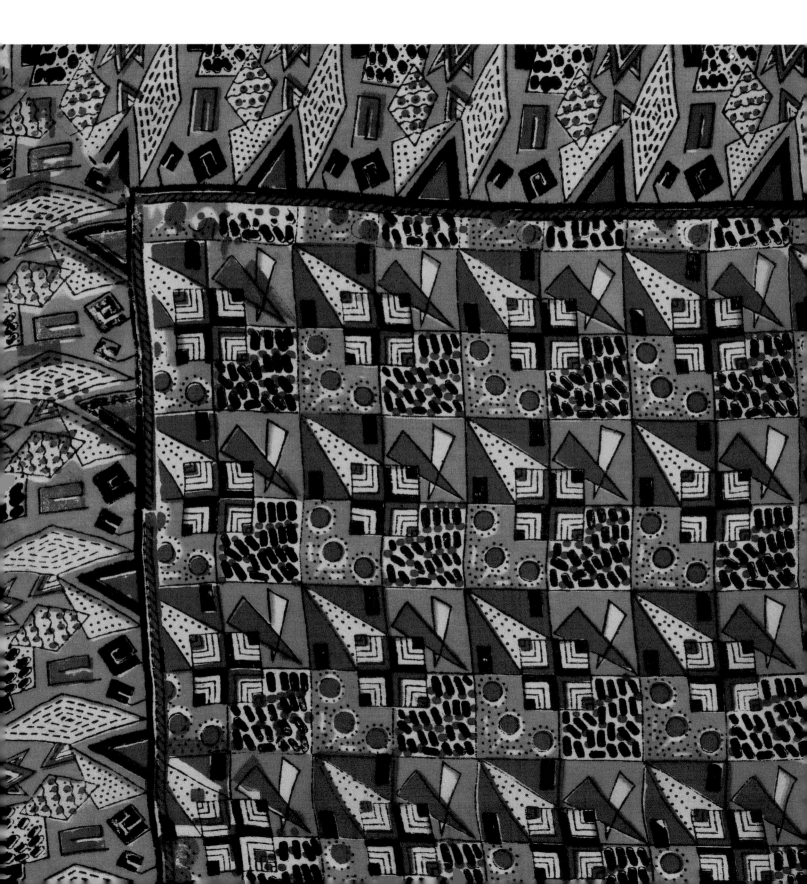

Paint, Resist and Print

Paint, Resist and Print

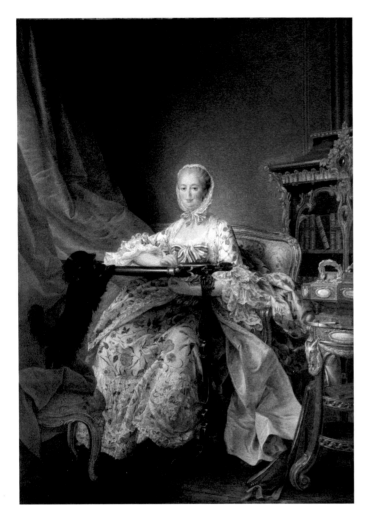

344 (ABOVE)
Madame de Pompadour at her Embroidery Frame by François-Hubert Drouais, France, 1763–4. Oil on canvas

National Gallery, London

Substances for colouring come in a wide variety of forms and may be applied to silk in different ways. Paints, inks or dyes can be applied directly to the surface with brush or pen, or using block, roller, copperplate, screen or inkjet. Alternatively, patterning may involve immersing warp and weft yarns or woven or knitted fabric in a dyebath. The immersion method is often called pattern-dyeing and is particularly important and sophisticated in Asia.[1] Decorative effects differ according to the method. The layering of effects has long enhanced the most luxurious silks (346).

Painting or drawing on the surface offers most freedom, echoing artists' practice on canvas. The tool, some form of paintbrush, is light to lift and entirely flexible when wielded with expertise to create a single painterly composition or a repeat pattern. The Chinese already used silk as a base for painting in the fourth century, and their goods were much appreciated farther afield. By the eighteenth century influential European women such as the French king's mistress Madame de Pompadour chose to be portrayed in these glorious floral silks, so different from the woven patterns made in their own countries (344).[2] The method of application was similar to that practised by skilled silk painters today (345).

Quite different from painting is resist-dyeing, a term which refers to different methods in which parts of yarns or woven cloth are protected in some way so as to resist the dye. In the case of ikat (in Europe *chiné* and in Japan *kasuri*), the yarns are bound with bast or cotton or silk threads, according to different regional practices (348 and 349).[3]

The protective binding is removed after dyeing, revealing areas that have not taken the colour. Binding, dyeing and unbinding may be undertaken several times to create multicoloured yarns. Complex designs can then be created in both single and double ikats. The former has a plain warp and resist-dyed weft, or vice versa, while in a double ikat, both warp and weft are resist-dyed. Great skill is required to ensure that warp and weft intersect correctly, and the outline of the patterns generally has a distinctive hazy appearance (347). In tie-dyeing, or Japanese *shibori*, fabric rather than yarn is tightly bound, or sewn and gathered, before immersion in a dyebath.[4] The dye cannot penetrate the bound sections and afterwards the fabric is untied to reveal the pattern.

In batik and stencilling, the resist is a substance that is applied to the textile, and elaborate effects can be built up through repeated applications of resist in different configurations. In tie-dyeing, the fabric is gathered together in portions and tied with string before immersion in the dyebath. The dye fails to penetrate the tied sections. After drying, the fabric is untied to reveal a pattern of irregular circles, dots and stripes. In batik, wax is either drawn in dots or lines with a spouted tool or printed with a copper stamp on the fabric. It resists the dye and is subsequently removed by boiling in water or scraping off. In contrast, for Japanese stencil-dyeing, *katazome*, a pattern is cut into a sheet of mulberry paper laminated in layers. The paper is placed on the fabric and rice paste is brushed through the stencil, thus blocking the pattern area from taking the colour subsequently applied to the rest of the fabric. A particularly

345 (TOP)
Silk painting by Artisans Angkor, Cambodia, 2013

346 (ABOVE)
Fragment of plain weave silk with clamp resist-dyeing and painting, probably Dunhuang, China, 750–900 CE

Stein Textile Loan Collection, on loan from the Government of India and the Archaeological Survey of India. V&A LOAN:STEIN.298.

Paint, Resist and Print   277

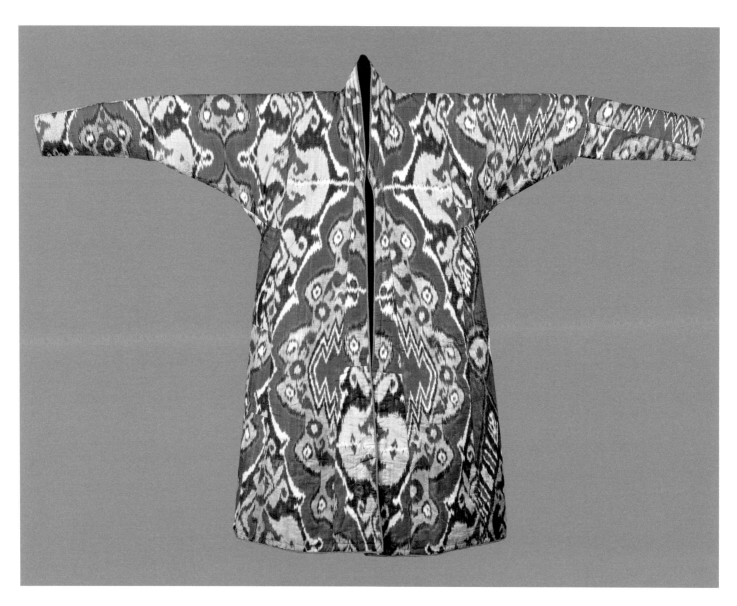

347 (ABOVE)
Man's robe of silk ikat, probably
Samarqand, Uzbekistan,
about 1860–70

V&A 9187(IS)

348 (FAR LEFT)
Making ikat: warp bundles
bound ready for second dyebath,
Marghilan, Uzbekistan, 2004

349 (LEFT)
Making ikat: partially dyed warp
threads with areas bound in
preparation for the next dyebath,
Marghilan, Uzbekistan, 2004

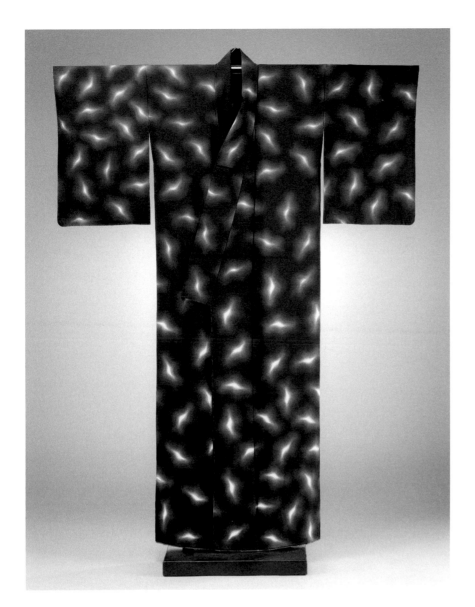

350 (LEFT)
Flight, kimono of plain weave silk crêpe with stencil-dyeing, by Matsubara Yoshichi, Tokyo, Japan, 1990

V&A FE.10:1-1995

351 (BELOW)
Twenty-nine stencils of mulberry paper laminated with the juice of persimmons

V&A FE.10:2 to 30-1995

fine kimono by Matsubara Yoshichi reveals his unique method of working in which stencils of the same shape, but of gradually diminishing size, are used in succession, the fabric being repeatedly dip-dyed after each application of rice paste (350 and 351). *Yūzen* is another specifically Japanese form of resist-dyeing in which an image is drawn on the surface of the fabric with rice paste. Dyes are then brushed within these paste boundaries, which prevent the colours bleeding into each other.

Printing may be used as either resist or direct method. In both cases, wood blocks or stamps are applied to the surface of the cloth. Direct printing was practised in Asia as early as the third century BCE and became widespread in Europe much later.[5] Areas of wooden blocks or stamps are carved away to leave the design for printing in relief. For fine lines, copper or brass strips or pins are hammered into

the block. Stamps – used particularly in South and South-East Asia – are relatively small and lightweight (352 and 353). European blocks are larger and heavier, but seldom more than 46 cm square and 6 cm deep because the printer must be able to lift each easily to place in the dye tub, lift out and press firmly onto the fabric.[6] Each new motif and colour requires a new block and cannot be superimposed on the textile until the previous colour is dry, so the process is relatively slow (354). It is highly skilled as the printer must place the blocks in exactly the correct position if the joins in the pattern are to be invisible. A sample from William Morris's experimentation with Thomas Wardle of Leek provides a fine example of a pattern that required five blocks because of the number of colours (355).[7] One American manufacturer in the 1920s printed different qualities of silks, two being the lowest number of colours, 22 the highest.[8] The more colours, the more expensive the printed silk will be. Block printing survives to the present day in artisan workshops across the globe, often used for exclusive craft textiles.

A European contribution to printing on silk came through adapting methods of printing maps on paper. Commemorative silk handkerchiefs (356) bear testimony to this development which generated finely drawn pictorial imagery from an intaglio-engraved copperplate. The latter was placed in a rolling-print press, coated in ink or dye that remained in the engraved decoration once the surface had been wiped clean of excess dye. The press did the heavy work of feeding the cloth to the plate.[9] Generally, printing in only one colour was possible, with any additional colours being hand painted or block printed. Copperplates allowed larger repeat compositions, varying from about 40 to 91 cm square.[10] From both block printing and copperplate printing, the first fully mechanized system using cylinders developed from the late eighteenth century, mainly for printing cottons.[11]

352 (TOP)
Man block printing, from a series of paintings depicting different occupations and conveyances, Varanasi, Uttar Pradesh, India, about 1815–20.
Watercolour on paper

V&A AL.8042:13

353 (ABOVE)
Printing stamps, carved wood, South and South–East Asia, about 1855–1920

V&A IPN.762, 6837A(IS), IPN.1750, IPN.665, IM.176-1914, IM.194-1914, 6800(IS), IPN.1757, 6791(IS)

Given by HH the Sultan of Selangor.
V&A IM.104-1925

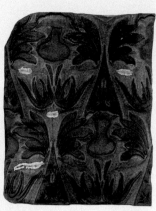

354 (TOP)
Set of woodblocks for printing on silk, two carved wood, one with inserted bronze strips (top right), David Evans, Essex, England, 1889–90

V&A T.41 to C-1981

355 (ABOVE LEFT)
Half width of *Honeysuckle* furnishing silk with woodblock printing, designed by William Morris for Morris & Co. and printed by Thomas Wardle, Leek, Staffordshire, England, 1876

V&A CIRC.491-1965

356 (ABOVE)
Handkerchief of plain weave silk with metal-plate printing by Robert Spofforth, England, 1707

Given by A.G. Munday.
V&A T.85-1934

Screen printing – initially attempted in Lyon in 1850 – has become the most widespread commercial printing process since the 1920s, either in its initial form as flat screen printing or in its more recent rotary or cylinder form. The screens are usually made of sheets of material with a cut design – not dissimilar to stencils. Unlike them, however, screens are supported on a framed woven mesh, through which the ink or dye can pass. Virtually any aesthetic quality from other printing methods can be achieved. Flat screens are usually the width of the printing table and require the printer to pass the squeegee holding the dye from side to side (357). There are no restrictions to the length of the design, and even mechanized cylinders can create a repeat of at least 64 cm square.[12] Screen printing continues even in businesses that have since the 1990s embraced the most recent direct printing process: digital printing (358). Designs are produced digitally, and then all colours are inkjet printed onto the fabric at once, whether for bulk production or single one-off pieces such as the *Plato's Atlantis* dress by Alexander McQueen (359).

Various techniques for dyeing or printing coexist today, practised industrially, in artisanal workshops and in some cases as a leisure activity. The natural lustre of silk and its easy absorption of colour allow for virtuoso and dramatic effects. ACL/KH

357 (ABOVE)
Screen printing tables at Beckford Silk Ltd, Tewkesbury, Gloucestershire, England, about 2018

358 (BELOW)
Digital inkjet printing, Beckford Silk Ltd, Tewkesbury, Gloucestershire, England, about 2018

PAINTING

Buddhist banners were hung both inside cave temples and outdoors, as well as being carried in processions. The head of this banner (360), beautifully painted on both sides with a haloed Buddha, may have been for indoor use and therefore more decorative than most other surviving examples. HP

360 (RIGHT)
Head of a banner of damask weave silk with painting
Probably Dunhuang, China, 800–900 CE

Stein Textile Loan Collection, on loan from the Government of India and the Archaeological Survey of India.
V&A LOAN:STEIN.490

Painted liturgical silks and vestments were made in China in the eighteenth century, not only to export to Europe but also to supply the requirements of newly established Catholic churches in China. The configuration of the naturalistic floral pattern and border in this example (361) reveals that it was made to the shape of the chasuble, so always intended for ecclesiastical use. HP

361 (OPPOSITE)
Back of chasuble of satin weave silk with painting
Probably Canton (now Guangzhou), China, 1700–1800

V&A CIRC.624-1923

From the seventeenth to the nineteenth centuries in Europe, decorative nightcaps were worn by men for relaxing at home, where they received informal visits. The brim and crown of this cap (362) are one piece, therefore the decoration on the former had to be painted on the reverse of the silk in order to be visible when the brim was turned up. OC

362 (LEFT)
Man's nightcap of plain weave silk with painting
Italy, 1700–25

Bequeathed by the Rev. Dr N.H.C. Ruddock.
V&A 528-1898

Among the most appealing
eighteenth-century Chinese
exports are hand-painted silks.
They were manufactured
specifically for Europe where they
were fashionable. Most of those
that survive have curvaceous
mid-century decoration on
pastel backgrounds, but other
colours were also available.
The British East India Company
sent patterns and samples of
textiles for artists in Canton
(now Guangzhou) to copy.
On the white satin of the gown
(364), fanciful combinations
of English roses and sunflowers
have been painted alongside
Chinese peonies and orchids.
SN/HP

363 (OPPOSITE)
**Detail of plain weave silk
with painting**
China, about 1770–80

Given by J. Gordon Deedes.
V&A T.121-1933

364 (RIGHT)
**Back of gown of satin weave silk
from China with painting and
silk braid**
Britain, 1735–60

V&A T.115-1953

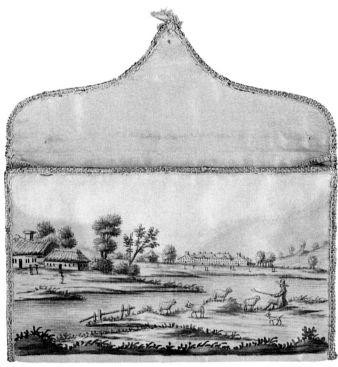

This chasuble (367) belongs to a set of vestments commissioned by the cardinal whose arms are incorporated into its design. A minuscule inscription on the front (368) reveals that the set was ornamented by Saverio Caselli, a priest, architect, cartographer and archaeologist. His remarkable talent and affection for antiquities are reflected in the impressive decorations minutely drawn on the silk with such precision that they appear printed. SB

367 (BELOW) & 368 (OPPOSITE)
Front and detail of a chasuble of plain weave silk, with pen and ink drawing and painting
By Saverio Caselli, possibly Benevento, Italy, 1776–82

V&A 268-1880

Seventeenth-century Dutch landscape prints inspired the scene on this eighteenth-century version of a wallet, showing on the left a pastoral scene with farmhouses and in the background a grand country house. Hand-painting in grey imitates the shading of an engraving or etching. A blush pink silk lining contrasts with the cream-coloured exterior, also highlighted by silver-gilt woven trimming. SN
ABOVE (365 & 366)

Pocket book or case of plain weave silk, with painting in grisaille, edged with ribbon of metal thread
France, 1750–60

Given by Miss Florence Kinkelin.
V&A T.143-1961

M.º Savario.   Casselli Archit.

1776 per tulta 1752

The design of this kimono (369) illustrates the close connection between painting and textile arts that existed in Japan. The silk crêpe of the garment has served like the surface of a hanging scroll for the creation of a hand-painted and resist-dyed auspicious image of cranes among pine trees and plum blossoms. AJ

369 (OPPOSITE)
Young woman's outer kimono of plain weave silk crêpe with painting in ink and colours, freehand paste resist-dyeing and touches of embroidery in silk and gold wrapped threads
Probably Kyoto, Japan, 1860–1900

Murray Bequest.
V&A T.389-1910

A number of techniques has been used to create the patterning on this kimono (370), including painting in ink directly on the surface and stencil paste resist-dyeing. The main motif is bamboo, while the various characters across the shoulders and sleeves are taken from the 'Poems of Congratulation' in the tenth-century *Kokinshū* anthology. Incorporating the written word into kimono design served to demonstrate the literary discernment of the wearer. AJ

370 (RIGHT)
Detail of woman's kimono of figured satin weave silk with hand-painting in ink, stencil-imitation tie-dyeing and embroidery in silk and gold wrapped threads
Probably Kyoto, Japan, 1780–1820

V&A FE.106 1982

On the Korean peninsula painting on textiles began in the Three Kingdoms period (57 BCE–668 CE) and was applied mainly to royal wrapping cloth and flags during the Joseon dynasty (1392–1910). Flags were important military equipment during the period, waved in different ways to command troops during battle. In these examples, the ground is blue, the directional colour for the east. The tiger in military attire represented courage while the war-deity provided leadership and protection. RK/EL

371 (OPPOSITE) & 372 (RIGHT)
Flags of damask weave silk with painting
Korea, 1700–1900 and 1800–1900

V&A FE.45-1999 & T.199-1920

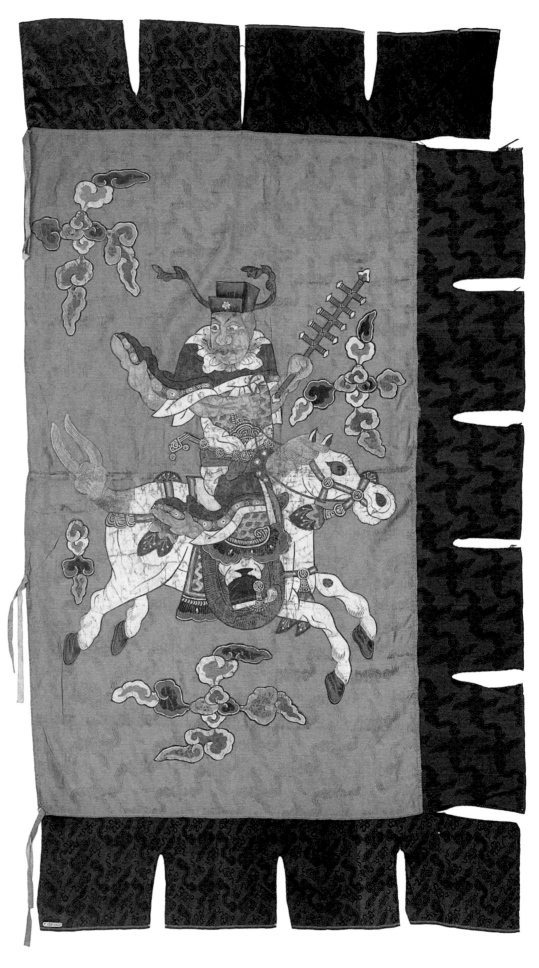

Traditional handcraft takes centre stage in this dress (373) which comes from Dolce & Gabbana's first foray into *alta costura* (haute couture). In this case three months of bespoke work included the hand-painting of the central burst of flowers and the application of chiffon adornments. RH

373 (OPPOSITE)
Detail of *Leonarda*, dress of silk faille with painting
By Dolce & Gabbana, Milan, Italy, 2015

Given by the designers.
V&A T.33:1-2015

Brisé fans are made of sticks held together with a silk cord or ribbon. This example (374) imitates feathers, its silk-covered sticks brightly painted in gouache with flowers, birds and insects. It is a foretaste of the increasing use of real feathers in fans from the 1870s. HF

374 (ABOVE)
Fan of plain weave silk with painting
Probably Netherlands, 1820–40

Given by Emily Beauclerk.
V&A T.120-1920

This Sun motif (375) is part of a much larger hanging with peacocks and geometrical patterns. The solar character of the face is marked by its perfect roundness and the red rays emanating from its perimeter, made by the ikat warps. The cross-shaped tattoo on its forehead and conjoined eyebrows were a mark of beauty in nineteenth-century Iran. They are hand painted. TS

375 (BELOW)
Detail from a hanging of plain weave silk with resist-dyeing (warp ikat) and painting
Iran, 1830–75

V&A 993-1886

In the 1980s and early 1990s Victoria Holton sold hand-painted neckties to high-end retailers such as Bergdorf Goodman in New York and Harrods in London. These examples are made from a woven silk frequently used for luxury ties. Holton's hand-painted aesthetic resulted in whimsical, one-of-a-kind accessories. SS

RIGHT (376, 377 & 378)
Neckties of plain weave silk with painting in an impasto technique and spirit-based paint
By Victoria Holton, Northampton, England, 1987

Given by the designer.
V&A T.43-1992, T.41-1992 & T.42-1992

In this sari (379), the hand-drawn design on the border and decorative end or *pallu* is in a style specific to Bihar, known as *Madhubani*. Such paintings traditionally decorated the interiors of village houses but in the late 1960s were transferred to paper and textiles to generate income for women painters. The motif of a woman under a tree symbolizes fertility, power and prosperity. DP

379 (OPPOSITE)
Detail of sari of plain weave tasar silk with painting
By Geeta Devi, Bihar, India, 1997

V&A IS.2-2000

RESIST-DYEING

This detailed landscape (380) was drawn on the surface of the fabric with rice paste extruded from a cloth tube fitted with a metal nozzle, a technique called *yūzen*. Dyes are normally then brushed on, but this example has been immersion-dyed, the resisted lines creating the pattern against the blue ground. The matte surface of silk crêpe provided the perfect ground fabric for such finely executed designs. AJ

380 (RIGHT)
Detail of young woman's outer kimono of plain weave silk crêpe with freehand paste resist-dyeing, stencil imitation tie-dyeing and embroidery in silk and gold wrapped threads
Probably Kyoto, Japan, 1800–50

V&A FE.188-2018

Moriguchi Kunihiko is known for his abstract, geometric designs executed in the freehand paste resist *yūzen* technique. Here waves decrease in number across the kimono from bottom to top and left to right (381). This is combined with tonal grading from dark to mid-green. Moriguchi was designated a Living National Treasure in 2007. AJ

381 (OPPOSITE)
Kimono of plain weave pongee silk with freehand paste resist-dyeing, entitled *Green Waves*
By Moriguchi Kunihiko, Kyoto, Japan, 1973

V&A FE.420-1992

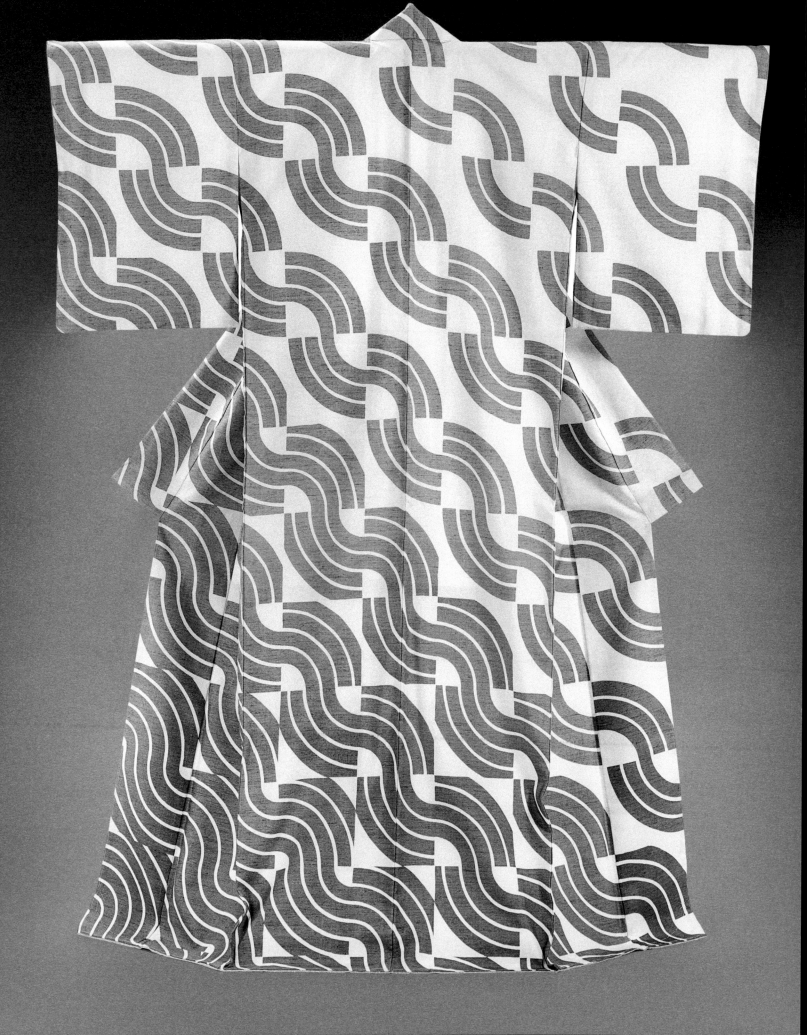

These are early examples of tie-dyeing and wax and lime resist-dyeing from China, clamp resist-dyeing being refined during the Tang dynasty (618–907 CE). The patterns on such silks were mostly small and usually in one colour. A set of symmetrically carved concave wooden boards with carved out spaces was used. Holes in the boards were opened to allow the dye to flow into the pattern spaces. When clamped to a folded fabric, the boards released dye on to the cloth according to the pattern areas into which the dye had flowed. Two sets of blocks were used for one of these fragments (384), one for blue, one for red. Where the two colours overlapped purplish brown appeared in the pattern. Subsequently, yellow was painted on to the blue and red to create greens and orange respectively. HP

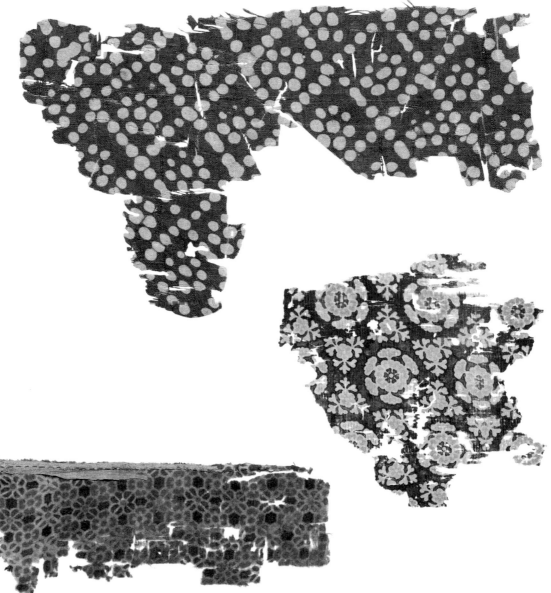

382 (TOP), 383 (ABOVE RIGHT), 384 (CENTRE LEFT) & 385 (BOTTOM)
Details of fragments of plain weave silk with clamp resist-dyeing
(382) Probably Astana, China, 200–800 CE
(383) Probably China, 800–1000 CE
(384) Probably China, 750–900 CE
(385) Probably China, 700–800 CE

Stein Textile Loan Collection, on loan from the Government of India and the Archaeological Survey of India.
V&A LOAN:STEIN.302, LOAN:STEIN.546, LOAN:STEIN.591 & LOAN:STEIN.544

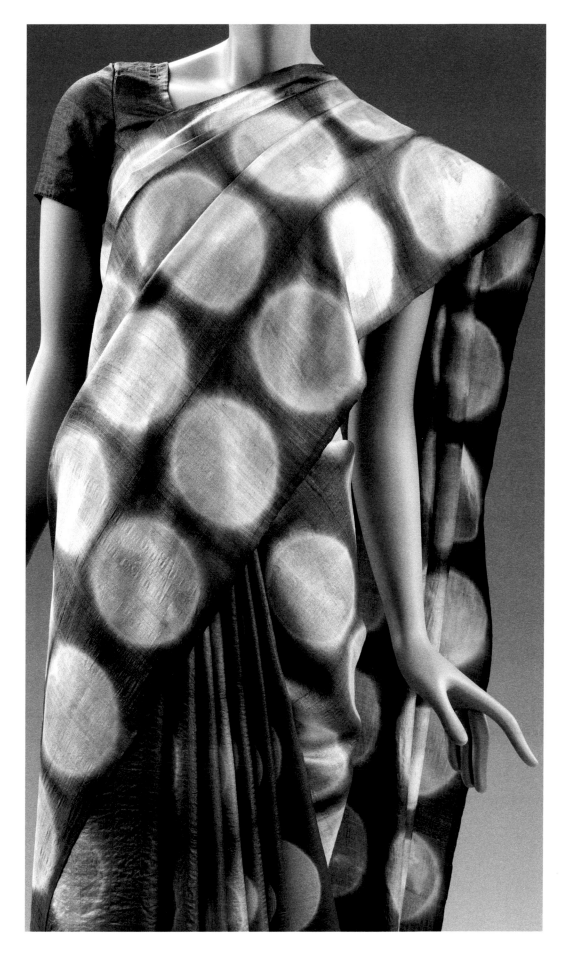

This bold design was made using the clamp-dyeing process. The designer-makers began by painting the silk base with swirls of grey and then folded it into squares, clamping it between pairs of wooden discs before dipping the cloth into dye. Undyed areas beneath the discs show the original painting which mimics the moon. The process left white halos around the disc, enhancing the lunar effect. DP

386
Detail of *Moon Sari* of plain weave tasar silk with clamp resist-dyeing
By Aziz Khatri and Suleman Khatri with NorBlack NorWhite, Bhadli, Kutch, Gujarat, India, 2012

V&A IS.3-2015

Both Malay people living in Indonesia and Cham people living in Cambodia create patterns in silk fabric using tie-dyeing and stitch-dyeing (387 and 388). They call this technique *plangi* which translates as rainbow, and possibly refers to the vibrant colours of the fabrics. FHP

387
Detail of sarong of plain weave silk with tie-dyeing and stitch resist-dyeing
Palembang, Sumatra, Indonesia, 1900–85

Given by Mrs L. Ryan.
V&A IS.45-1985

388
Detail of shawl or head covering
of plain weave silk with tie-dyeing
and stitch resist-dyeing
Cambodia, 1900–50

V&A IS.4-2001

In Gujarat head covers, saris, hangings and lengths of fabric were traditionally worked on locally woven satin, which is a base for some of the finest tie-dyeing work in India. The patterns are made up of rings of colour, produced by the pinching and binding of thousands of individual puckers of fabric. To produce large *bandhani* pieces like the head cover opposite (390), the fabric was folded in half, quarters, or even eighths, to allow multiple layers of cloth to be pinched and bound simultaneously. The field of the other cover (389) has been worked with a garden scene filled with elephants, tigers and birds. The dyer dip-dyed the head cover's edges to frame the red ground in indigo blue. AF

389 (ABOVE)
Detail of head cover of satin weave silk with tie-dyeing
Possibly Jamnagar, Gujarat, India, about 1870–1930

V&A IS.142-1953

390 (OPPOSITE)
Detail of head cover of satin weave silk with tie-dyeing
Gujarat, India, about 1900–30

Given by Mr A. Hennessy.
V&A IS.6-1976

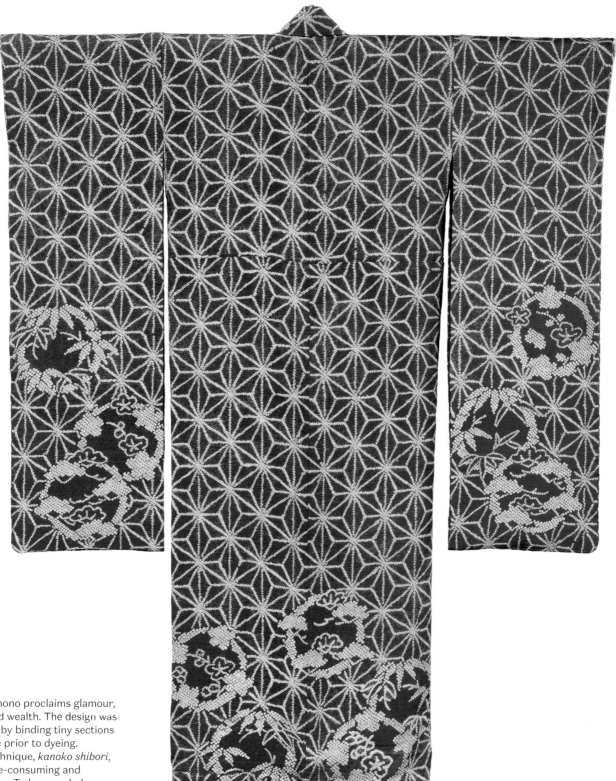

This kimono proclaims glamour, style and wealth. The design was created by binding tiny sections of fabric prior to dyeing. This technique, *kanoko shibori*, was time-consuming and expensive. To have a whole garment patterned in this way was extremely extravagant. Red, symbolic of youth and passion, derives from safflower, which was also costly. AJ

391 (OPPOSITE) & 392 (ABOVE)
Young woman's kimono of figured satin weave silk with tie-dyeing
Probably Kyoto, Japan, 1800–40

V&A FE.32-1982

This sumptuous kimono
was worn by a bride. The
folded paper male and female
butterflies, created using the
kanoko shibori technique,
symbolize harmony for the
new couple. The pattern has
been further embellished by
embroidery in glossy, untwisted
silk and shimmering gold
wrapped threads. AJ

393
Young woman's outer kimono
of figured satin weave silk with
tie-dyeing and embroidery in silk
and gold wrapped threads
Probably Kyoto, Japan, 1800–50

V&A FE.28-1984

Many early twentieth-century kimono were made from *meisen*, a thick pongee silk that was both long-lasting and relatively inexpensive but still lustrous. *Meisen* was patterned with chemical dyes applied through stencils on to the threads before weaving, a speeding-up of the hand-tie *kasuri* method. These informal garments were decorated with striking patterns that provided an exuberant visual statement for the stylish, urban woman. AJ

394
Woman's kimono of machine-spun plain weave pongee silk, with stencil dyeing of warps and wefts
Possibly Isesaki, Japan, 1920–40
V&A FE.28-2014

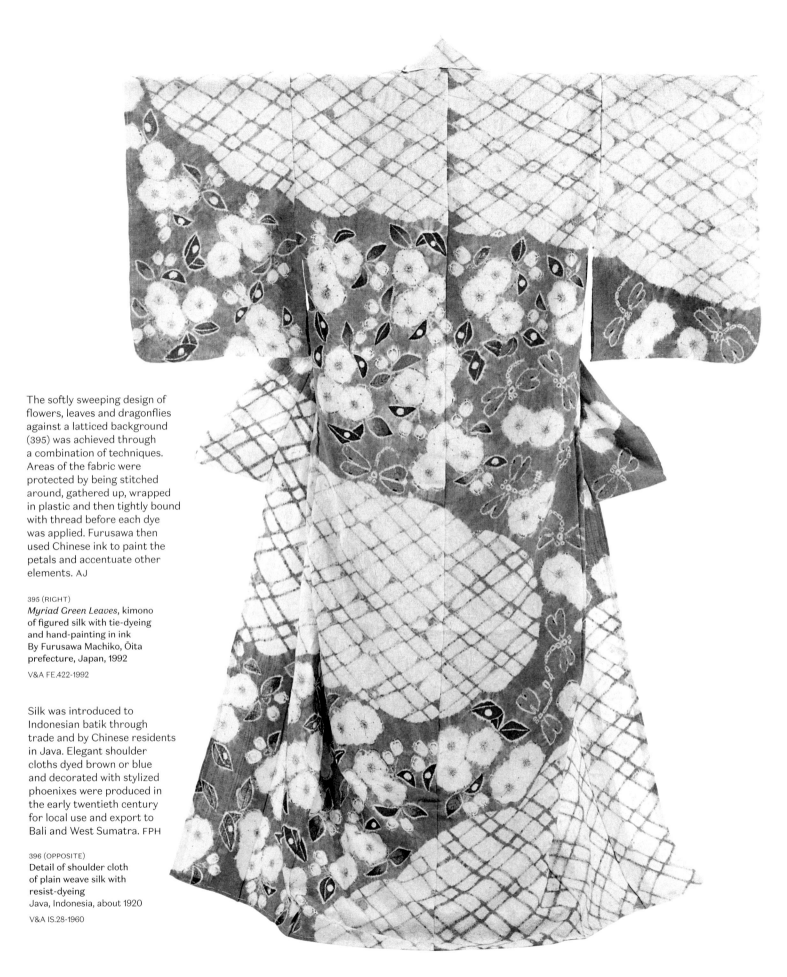

The softly sweeping design of flowers, leaves and dragonflies against a latticed background (395) was achieved through a combination of techniques. Areas of the fabric were protected by being stitched around, gathered up, wrapped in plastic and then tightly bound with thread before each dye was applied. Furusawa then used Chinese ink to paint the petals and accentuate other elements. AJ

395 (RIGHT)
Myriad Green Leaves, kimono of figured silk with tie-dyeing and hand-painting in ink
By Furusawa Machiko, Ōita prefecture, Japan, 1992
V&A FE.422-1992

Silk was introduced to Indonesian batik through trade and by Chinese residents in Java. Elegant shoulder cloths dyed brown or blue and decorated with stylized phoenixes were produced in the early twentieth century for local use and export to Bali and West Sumatra. FPH

396 (OPPOSITE)
Detail of shoulder cloth of plain weave silk with resist-dyeing
Java, Indonesia, about 1920
V&A IS.28-1960

Batik-dyeing became popular in Europe in the 1920s. In Britain, Scottish designer Winifred Kennedy Scott used the characteristic lines made by cracks in the wax during the dyeing process to ornamental effect in her designs. EM

397 (RIGHT)
Detail of shawl of silk crêpe de Chine with resist-dyeing
By Winifred Kennedy Scott, Britain, 1924–6

Given by Mrs E. Macqueen.
V&A T.114-1975

Simpsons of Piccadilly was proudly modern when it opened in 1936. After supplying uniforms during the Second World War (1939–45) and experiencing rationing and post-war austerity, the store embraced the Swinging Sixties. These bright trousers (398), tie-dyed in an idiom designed to appeal to modern European taste, are characteristic of this era. CAJ

398 (OPPOSITE)
Detail of trousers of twill weave silk with tie-dyeing
By Gordon Deighton for Simpsons of Piccadilly, London, England, 1968

Given by Gordon Deighton.
V&A T.881-2000

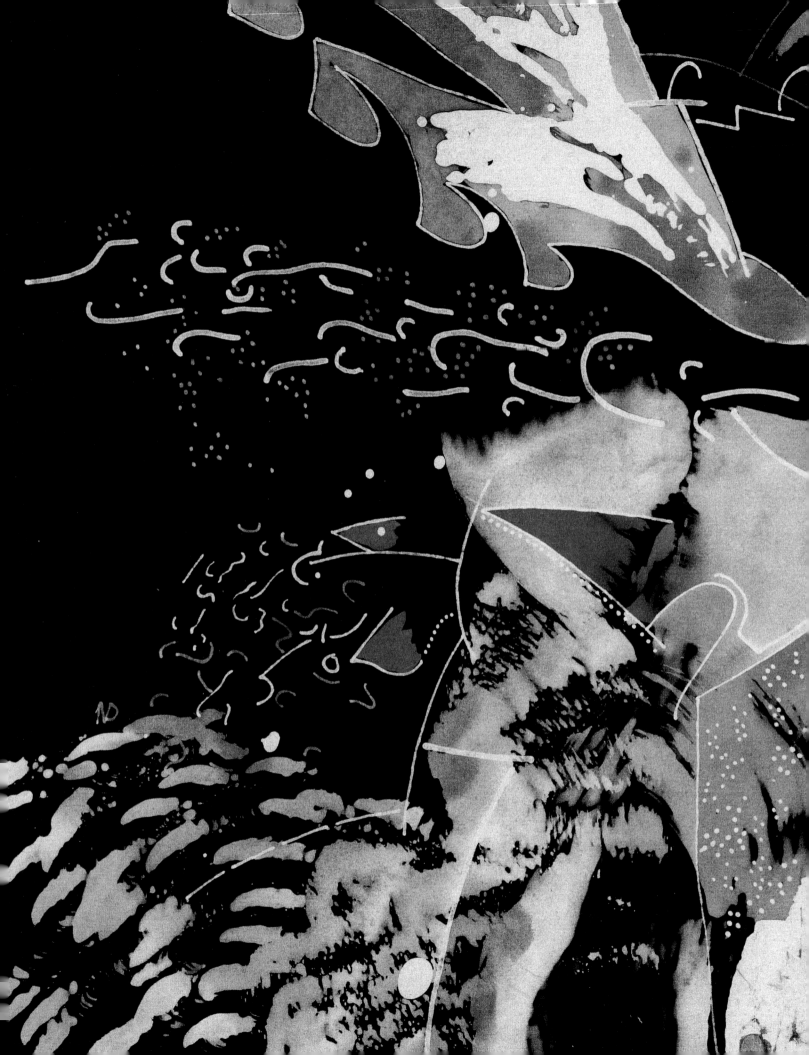

Noel Dyrenforth has
experimented with batik
since 1962. He believes that
his renown in this craft was
partly a result of attempts to
blur boundaries between art
and craft in Britain after the
Second World War. VB

Bingata, usually translated as 'scarlet colours', refers to the bright, stencil-dyed fabrics used exclusively by rulers of the Ryūkyū Islands. This archipelago stretches south-west of the main islands of Japan and was an independent kingdom until 1879. The vivid hues derive from mineral pigments, and although mainly applied to cotton, they were also used on silk such as this undergarment. AJ

400
Undergarment of plain weave silk with stencil-dyeing
Shuri, Okinawa, Japan, 1800–80

V&A T.20-1963

The fabric of this kimono (401) is *ro*, in which stripes of plain weave alternate with gauze to create a sheer silk fabric well-suited to Japan's humid summer climate. The bold visual rhythm of the cooling water motif was produced with one large stencil used repeatedly along the length of cloth. AJ

401 (OPPOSITE)
Summer kimono of plain and gauze weave silk with stencil-dyeing
Japan, 1910–30

Given by Moe Co. Ltd.
V&A FE.146-2002

In early twentieth-century Japan, chemical dyes were mixed with rice paste allowing colour to be applied directly through stencils. The new technique, called *kata-yūzen*, speeded up freehand patterning methods. Multiple stencils were used to create this design of cranes flying over a landscape. Small elements, such as the wing feathers and crests of the birds, have been highlighted with embroidery. AJ

402
Detail of young woman's kimono of plain weave silk crêpe with freehand paste resist- and stencil-dyeing, and touches of embroidery in silk and gold wrapped threads
Probably Kyoto, Japan, 1910–30

Given by Miss Christobel Hardcastle.
V&A FE.233-1974

Lightweight plain silk or silk and cotton warp ikat from Varanasi tended towards subtler patterns and colour combinations than ikats produced further south in India. Typically patterned with close-set dagger-like zigzags, such silk was often used for women's garments. These *paijama* trousers still have their silk sprang drawstring. AF

403 (BELOW) & 404 (RIGHT)
Trousers and detail of plain weave silk with warp resist-dyeing
Probably Varanasi, Uttar Pradesh, India (silk woven) and north India (garment made up), 1790–1850

V&A IS.32-1995

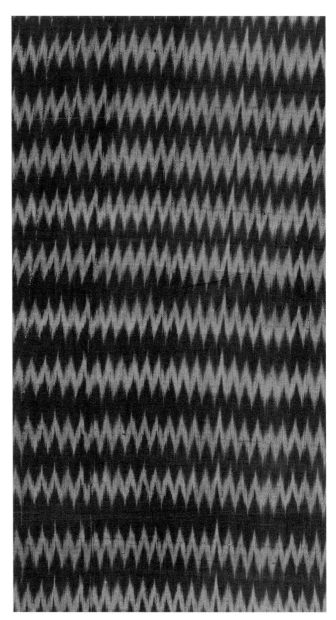

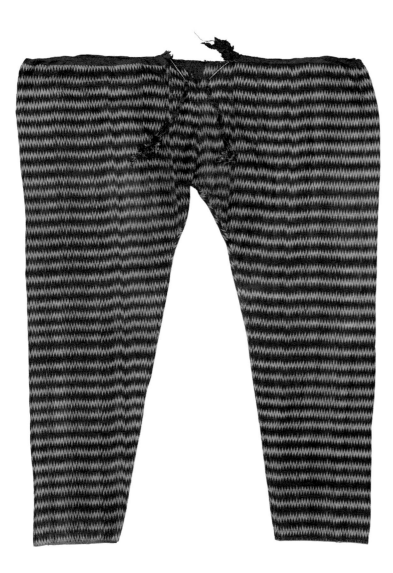

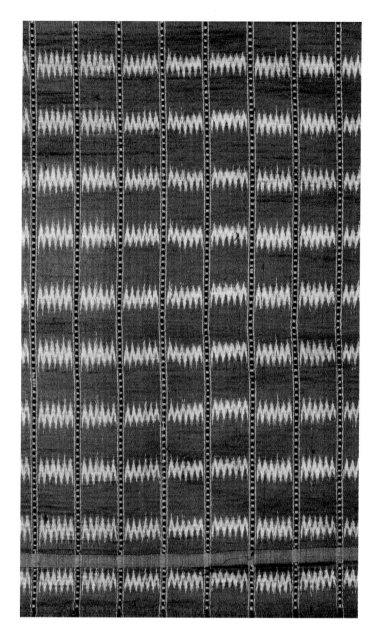

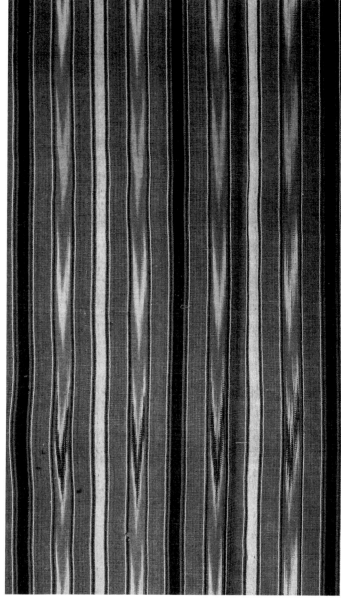

Thanjavur was a renowned centre for ikat *mashru* (silk and cotton) with chevron patterns worked by selectively dyeing the silk warps before weaving and staggering their arrangement on the loom. Such fabrics were used for both furnishings and garments, particularly as linings for mats and saddle cloths and for tailored *paijama* trousers and skirts. AF

405 (ABOVE)
Detail of length of satin weave of silk warp and cotton wefts with warp resist-dyeing
Thanjavur, Tamil Nadu, India, about 1855

V&A 6982(IS)

Female aristocrats in Aceh wore a striped silk hip cloth over trousers as ceremonial clothing. They covered their crotches to abide by Muslim rules on propriety. The warp threads are resist-dyed to create the chevron patterns. This warp ikat is typical of Acehnese silk textiles. SFC

406 (ABOVE)
Detail of woman's hip cloth of plain weave silk with warp resist-dyeing
Aceh, Sumatra, Indonesia, about 1900

V&A IS.61-1961

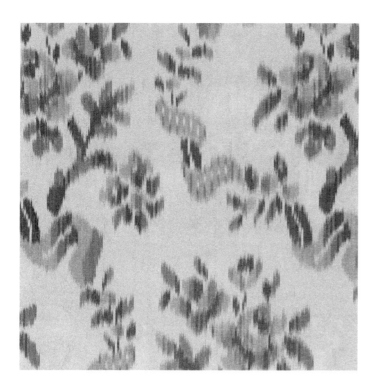

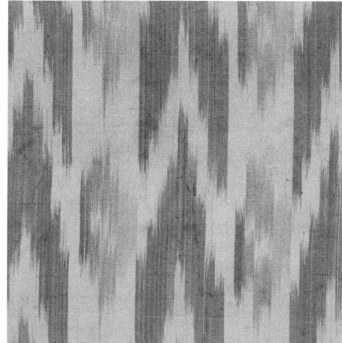

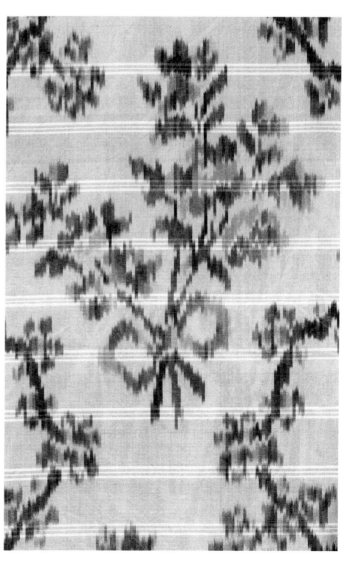

Christian Dior originally designed this haute couture cocktail dress (407) in a plain ivory taffeta, but client Laurie Newton Sharp, Harrods News editor and fashion consultant, ordered it in a lively *chiné* to wear with a pale pink silk coat. The stiffness of the taffeta complements the flared silhouette. In the *News Chronicle*, its wearer said she had chosen this dress 'for grand summer occasions'. CKB

407 (OPPOSITE)
Monte Carlo, evening gown of plain weave silk with warp and weft resist-dyeing, from 'La Ligne Flèche' collection
By Christian Dior, Paris, France, Spring/Summer 1956

Given by Mrs Laurie Newton Sharp.
V&A T.216-1968

In eighteenth-century Europe, these elegant lightweight silks (408–10), especially favoured for women's summer dresses, were described as '*chinés*' in France and 'clouded' in England, the latter a reference to the hazy outline. These patterns were achieved by a technique similar to ikat in which groups of warp threads were dyed before weaving. They were expensive because the dyeing was a slow, delicate process. The price increased with the complexity of the motifs, which ranged from simple, V-shaped elements to elaborate meanders of floral garlands and festoons. The most intricate examples have woven stripes or checks in the background. SB

408 (ABOVE)
Detail of lining of cope hood of plain weave silk with warp and weft resist-dyeing
France, 1760–70

V&A 730H-1864

409 (ABOVE RIGHT)
Fragment of satin weave silk with warp and weft resist-dyeing
Probably Italy, 1750–1800

Given by Sydney Vacher.
V&A T.268-1921

410 (RIGHT)
Detail of petticoat of plain weave silk with warp and weft resist-dyeing
France, 1760–70

V&A T.48-2018

In the nineteenth century, Bukhara was the capital the largest of the khanates of Central Asia. The city became a centre for the production of ikat textiles, which were used for court dress and 'robes of honour'. Silk velvets were the most luxurious and expensive of the fabrics made in this technique (411). TS

411 (FAR LEFT)
Detail of cut silk velvet with warp and weft resist-dyeing
Probably Bukhara, Uzbekistan, before 1875
V&A 2145(IS)

From 1865 to 1877, Yarkand in western Xinjiang province of China was the centre of an independent khanate ruled by an Uzbek military leader. This man, Ya'qub Beg, introduced the court practices of his homeland, including the production of ikat for court dress and 'robes of honour'. TS

412 (LEFT)
Length of plain weave silk and cotton with warp and weft resist-dyeing
Probably Yarkand (now Shache county, Xinjiang province), China, 1866–73
V&A 2110(IS)

The border of the waistcoat opposite (413) has been woven to shape, its 'clouded' pattern of swagged draperies and floral garlands in velvet contrasting with the sharply defined ribbed and alternating velvet stripes. The complexity of designing for such silks merited a chapter in the first manual of silk design published in 1765 and a detailed description and plates in Diderot and d'Alembert's *Encyclopédie*, vol. 28 (Paris 1772). LEM

413 (OPPOSITE)
Detail of waistcoat of cut silk velvet and *cannelé* weave with warp and weft resist-dyeing (border)
Probably France, 1790–1800
Given by Mrs M. Sidwell.
V&A T.173-1966

Mary Restieaux's ikat hangings
require bespoke dyed yarns
and are woven individually on
a handloom. Her designs have
also been adapted for use
in the fashion industry. She
chooses tasar silk for her work
because of its strength and
matte finish. VB

414
**Hanging of plain weave tasar silk
with warp resist-dyeing**
By Mary Restieaux, England, 1980

V&A T.432-1980

This striking abstract pattern was the result of a collaborative project between designers and artisans. Pochampally in south India is famous for its ikat dyeing and weaving and the project aimed to bring a fresh and contemporary design aesthetic to traditional techniques. DP

415 (BELOW) & 416 (RIGHT)
Sari of plain weave silk with warp resist-dyeing
Designed by Hitesh Rawat and Avanish Kumar for Jiyo!, woven by Jella Sudhakar, Pochampally, Telangala, India, 2011

V&A IS.20-2012

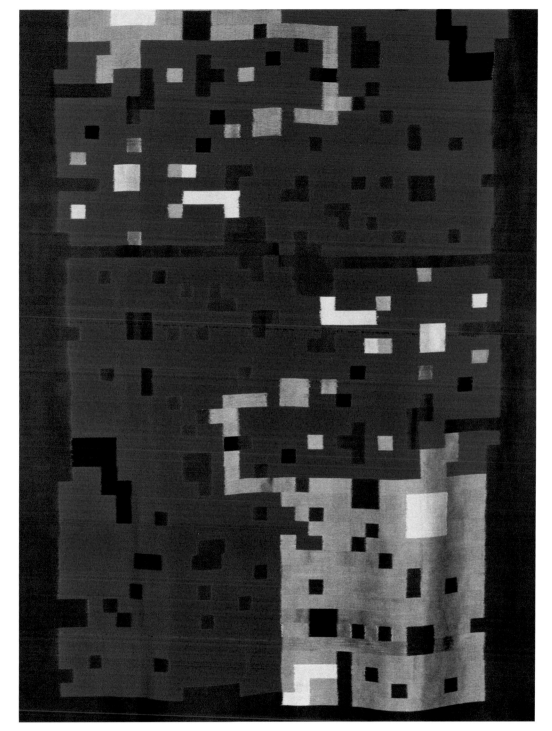

The complex technique of
double ikat is practised in only
a few select production centres
in India. Most famous is Patan,
Gujarat, which is home to India's
most intricate double ikats,
silk *patola*. They are worked
with extraordinary precision.
Both the warps and wefts are
pre-dyed with complex patterns
before being carefully woven
together. AF

417 (ABOVE)
Detail from a sari of plain weave silk
with warp and weft resist-dyeing
and metal wrapped thread
Probably Patan, Gujarat, India,
about 1900–20

V&A IS.189-1960

Khmer weavers in Cambodia
use weft ikat to decorate
lustrous temple hangings with
Buddhist imagery. The clarity
of the pictorial scenes depicting
the life of Buddha on this
example (418) demonstrates
the maker's technical virtuosity
in dyeing and weaving the weft
threads. The use of twill weave
heightens the brilliance of the
cloth's surface. FHP

418 (OPPOSITE)
Detail of temple hanging of twill
weave silk with weft resist-dyeing
Cambodia, 1900–93

V&A IS.205-1993

The technique of weaving with selectively pre-dyed threads is known as *kasuri* in Japan and is closely associated with indigo-dyed cotton, ramie and hemp produced in rural areas. This child's kimono (419) has been woven with silk, however, giving the otherwise simple, soft stripes a lustrous appearance. AJ

419 (LEFT)
Child's kimono of plain weave silk with selectively pre-dyed threads
Japan, 1870–1910
V&A FE.51-1982

The design of this chic outfit (420) with its long-sleeved shirt was inspired by western office wear. It was made using ikat hand dyeing and weaving techniques in the workshops of Shri Govardhana, renowned for its high quality craftsmanship. A black-and-white weft ikat houndstooth pattern leads to a warp-ikat transition into a plain chartreuse section. DP

420 (OPPOSITE)
Detail of sari of plain weave silk with warp and weft resist-dyeing
Designed by Abraham & Thakore, woven by Shri Govardhana, Puttapaka, Telangana, India, 2011

Given by the designers.
V&A IS.3-2013

PRINTING

Twirling bouquets of tulips, irises, carnations, roses and sunflowers arranged in vases give this silk – probably originally intended for a woman's dress – an air of cheerfulness. The ivory damask was vibrantly patterned by block printing and hand colouring, probably in Amsterdam, a city where master craftsmen specialized in this technique from the early eighteenth century. SB

421
Detail of a chasuble of damask weave silk with block printing and hand painting
Probably Amsterdam, Netherlands, 1730–40
V&A 1582-1899

This silk was woven in India and subsequently block printed in England. It was probably shown at the 'Exposition Universelle' in Paris in 1878 by dyer and printer Thomas Wardle, who championed the dyeing and printing of this kind of wild silk. The natural gold sheen of the ground reveals that it dates from before Wardle succeeded in perfecting the process of bleaching out the colour. HF

422
Length of plain weave tasar silk with block printing
Woven in India, printed by Thomas Wardle, Leek, Staffordshire, England, 1878

V&A CIRC.502-1965

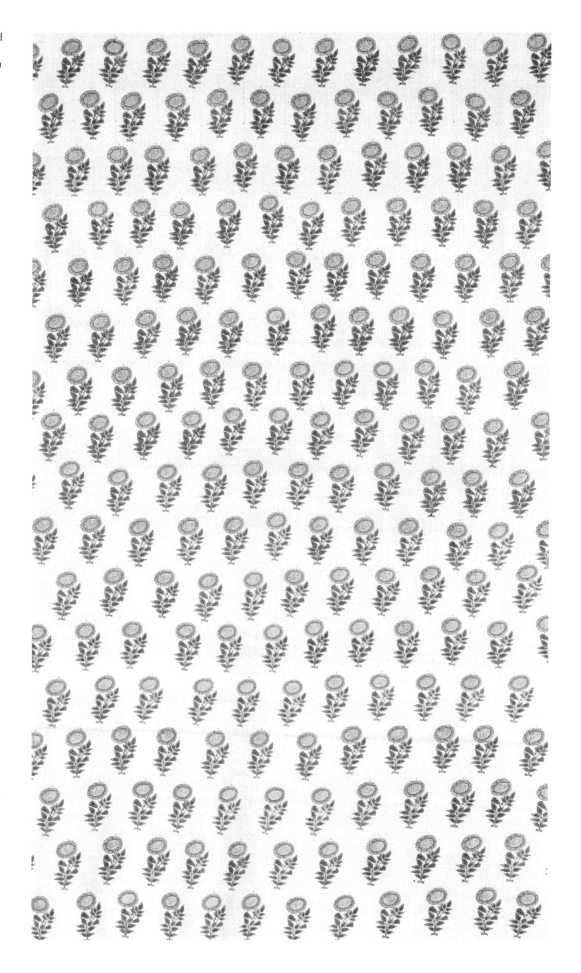

These head covers are woven in the same technique but coloured differently. The first (423) is made of Chinese silk lengths, the stock-taking inscriptions still visible. Wooden blocks carved with motifs imitating Gujarati tie-dyed patterns were then used to print the design, a quicker process than genuine tie-dyeing. The second head cover (424) was more time-consuming, being dyed in magenta, then block printed with wax resist, before being dyed again in deep indigo blue. AF/DP

423 (OPPOSITE)
Detail of head cover of satin weave silk with block printing
Gujarat, India, about 1855

V&A 4903(IS)

424 (ABOVE)
Detail of head cover of satin weave silk with resist printing and over-dyeing
Saurashtra, Gujarat, India, 1900–40

Given by Ann French and Lynda Hillyer.
V&A IS.5-2014

Silk chiffon is a soft sheer fabric woven from single yarns in a plain weave open structure. Its fine lightweight quality suits draping styles such as saris. In this unusual example (425) the sari has a woven pattern onto which colour has been screen printed. DP

425 (OPPOSITE)
Detail of sari of silk chiffon with screen printing
Probably woven and printed in Europe, about 1930
Worn by Mrs Mayura Brown
Given by the wearer.
V&A IS.49-1998

First produced in Bengal in the late seventeenth century, the carliest bandannas were simply made in low-grade silk and patterned with tie-dyed spots. Millions of Bengali silk bandannas were exported worldwide before western industrially printed cotton versions took over the market in the nineteenth century. This length (426) shows how Indian makers attempted to compete with machine printing: they used printing blocks to create more complex designs than the previous hand-tied and dyed spots. AF

426 (RIGHT)
Length of bandanna handkerchiefs of plain weave silk, with resist block printing
Murshidabad, West Bengal, India, about 1867
V&A 4909(IS)

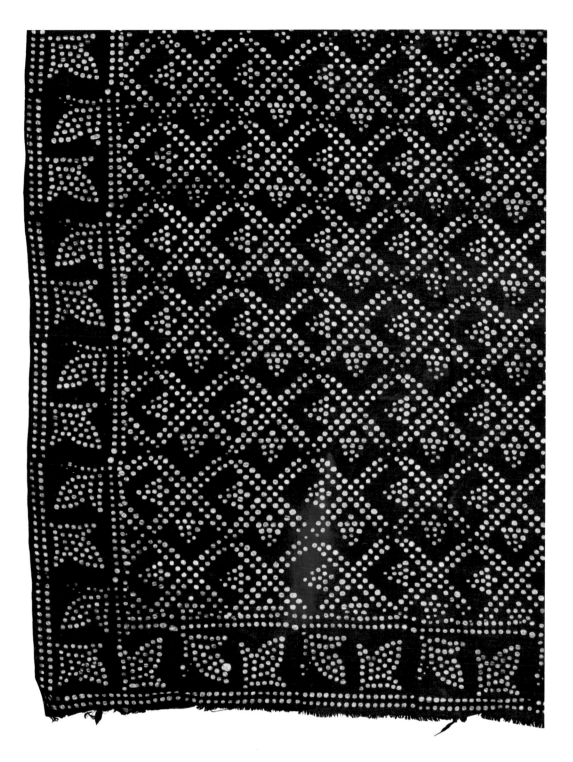

Artist and designer Paul Nash was dismissive of the quality of British pattern design in the 1920s and 1930s. He enjoyed the technique of block printing and also believed in the possibility of high quality industrially manufactured design. The production of this design, *Cherry Orchard*, was first outsourced to Footprints (427) where it was hand block printed onto silk crêpe de Chine. Dissatisfied with the colours and production, Nash then supplied the design to the larger enterprise Cresta Silks where it was screen printed from 1932 onwards (428). The difference in the production techniques is evident when the two fabrics are compared. VB

427 (RIGHT)
Top of silk crêpe de Chine with block printing
Designed by Paul Nash, printed by Footprints, Britain, 1925–9

Given by Valerie Mendes.
V&A T.358-1990

428 (BELOW)
Length of silk crêpe de Chine with screen printing
Printed by Cresta Silks, England, after 1932

Given by the Paul Nash Trust.
V&A CIRC.465-1962

Alec Walker was inspired by his contact with French artist Raoul Dufy who also designed fashion textiles. Walker's own painterly designs were often based on landscapes in Cornwall where he produced his textiles. This sample is stamped with its 1930 Design Registry number that protected it from use by other manufacturers. VB

429
Length of silk crêpe de Chine with block printing
By Alec Walker for Cryséde, St Ives, Cornwall, England, 1930

Given by Manchester Design Registry.
V&A T.67-1979

This textured fabric, known as raw silk or dupion, is made from a smooth fine yarn warp woven with a slightly slubby yarn weft. This uneven yarn results from the tangled fibres that occur when two silkworms build a single cocoon or when they build their cocoons close together. Here, the irregularities in the fabric complement the rough nature of the block printed design. DP

430
Detail of sari of plain weave raw silk with block printing
By Masaba Gupta, Mumbai, Maharastra, India, 2012

V&A IS.22-2012

This bag was produced and sold by the Female Society for Birmingham, West Bromwich, Walsall and their Respective Neighbourhoods, for the Relief of British Negro Slaves, the first and most influential group of women campaigning for the abolition of slavery in Britain. Bags, pin cushions and jewellery were sold, particularly in the late 1820s when women became increasingly significant in the movement. Such items were accompanied by a card explaining their purpose. KH

431 (RIGHT)
Bag of satin weave silk with copperplate printing after design by Samuel Lines
Birmingham, England, about 1825

Given by Mrs Foster.
V&A T.227-1966

In the years before and following the French Revolution (1789–99), French manufacturers fed patriotic appetite with topical fashionable goods. This set of buttons (432) depicts 18 political figures, their portraits taken from engravings. They include an early revolutionary leader, Honoré-Gabriel Riqueti, Count of Mirabeau, and the younger Jacobin leader Louis-Antoine de Saint Just. SB/KH

432 (LEFT)
Part of a set of 18 buttons of satin weave silk with copperplate printing, framed in glass and gilt metal
France, about 1790

Given by C.W. Dyson Perrins.
V&A T.39-1948

433 (NEAR LEFT)
Top of button from similar set, ready to frame

V&A 1869-1899

Many theatres produced silk programmes around the turn of the twentieth century (434). Typically, they celebrated special occasions, here the state visit of Wilhelm II, the last German emperor and king of Prussia, and his wife, Princess Augusta Viktoria, to London's Royal Italian Opera House on 8 July 1891. Luxurious and less fragile than paper bills, they were sold as souvenirs. CAJ

434 (OPPOSITE)
Playbill of satin weave silk with copperplate printing
By the London Stereoscopic and Photographic Company, England, 1891

V&A S.201-1981

This scarf was probably associated with the Women's Social and Political Union (1903–17), a British suffrage group which adopted a purple, white and green colour scheme in 1908. Featuring a hard-hitting slogan woven in soft silk, it embodies the WSPU's tactical attempt to blend feminism with femininity in its fight for votes for women. CAJ

435 (RIGHT)
Commemorative scarf of satin weave silk with roller printing
Britain, about 1910
Given by G. Brett, Esq.
V&A T.20-1946

436 (BELOW)
Suffragette Delivering a Speech at the Earl's Court Exhibition
Photograph, England, 1908
Museum of London

Reproduced following an eighteenth-century fabric, this silk is appropriate for this daybed because the pattern echoes those favoured from the mid-eighteenth century by the French queen. The warp threads in the original would have been hand-dyed, while this contemporary version is screen printed on a loosely woven silk fabric from which loose weft threads are subsequently removed and the warps then rewoven using plain wefts, thus creating the 'clouded' effect. LEM

437 (RIGHT) & 438 (BELOW)
Cover of plain weave silk with screen printing, entitled *Menuet*
By La Manufacture Prelle, Lyon, France, 2014
Daybed
By Jean-Baptiste Tilliard, Paris, France, about 1750

Given by Sir Alfred Chester Beatty in memory of his wife.
V&A W.5-1956

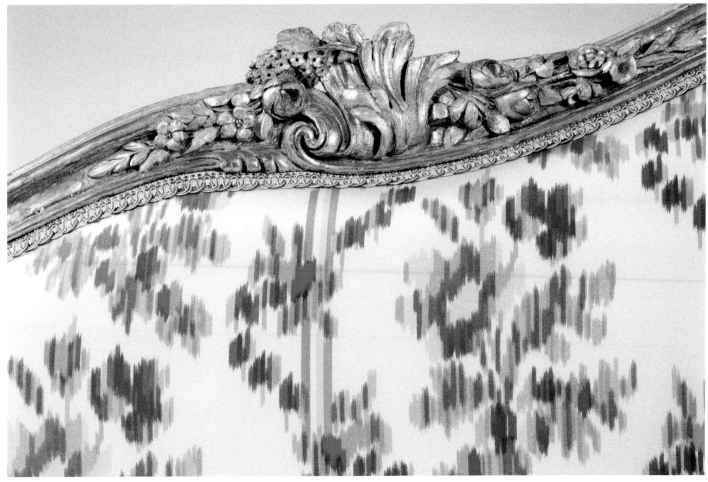

This Liberty & Co. headscarf (439) prominently features the *buta* motif, which is strongly associated with Indian design. In this way it gestures towards the company's earliest phase. When Arthur Lasenby Liberty opened his shop in London in 1875, it was called East India House. It traded exclusively in silk that had been imported from countries including India and dyed in England. CAJ

439
Head scarf of twill weave silk with block printing
Retailed by Liberty & Co., London, England, 1930–40

Given by Miss Mary Peerless.
V&A T.511-1974

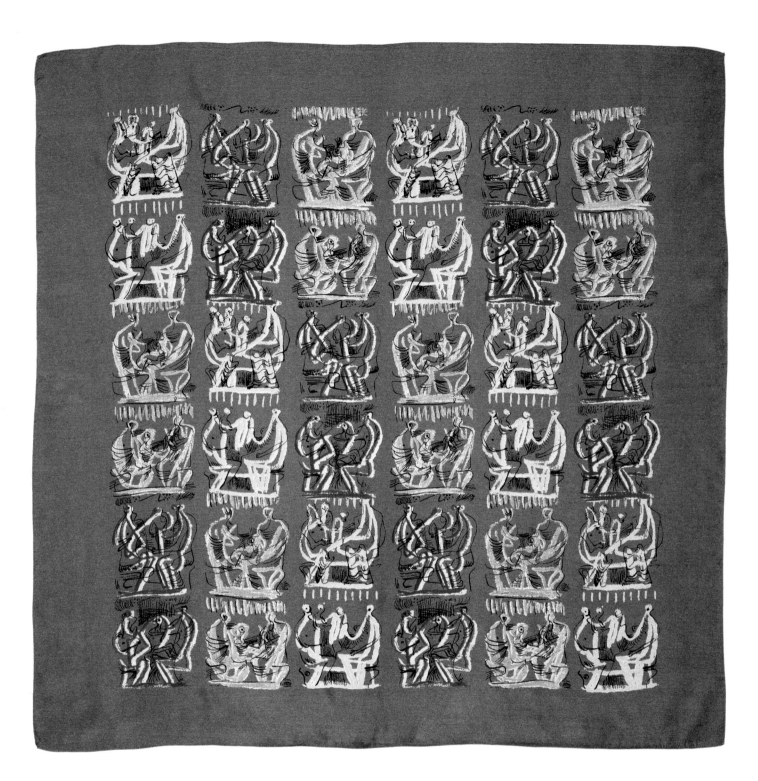

In the early twentieth century European textile manufacturers revealed the painterly qualities of screen printing by commissioning designs from contemporary fine artists (440–2). The London-based firm Ascher was one such company producing head scarves valued for both their artistic and fashionable qualities. Some designs were limited editions and the printing screens were destroyed once the allotted number (between two and 600) had been produced. CKB

440
Family Group, head scarf of twill weave silk with block printing
Designed by Henry Moore for Ascher Ltd, London, England, 1945–6

V&A CIRC.331-1961

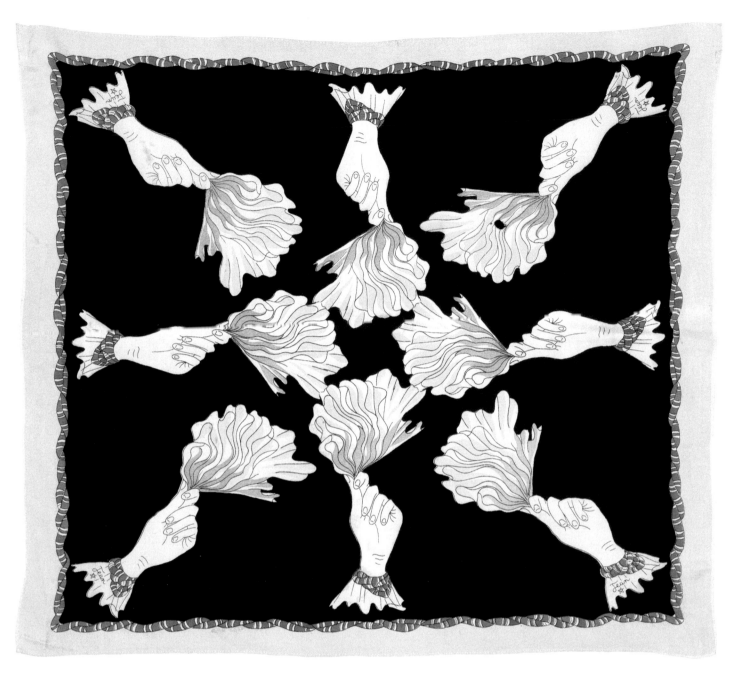

441 (ABOVE)
Head scarf of plain weave silk
with screen printing
Designed by Jean Cocteau,
France, 1937–9

V&A T.220–1979

442 (OPPOSITE)
Head scarf of twill weave silk
with screen printing
Designed by André Derain for
Ascher Ltd, London, England, 1947

V&A T.719-1997

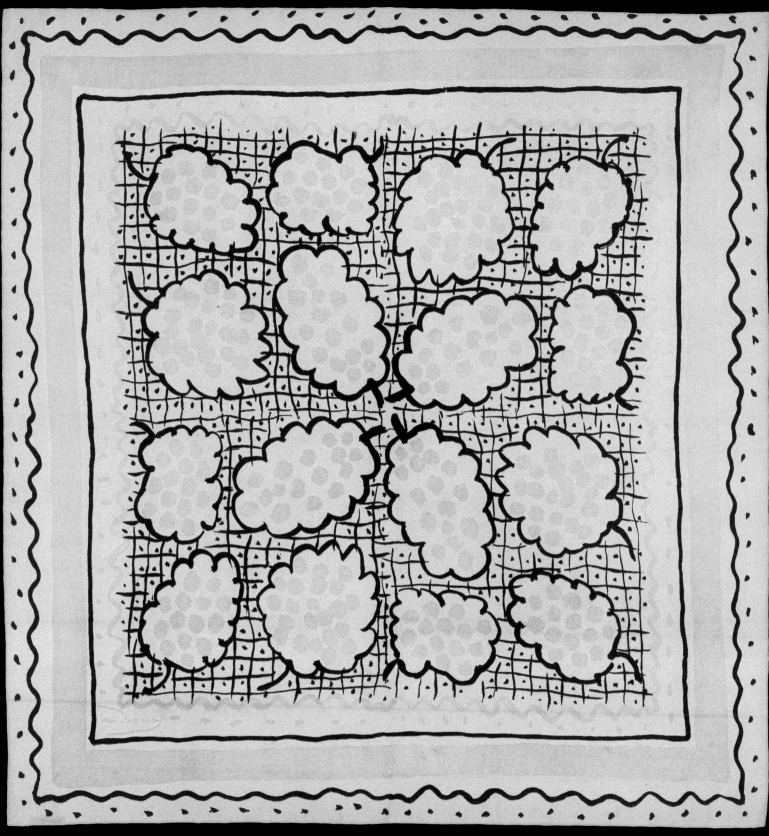

Established in Paris in 1837 as a harness maker, Hermès was known by the mid-twentieth century for its luxury accessories as well as leather goods. These included silk scarves, designed in conjunction with well-known artists, referencing Hermès' equestrian heritage. Swiss artist Jean-Louis Clerc designed 10 scarves for the house during the 1950s and 1960s, frequently featuring fashionable crowds (444). In contrast, the British head scarf (443), decorated with advertising slogans for goods as diverse as alcoholic drinks, clothing and vacuum cleaners, reveals how one advertising agency promised an exciting new world free from the restraints of wartime austerity to less wealthy consumers. OC/JR

443 (ABOVE)
Head scarf of twill weave silk with screen printing
Designed for C.J. Lytle Advertising, Britain, 1950–60

Given by Mrs Greta Edwards.
V&A T.384-1988

444 (OPPOSITE)
Paddock, head scarf of twill weave silk with screen printing
By Jean-Louis Clerc for Hermès, Paris, 1955

Given by Rosemary D. Hammond.
V&A T.55-2016

The pattern on this sari (445) was probably screen rather than block printed as the printing appears very regular. The all-over geometric design reflects the rise of a modern aesthetic from the 1920s and a fashion for lightweight silks that drape easily. Heavy woven and embellished saris continued to be worn alongside such new styles. DP

445 (RIGHT)
Detail of sari of plain weave silk probably with screen printing
Kolkata, India, about 1930
Worn by Mrs Mayura Brown

Given by the wearer.
V&A IS.46-1998

Playful and subversive prints were a mainstay of Red or Dead's fashion collections. Here the decorative motif of the sunflower is reimagined in a haphazardly arranged collage of imperfectly exposed photos (446). The fabric appeared in the 1994 Spring/Summer collection which included a billowing kimono-style garment that made full use of the large-scale print. VB

446 (OPPOSITE)
Detail of dress fabric of satin weave silk with screen printing
By Gary Page for Red or Dead, London, England, 1994

Given by the designer.
V&A T.7-2007

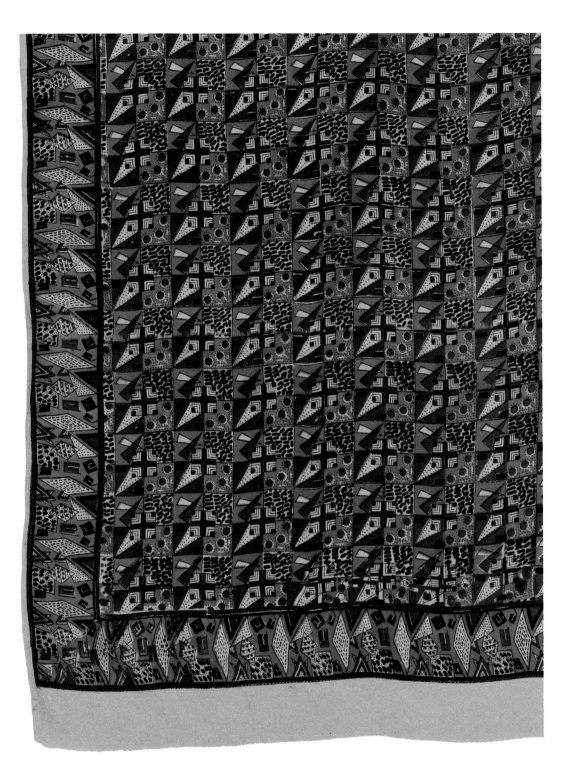

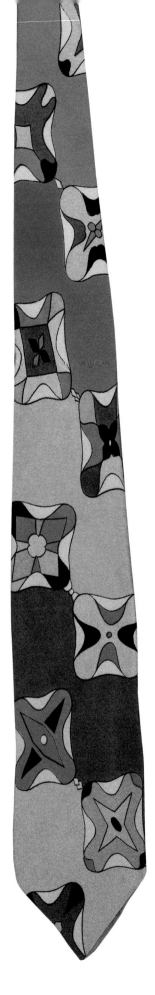

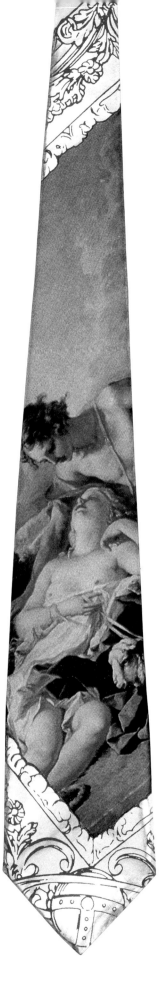

A colourfully printed necktie can be an effective vehicle for self-expression. These examples illustrate a range of prints in vibrant hues depicting inventive motifs. A quintessentially kaleidoscopic textile design (447) from the Italian fashion house Emilio Pucci contrasts with the more sombre, striated pattern seen in the design by Christian Dior (448), a firm which early in its history extended global licensing agreements to a range of luxury goods, including ties. In contrast, Vivienne Westwood, a fashion designer known for borrowing imagery from fine art, chose details from *Daphnis and Chloe* (449), painted by the French artist François Boucher in 1743. SS

447 (FAR LEFT), 448 (CENTRE LEFT) & 449 (NEAR LEFT)
Neckties of plain weave silk with screen printing

(447) By Emilio Pucci, Italy, 1960–70
Given by G.A. Browning.
V&A T.461-1985

(448) By Christian Dior, France, about 1970
Worn by Kenneth Tynan
Given by the Department of Manuscripts, British Library.
V&A T.532-1995

(449) By Vivienne Westwood, London, England, 1991
Given by the designer.
V&A T.24-1992

The bustier of this evening dress (450) is embellished with an enlarged floral motif in *dancheong* style, a colourful art used for decorating and protecting wooden structures of traditional Korean palaces and temples. *Dancheong* uses the five directional colours red (south), blue (east), yellow (centre), white (west) and black (north), symbolically protecting the building from evil spirits in these cardinal directions. RK

450 (OPPOSITE)
Detail of *Dancheong Bustier Dress,* evening dress of plain weave silk with screen printing on bodice
By Lie Sangbong, South Korea, Spring/Summer 2012
Given by the designer.
V&A FE.65-2012

Traditional Korean costume (*hanbok*) comprises a jacket (*jeogori*) and a skirt (*chima*). Here the *jeogori*'s design is based on eighteenth-century models, characterized by narrow sleeves and short sashes. Its modern twist lies in the lively floral pattern, in contrast to the modest, monochromatic silk of traditional jackets. RK

451 (LEFT) & 452 (RIGHT)
Modern Girl, ensemble of silk organza with screen printing
By Kim Young Jin, Seoul, South Korea, 2009

Purchase funded by Samsung.
V&A FE.17:1 to 11-2015

Greek-born fashion and textile designer Mary Katrantzou uses ground-breaking digital printing technology to transpose the stylized aesthetic of 1970s fashion photography onto the body (453). The illusion is completed by the structured pelmet across the shoulders, mimicking the line of ceiling arches. The monochrome silk chiffon falls like curtains of sheer fabric to frame the legs. RH

453 (RIGHT)
Vila Pong, evening dress of plain weave ribbed silk with digital printing and silk chiffon
By Mary Katrantzou, London, England, 2011
Given by the designer.
V&A T.31:1 to 3-2015

The complex design on this kimono (454) has been digitally printed on silk woven with a spotted pattern. The bright blues and pinks, and motifs of roses, butterflies and ribbon, are suitable for a young woman's garment. However, the oversize swans and seashells, the curious figures, and the fairy-tale castle on a chequered ground are more disconcerting and reveal Shigemune's interest in Surrealism. AJ

454 (OPPOSITE)
Engagement Ribbon, young woman's kimono of figured satin weave silk with digital printing
By Shigemune Tamao, designed in Tokyo, made in Kyoto, Japan, 2016
V&A FE.43-2018

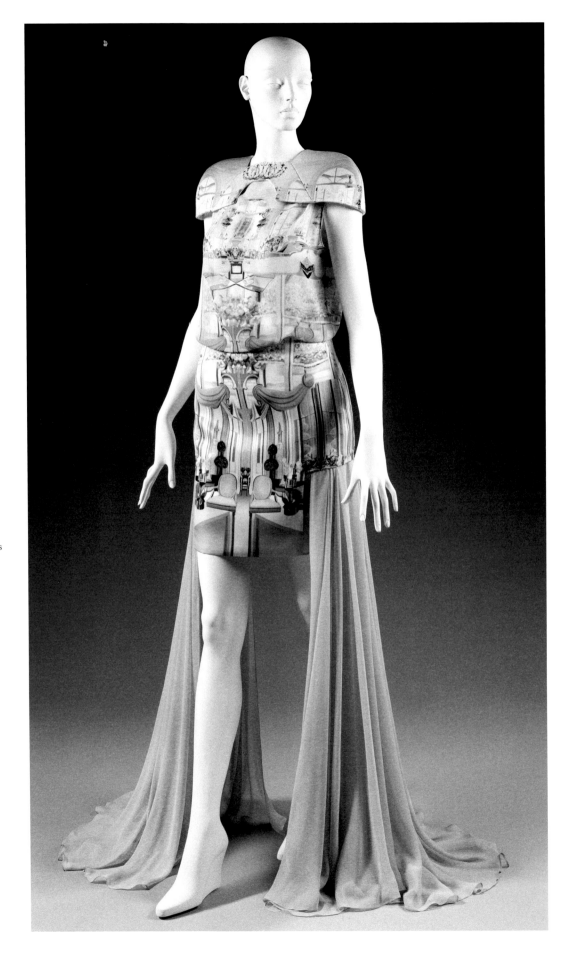

GOLD AND SILVER

Like many kimono fabrics, this example is patterned with a number of different techniques including applied gold leaf, which has been fixed to the figured satin with paste. The use of gold, with small-scale embroidery and tie-dyeing against a dark ground, is a feature of kimono from the early seventeenth century. AJ

455
Fragment of a kimono of damask weave silk with applied gold leaf, tie-dyeing and embroidery in silk and gold wrapped threads
Kyoto, Japan, 1596–1615

V&A 1588-1899

Doturak daenggi, a Korean bridal hair ribbon, has its origins in a ceremonial ribbon worn by royal and noble women of the Joseon dynasty (1392–1910). This example of silk gauze is ornamented with auspicious motifs stamped in gold leaf. Gold expressed stability, eternity and prosperity. RK/EL

456
Hair ribbon of silk gauze with stamping in gold
By Lee Young Hee, Seoul, South Korea, 1992

Given by the designer.
V&A FE.431:6-1992

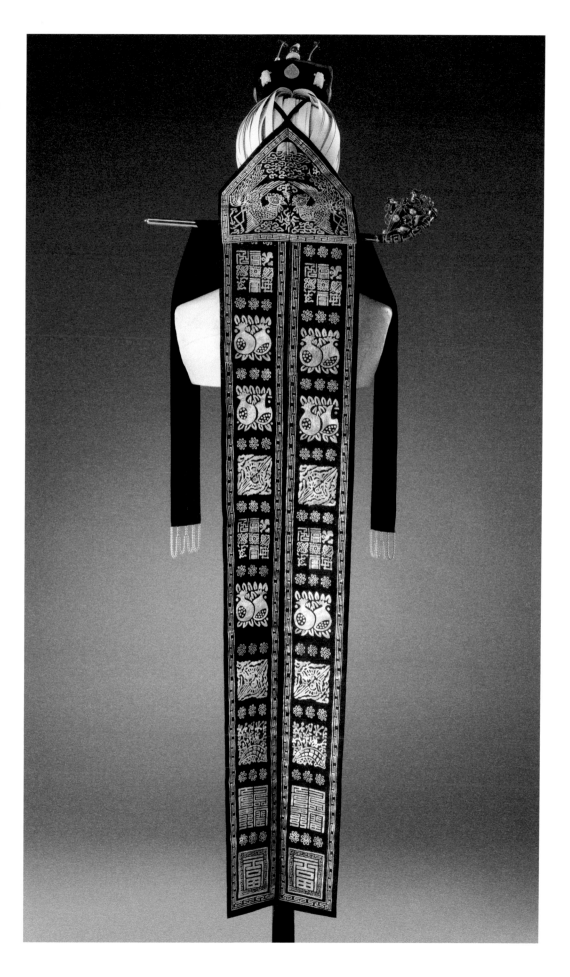

This courtly woman's skirt (457) is voluminous and particularly rich because it is made of silk, as opposed to the more common muslin. The 68-metre-long hem is weighted down by a broad band of silver-gilt tinsel ribbon, which helps the fabric fall evenly around the body. Large skirts of this style were fashionable in nineteenth-century Rajasthan. AF

457 (OPPOSITE)
Detail of skirt of plain weave silk with block printing of adhesive gum overlaid with gold leaf
Possibly Bharatpur, Rajasthan, India, about 1855–80

V&A 05846(IS)

The main feature of a Malaysian sarong is a broad band known as the *kepala* (head). It contains triangular *tumpal* motifs derived from bamboo shoots that symbolized fertility. This sarong (458) is polished on one side with a cowrie-shell and printed with gum-treated wooden stamps, such as the examples on the right (459). The pattern was then overlaid with gold leaf. SFC

458 (ABOVE)
Detail of sarong of plain weave silk with stamping in gold leaf
Terengganu, Malaysia, 1924

V&A IM.271-1924

459 (RIGHT)
Printing blocks of *tumpal* motifs for textile printing, carved wood
Selangor, Malaysia, 1920–3

Given by HH the Sultan of Selangor.
V&A IM.66 to 68-1925

Gold and Silver   361

Like many of Spanish designer Mariano Fortuny's creations, this jacket was inspired by history and international design. Silk velvet had its heyday in the Renaissance, and the formal gold leaf design, printed to replicate woven decoration, resembles both Renaissance and Persian motifs. The jacket's cut evokes nineteenth-century dolmans and Japanese kimono. CAJ

460
Detail of evening jacket of cut silk velvet with roller printing
Probably printed by Mariano Fortuny, Venice, Italy, about 1920

Given by Mrs Hollond.
V&A T.424-1976

Surviving tent panels give a taste of the opulence of India's courtly tents, which were erected during journeys between capitals and on military campaigns. This example is one of a set of dozens that together formed the wall of a tent belonging to a Maharaja of Jaipur. AF

461
Tent hanging of cut silk velvet with stencilling with gum and gold leaf
Probably Jaipur, Rajasthan, India, 1700–1800
V&A IM.30–1936

Graduated garlands of painted ribbons and bows encircle the voluminous skirt of this evening dress. The pattern is applied in a gold metallic paint. Designer Marcelle Chaumont (1891–1990) was a highly skilled former head-of-workroom at the Parisian couture houses of Jeanne Lanvin and Madeleine Vionnet and ran her own house from 1939 to 1953. OC

462 (LEFT) & 463 (OPPOSITE)
Evening dress of silk organza with hand-painting
By Marcelle Chaumont, Paris, France, 1949
Worn by Mrs Loel Guinness

Given by the wearer.
V&A T.92 to B-1974

DYERS' SECRETS

Dyers leave their recipes hidden in the fibres of historical silk fabrics. Only scientific analysis can unveil those secrets, allowing conservators to choose the most appropriate storage conditions for the silk and unlocking information for historians about the trade in dyestuffs.

Chromatography is a laboratory technique in use since the end of the twentieth century to separate mixtures of substances into their component parts.[13] Through high pressure (or performance) liquid chromatography (HPLC) scientists can usually identify the dyes and through the scanning electron microscope (SEM) or X-ray fluorescence (XRF) the metal salts (alum, iron or copper) that fix the dye or darken the colour. Only an uncontaminated sample of fibres may be used, one that has not degraded due to exposure to light or damp or earlier repair or conservation.

Dye samples from the five medieval silks pictured here, originating in Central Asia, Iberia and Sicily between 600 and 1400 CE, were identified on the basis of their weave structure and iconography, and threads of 1 to 5 mm in thickness were analysed. They revealed the use of three different dyes for red (madder [469], cochineal and kermes), and one for green (indigotine), yellow (Persian berries) and blue (indigotine from either indigo or woad).[14] Two samples contain some undyed white silk threads (464 and 466).

Kermes is native to Iberia, madder to the Mediterranean basin, and both were used not only for the pieces made there (467 and 468) but also for a silk made in Central Asia (464–466). Cochineal usually came from Armenia so travelled to Sicily or the western Mediterranean to dye the red threads, as in the fragment opposite (468). These findings suggest that trade in these red dyestuffs between these regions already existed in this early period. ACL

Three fragments of silk samite or compound twill with silk embroidery, probably Central Asia, 650–700 ce, with inscription embroidered in Ifriqiya (now Tunisia), about 750 ce

464 (ABOVE LEFT)
Undyed white silk, dyed red with madder and kermes (two samples taken), yellow with Persian berries; metallic salts detected aluminium, sulphur, copper and iron

V&A T.13-1960

465 (ABOVE RIGHT)
Dyed red and orange with madder, green with indigotine and madder, yellow inconclusive because faded

V&A 1385-1888

466 (BELOW RIGHT)
Undyed white silk from embroidery, dyed red with madder, green with indigotine, yellow inconclusive because faded

V&A 1314-1888

467 (OPPOSITE)
Fragment of silk samite or
compound twill weave, made in
Al-Andalus, Iberia, 1100–50. Undyed
white silk and dyed light blue with
indigotine. It was not possible
to take a sample for the red for
conservation reasons.

V&A 828-1894

468 (ABOVE)
Fragment of tapestry weave silk
with gilt-metal threads, Sicily or the
western Mediterranean, 1100–1200.
Dyed dark red with a bath of
cochineal and then of kermes and
black/brown with ellagic acid from
tannins such as oak galls.

V&A 8229-1863

469 (BELOW)
Fragment of lampas weave silk
with silver-gilt thread, probably
Granada, Spain, about 1230–70.
Dyed blue with indigotine and
red with madder.

V&A 796-1893

KIMONO STORIES

The images used to decorate kimono often have complex levels of meaning and auspicious significance. Some have poetic associations or refer to classical literature or popular myths. The animated motif on this kimono relates to a famous Japanese fairy-tale about the value of friendship and the perils of avarice (470, 472–4).

The story tells of a kind woodcutter who lived with his mean-spirited wife. One day he found an injured sparrow which he took home and nursed back to health. His wife resented the care her husband lavished on the bird, so she cut out its tongue and sent it flying back to the mountains. The man went searching for the bird and found his way to the bamboo grove where it lived. Here his feathered friend gave him food, while other birds sang and danced for him. Upon his departure the sparrow offered the man the choice of two baskets, one large and heavy, the other small and light. Not wishing to be greedy, the woodcutter chose the latter and when he got home was amazed to find it full of treasure.

His wife, annoyed that he had not chosen the bigger basket, went herself in search of the sparrow she had harmed. She was greeted kindly by the birds and given the large basket. Eager for the wealth she assumed it contained, the woman opened the basket on the way home only to discover it was full of monsters and ghosts. She was so surprised and scared that she tumbled to her death.

The scene on this garment shows the sparrows in the bamboo grove, dressed in kimono (473) and dancing for the woodcutter who is enjoying food and *sake* (472). The detailed depiction is executed in freehand paste resist-dyeing and embroidery, while the bamboo is tie-dyed. One tree rises dramatically from the green shading of the scene into the black of the upper garment. Interestingly, the Victoria and Albert Museum has in its collection an album of photographs of kimono published in Kyoto in 1932 which includes an image of a very similar garment, enabling us to date this example accurately (471). AJ

敬
老

15

470 (OPPOSITE LEFT)
Woman's kimono of plain weave
silk crêpe with tie-dyeing, freehand
paste resist-dyeing and embroidery
in silk and gold wrapped threads,
Japan, 1930–5

V&A FE.19-2014

471 (OPPOSITE RIGHT)
Photograph from an album of
kimono by Kawamoto Bijutsushoshi,
Kyoto, Japan, 1932

V&A FE.3-1987

472 (RIGHT)
Detail of the woodcutter

473 (OPPOSITE)
Detail of the sparrows dancing

474 (RIGHT)
Back of a woman's kimono of plain
weave silk crêpe with tie-dyeing,
freehand paste resist-dyeing and
embroidery in silk and gold wrapped
threads, Japan, 1930–5

V&A FE.19-2014

Stitch, Slash, Stamp and Pleat

5

Stitch, Slash, Stamp and Pleat

Silks have been embellished, either through the addition of decorative effects or through other modifications of their surface, since at least 1000 BCE.[1] Embroidery is the best-known and most widespread form of adding ornamentation, and the one that allows the most freedom of expression and artistry. It is achieved by using a needle or hook to stitch through a fabric. Methods of modifying the surface by making cuts, slits or holes or by applying heat and pressure to create embossed and watered effects or pleats are usually associated with particular periods, places and fashions and employed less globally.

Embroidery can be made by hand or machine and is used worldwide, practised by men, women and children. In a domestic sphere, it has been a home-making, leisure or income-generating activity; in religious establishments, it has furnished buildings, dressed celebrants and prepared girls for marriage or to earn a living; in commercial workshops, it has been both a small- or large-scale business. Until the nineteenth century, all was handmade. As European engravings of domestic and professional activity, and a drawing and photograph of embroiderers at work in India (475–8) suggest relatively simple equipment is required – needle and thread, and optionally a frame. Such

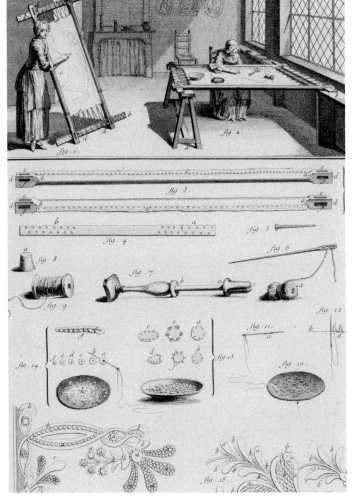

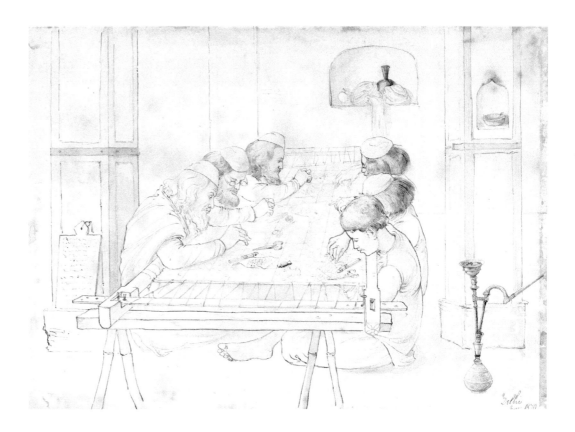

475 (OPPOSITE LEFT)
Woman embroidering by Abraham Bosse, France, about 1635. Engraving

V&A E.6052-1911

476 (OPPOSITE RIGHT)
The Embroiderer, published in Diderot and d'Alembert, vol. 19 (Paris 1763), pl. I. Engraving

National Art Library, V&A 38041800786170

477 (TOP RIGHT)
Five men and a boy working on an embroidery frame to produce jewelled and spangled cloth by John Lockwood Kipling, Delhi, India, 1870. Pen, pencil and wash on paper

V&A 0929:31/(IS)

478 (ABOVE)
Women stitching with embroidery hoops, Kutch, India, 2015

tools do not require major capital investment, nor do they necessarily take up a large amount of space.

While needles have long been used worldwide, tambour embroidery with a hook – a faster method – only arrived in Europe from Asia in the middle of the eighteenth century. Mechanization dates to the 1850s in St Gallen in Switzerland, where the Schiffli and Cornély machines were launched commercially by Isaac Groebli and Émile Cornély in 1863 and 1868 respectively (479). At first, they were hand operated, but by the late nineteenth century an automatic Schiffli machine had been invented, the embroiderer replaced by cards (as in the Jacquard system discussed in Chapter 2).[2]

Just as hand embroidery equipment has remained largely constant through the centuries and across the globe, so, too, has the basic process. The embroiderer selects a base fabric and an appropriate range of threads, chooses a design motif, and draws or transfers its outline onto the fabric to stitch. For the best results the fabric is held taut in a frame (476–8) in order to avoid the distortion that naturally occurs when holding the fabric. Tautness facilitates the passing of the needle or hook through from one side to the other.

Embroiderers use a variety of base fabrics, threads and stitches. Grounds other than silk are often embroidered

479 (LEFT)
Embroidery machine, Calais,
France, about 1900
Photographic post card

480 (BELOW)
Edge of woman's blouse of plain
weave cotton with machine-made
polychrome silk embroidery,
Sisak, Croatia, 1870–1920

Given by Mr and Mrs C.O.
Wakefield-Harvey.
V&A T.29A-1958

481 (OPPOSITE) & 482
Back and front of orphrey of silk
velvet, with appliqué of silk satin,
silk cord and metal threads with
traces of embroidery design drawn
out on plain weave linen on the
back, Spain, about 1550

V&A 248-1880

483 (LEFT)
Shawl of silk crêpe with embroidery in silk and silk knotted fringe, possibly Guangdong, China, 1880–1920
Given by Mrs. N. Iliffe.
V&A FE.29-1983

484 (ABOVE)
Small Rose, unfinished embroidery-kit panel of plain weave cotton with design in ink and embroidery in silks, designed by May Morris for Morris & Co., London, England, about 1890
Given by Miss Vere Roberts.
V&A CIRC.302-1960

with silk, sometimes to the point where the ground is entirely hidden by stitching. The best-known stitches are different forms of knots, satin stitch, cross stitch and chain stitch, the latter created using needle or hook. Some stitches are generally used for outlines (back or running stitches), others to fill in motifs (satin and knot stitches), and others to hold down silk or metal threads laid on the surface (couching stitches). They are so various that one influential embroidery dictionary, published in 1934, referred to stitches as 'the "scales and exercises" of embroidery', noting that 'a good working knowledge of them was the essential foundation of the art'.[3]

Other techniques that are related to embroidery are appliqué and raised work. The first is the sewing down of pieces of textile that have been cut into distinctive shapes, often covering the stitching around the outline with a fine cord, sometimes with metal threads (482). The second creates a relief pattern, by covering a mould or wadding with threads that are secured by couching. The quantity, distribution and finesse of embellishment are determined by the intended purpose of the embroidery – secular or religious, decorative or narrative – and may indicate status or express other identities. Beads, precious stones and metal, and sequins may enhance the most richly adorned pieces.

Many types of embroidery are associated with their place of making, because they share characteristics in design, materials or technique that are typical of their region or centre of production. As with other techniques, from the sixteenth century hybrid designs and methods were evident, especially in silks embroidered in Bengal and China for western markets (483).[4] Cross-fertilization was further facilitated later by publications, from the sheets of designs familiar since the sixteenth century to 'how to' manuals, and more recently fashion and craft magazines.[5] Other printed productions, such as embroidery kits, aided amateur embroiderers (484). One well-known nineteenth-century designer of kits was May Morris, who ran the professional embroidery workshops of her father, William Morris.

Embroidery – sometimes considered 'painting with the needle' – adds to the surface of a textile. In contrast, various other procedures modify the texture to create a decorative effect. The most destructive were slashing or punching – fashionable in Europe in the sixteenth and seventeenth centuries – in which a metal tool cut slits or punched

holes in the silk (485). Some silks were woven to facilitate this process. The resultant slits allowed glimpses of the contrasting lining or the undergarments of the wearer.

Less dramatic but also destructive was the application of heat or chemical substances to areas to be patterned. One example was the technique of stamping velvets. Imported to France from Italy about 1500, it involved applying heated dies or stamps, and later small heated metal rollers, to silk.[6] In the case of velvet, they crushed or flattened the pile, usually creating a small and simple repeating motif. This method was cheaper than weaving a similar pattern. A more recent version of this 'eating out' of the pile is a technique called devoré (devoured), which uses a substance such as caustic soda to burn out the areas selected for patterning. Depending on how the velvet has been woven, the 'bald' areas of the ground are often transparent as chiffon is used as the base weave. This process was developed in Lyon in France and by the end of the nineteenth century it had been mechanized. It was very much in fashion in Britain in the 1980s and 1990s.

Calendering – the application of heat and pressure as a silk is passed between rollers – is less destructive and has two possible outcomes. If the fabric has a plain weave and is fed through unfolded, the calendering will enhance the lustre, making it very shiny and smooth. If the fabric has a ribbed weave, the warp and weft have different thicknesses. When it is folded and passed between rollers, the friction and rubbing will create a watered (moiré) effect on the surface.[7] The writer Cesare Vecellio described young Venetians wearing hats in this type of silk in summer in his publication on ancient and modern dress of the world (1590).[8] Many European silk manufacturers sought excellence in watering silks in the eighteenth century, with the French importing English knowhow in the 1750s and the first manual on the subject being published in Spain in 1790 (486).[9]

Permanent pleating in silk is a different textural effect, one patented by textile and fashion designer Mariano Fortuny in 1909. His sinuous, soft and shiny, vertically pleated silks are still admired, yet the process is little understood.[10] It was a semi-mechanical pressing of damp

485
Doublet and breeches, slashed white satin over blue taffeta, England, about 1618. Probably worn by Sir Rowland Cotton

V&A T.28&A-1938

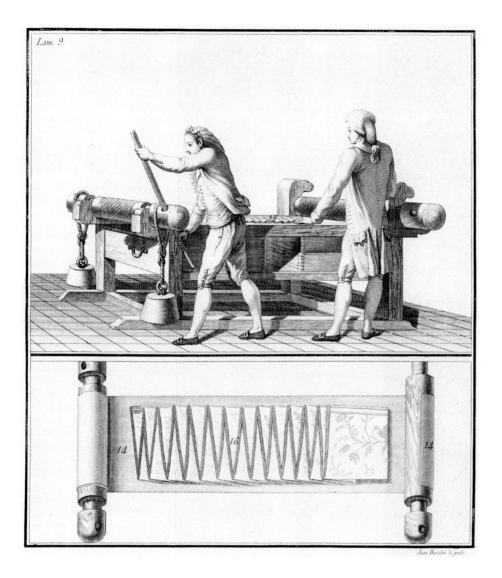

486 (LEFT)
Preparation of silk for watering,
published in Joaquín Manuel Fos,
*Instrucción metódica sobre
los mueres* (Valencia 1790),
pl. 9. Engraving

National Art Library, V&A L.944-1973

487 (BELOW)
Fragment of smocked silk velvet
from an evening dress, Jean Patou,
Paris, about 1925

Given by Mrs J.E.O. Morgan.
V&A T.1599-2017

silk, which was weighted down and passed between heated
vertical rollers.

Smocking brings the range of applied decorative
finishes full circle. It is a combination of stitching and
pleating that changes the surface and drape of the fabric,
and sometimes adds colour through the use of contrasting
threads or patterns of stitching. It is also functional, in that it
holds the fullness of the fabric evenly in certain areas of the
garment, shaping it without the fabric being cut or darted.
Cuffs, collars, headdresses and yokes have been treated in
this way, with the stitching keeping the pleats in place. Often
associated with light fabrics, it is also effective with other
weights, including certain silk velvets (487). ACL

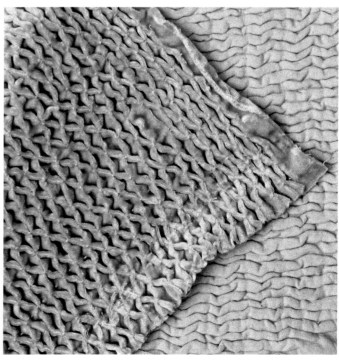

EMBROIDERY AND APPLIQUÉ

The solemn and serene head of Buddha below (489) was originally part of a much larger hanging of *A Thousand Buddhas*. The silk ground is completely covered with split stitch silk embroidery. By the seventh century this stitch was complemented by others, with the later panel (488) embroidered in stem, satin and long and short stitches and the rest painted. Made in the middle of the Qing dynasty (1644–1911), it is typical of a celebrated style pioneered during the Ming dynasty (1368–1644) by the Gu family in Shanghai, who reproduced earlier paintings with great delicacy. HP

488 (RIGHT)
Panel of plain weave silk with embroidery in silk and painting
China, 1700–1850

Purchased with Art Fund support.
V&A T.92-1948

489 (BELOW)
Fragment of plain weave silk with embroidery in silk
Dunhuang, China, 800–900 CE

Stein Textile Loan Collection, on loan from the Government of India and the Archaeological Survey of India.
V&A LOAN:STEIN.559

This medallion (490) depicts in stem stitch two scenes from the life of the Virgin Mary – the Visitation and the Annunciation. Discovered in Egypt, the embroidery is evidence that silk was arriving there along trade routes from China, Khotan or India by the eighth century. While the environmental conditions in this part of Africa are not suitable for sericulture, they are excellent for the preservation of historical textiles. ACL

490 (OPPOSITE)
Roundel of plain weave linen with embroidery in silk
Probably Egypt, 700 CE

V&A 814-1903

The decoration of geometric interlacing and inscriptions, made with stem and chain stitches on these panels, recalls the architectural decoration of monuments from the Nasrid dynasty (1238–1492). After the fall of Granada to Queen Isabella I of Castile and King Ferdinand II of Aragon in 1492, many of its inhabitants fled to North Africa, taking with them their traditions and crafts, such as this style of embroidery, which was used in the Chefchaouen region of north-western Morocco until the early twentieth century. ACL

491 (LEFT)
Detail of a panel of plain weave linen with embroidery in silk
Granada, Spain or Chefchaouen region, Morocco, 1400–1600

V&A T.243-1910

492 (BELOW) & 493 (OPPOSITE)
Panel of plain weave linen with embroidery in silk, with detail
Granada, Spain or Chefchaouen region, Morocco, 1400–1600

V&A 882-1892

Extremely fine chain stitch embroidery worked with a needle was produced by professional male embroiderers in Gujarat, who stitched the highest quality chain stitch embroideries for both the Mughal court and the western market throughout the seventeenth and eighteenth centuries. The length below (497 and 498) imitates European woven silks by including vaguely architectural forms and large abstract motifs in a diagonal repeat pattern. In contrast, the chain-stitched roses on the French shape (494, 495 and 496) have been tamboured – worked with a hook rather than a needle, a faster technique introduced to Europe by the mid-eighteenth century. The British Customs' stamp (not shown) indicates that it was confiscated when someone tried to smuggle it into Britain. French embroideries were highly valued throughout Europe. AF/SN

494 (RIGHT) & 495 & 496 (OPPOSITE)
The shape of the right side of a man's waistcoat of plain weave wilk with embroidery in silk, showing details of front and back of fabric
France, 1750–60

V&A T.12-1984

497 (BELOW LEFT) & 498 (BELOW RIGHT)
Length of plain weave cotton with embroidery in silk and detail of back
Gujarat, India, about 1710

V&A T.20-1947

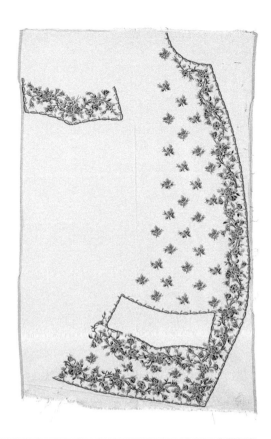

In both Europe and China, metal thread was couched onto lavish garments in fashionable or symbolic patterns. The generous length of this European man's court waistcoat of the 1730s (499) and its pocket flaps are richly decorated in a fashionably scrolling pattern in different qualities of metal and silk. During the Qing dynasty (1644–1911) in China, the sleeve-bands around the cuff edges of women's garments were similarly decorative (500 and 501). Like the waistcoat, they were probably created in professional workshops. The butterflies on the embroidery and in the pattern of the figured silk were common motifs symbolizing marital happiness. LFM/YC

499 (OPPOSITE)
Detail of waistcoat of satin weave silk with embroidery in silver, silk, strip and spangles
Probably France, 1730–40

V&A 252-1906

500 (RIGHT) & 501 (FAR RIGHT)
Pair of sleeve-bands for a woman's robe of figured silk gauze with embroidery in couched gold thread
China, 1875–1900

Purchased with Art Fund support.
V&A T.149&A-1948

In medieval Europe embroidered textiles from England were renowned for their complex designs and exceptional craftsmanship. In inventories of church goods, objects such as this luxurious vestment were referred to as *Opus Anglicanum* (Latin for 'English work'). Its linen ground is completely covered with minute stitches in coloured silks and metal threads in underside couching, split stitch, cross stitch and plait stitch, with laid and couched work. MZ

502
The Syon Cope of plain weave linen with embroidery in silk, silver-gilt and silver thread
England, 1310–20

V&A 83-1864

This cross-shaped panel (503) embroidered with scenes from Christ's Passion would once have decorated a church vestment. For the figures and some architectural details the embroiderers used coloured silks worked in split stitch, a technique particularly suited to rendering the fine details of facial expressions and subtly shading garments and hair. MZ

OPPOSITE (503–505)
The Marnhull Orphrey, plain weave linen with embroidery in silk, silver-gilt and silver thread with back and front details of central section
England, 1310–25

Purchased with Art Fund support.
V&A T.31-1936

In the later fourteenth century luxurious woven silk fabrics from Italy became increasingly available to wider sections of English society. This affected the production methods of English embroiderers, who by this stage also specialized in working motifs separately, to be applied to woven silk grounds such as this black velvet. Here satin stitch, brick stitch and split stitch, with laid and couched work, have been used (506). MZ

506 (RIGHT)
Chasuble of cut silk velvet with embroidery in silk, silver-gilt and silver threads
Possibly Italy or Spain (silk woven) and England (garment made up and embroidered), about 1510–33

V&A 697-1902

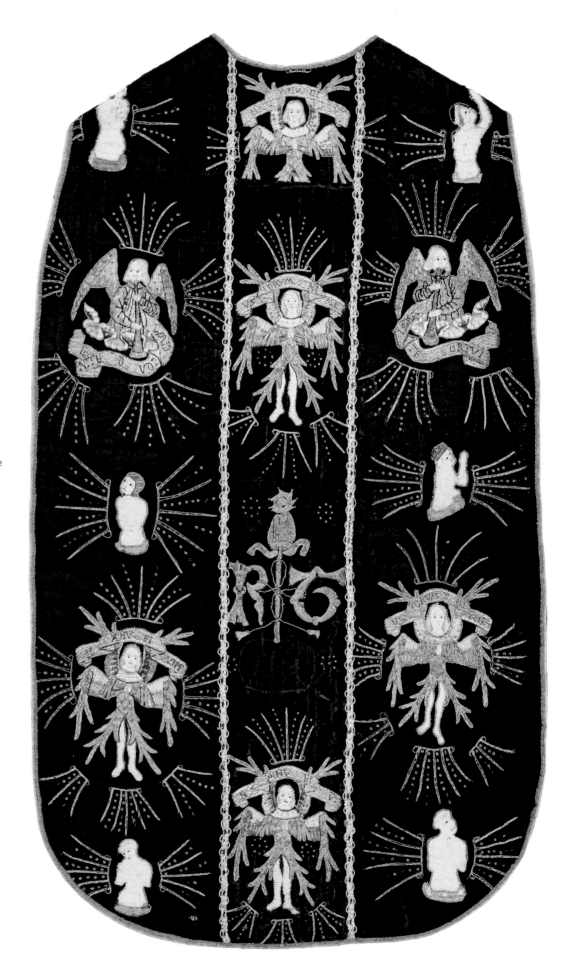

Officers of Arms employed by monarchs or noblemen read proclamations and conveyed messages. Over the centuries, their official dress was a tabard, a short, T-shaped surcoat emblazoned with heraldry. This tabard (508) was made for the Lord Lyon King of Arms, the head of Lyon Court. It includes the Scottish lion rampant, the Irish harp, English lions couchant and French fleurs-de-lis. Blue plain cut velvet was used as the ground for the harp and three fleurs-de-lis, while the three lions are applied on crimson velvet. The embroidery uses couching stitches, laid and raised work. Only Kings of Arms wore velvet, the two ranks below them wearing damask and satin. SB

507 (OPPOSITE)
Detail of the Neville altar frontal of plain weave linen with embroidery in silk, silver and silver-gilt threads applied to silk velvet
England, 1535–55

V&A 35-1888

508 (LEFT)
Back of Lord Lyon King of Arms' tabard, with the Scottish Royal Arms of Queen Anne of silk velvet with embroidery in silk, silver and silver-gilt threads and black glass beads
Edinburgh, Scotland, 1702–7

Bequeathed by Alfred Williams Hearn.
V&A T.174-1923

509 (ABOVE)
Drawing of *A Pursuivant from the Garter Procession* by Sir Peter Lely,
England, 1660–70
Black chalk, heightened with white, on paper

V&A 2166

People of Jewish faith have long created magnificent ritual decorations in silk, ranging from binders for the Bible to wedding canopies. Their most sacred objects are the Torah scrolls which contain the first five books of the Bible. When not in use, they are placed in a rigid case, covered by a rich mantle and kept inside the Holy Ark, the focal point in the synagogue. The doors of the Ark are then covered with a parochet, a curtain usually made of velvet or brocaded silks, decorated with symbols and inscriptions of the faith. SB

510 (LEFT)
Torah mantle of cut silk velvet and silk with brocading, with embroidery and trimmings in metal threads
Amsterdam, Netherlands, about 1675
V&A 349-1870

511 (OPPOSITE)
Parochet of plain weave linen with embroidery in silk and silver-gilt thread and with border of silver-gilt fringe
Possibly embroidered by Rikah Polacko, probably Venice, Italy, 1676
V&A 511-1877

Parasols are an ancient symbol of kingship in India. Held over rulers on public occasions, they were richly made and conveyed status. This example (512) is patterned with the 'thousand nails' technique, in which the design is formed by tiny gilt brass studs driven into a velvet ground. It was given by Maharana Bhim Singh of Mewar to Lord Amherst, governor-general of the East India Company. AF

512 (BELOW)
Parasol of silk velvet studded with brass
Udaipur, Rajasthan, India, about 1800–26

Given by the 5th Earl Amherst of Arracan.
V&A IS.17-1991

Huqqa or water pipes of precious materials had correspondingly rich mats and covers. This mat (513) is heavily embellished with silver and silver-gilt strips and sequins, with silk velvet used for the centre and as flower petals. The centres of the flowers are inset with clipped jewel beetle-wing cases, and their stems and leaves are embroidered in silk thread. AF

513 (OPPOSITE)
Water-pipe mat of cut silk velvet with silver and silver-gilt and beetle-wing case embellishments and silk embroidery
Probably north India, 1800–50

V&A IS.1:1-1999

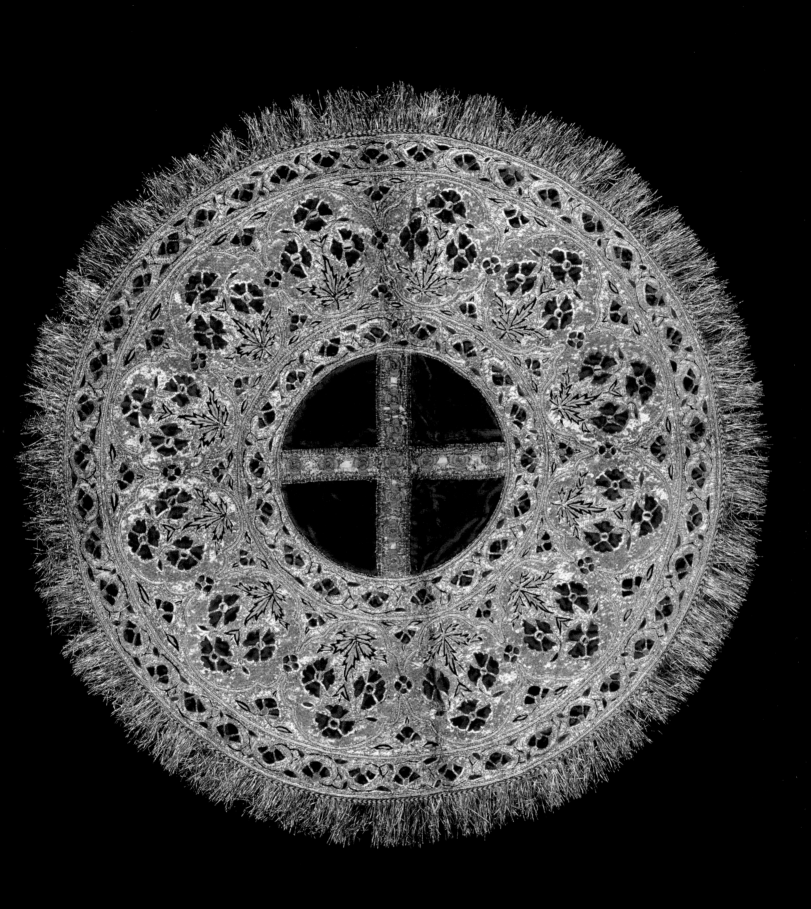

This panel formed part of the huge door curtain made each year for the Ka'bah in Mecca, Saudi Arabia, the cube-shaped building that is the holiest site in the Islamic world. This section surrounded the vertical slit at the bottom of the curtain. It is embroidered with *al-Ikhlas*, one of the shortest *surahs* (chapters) of the Qur'an, the central religious text of Islam. TS

514
Section of the door curtain from the Ka'bah of satin weave silk with embroidery of couched metal wire
Egypt, about 1910

V&A T.113-1932

A.W.N. Pugin was a Roman Catholic architect who championed the revival of the medieval Gothic style for the new churches built in England in the mid-nineteenth century. His many designs for embroidered textiles emulated fine English medieval embroidery (*Opus Anglicanum*). JL

515
Cope hood of silk velvet with embroidery in silk and silver-gilt wire thread and purl
Designed by A.W.N. Pugin for St Augustine's Church, Ramsgate, Kent, England; made by Lonsdale & Tyler, London, England; possibly embroidered by Lucy Powell, Birmingham, England, 1848–50

V&A T.287-1989

The Arts and Crafts movement, which developed in late nineteenth-century Britain, encouraged creative design and the use of an ambitious range of materials and techniques in embroidery. It led to artistic recognition for practitioners of the discipline, many of whom were women associated with the Glasgow School of Art. A specific style of embroidery flourished at this institution. Typical features were natural linen grounds, stylized flowers, and curves juxtaposed with straight lines. Helen Adelaide Lamb and Ann Macbeth both studied at the Glasgow School of Art, where Macbeth worked from 1901. The piece opposite (517), designed by Lamb, is particularly characteristic of the Glasgow Style. CAJ

516 (LEFT)
St Elizabeth of Hungary, picture of satin weave silk with embroidery in silk and metal threads, with beads and faux pearls
Designed by Ann Macbeth and embroidered by Elizabeth Jackson, Glasgow, Scotland, about 1910

Given by Mrs Ann Bowles, née Sawford. V&A T.359-1967

517 (OPPOSITE)
Picture of plain weave linen with embroidery in silk threads and beads
Designed by Helen Adelaide Lamb, Glasgow, Scotland, 1909 and probably made in the early 20th century

Purchase funded by Ivor and Sarah Braka. V&A T.25-2019

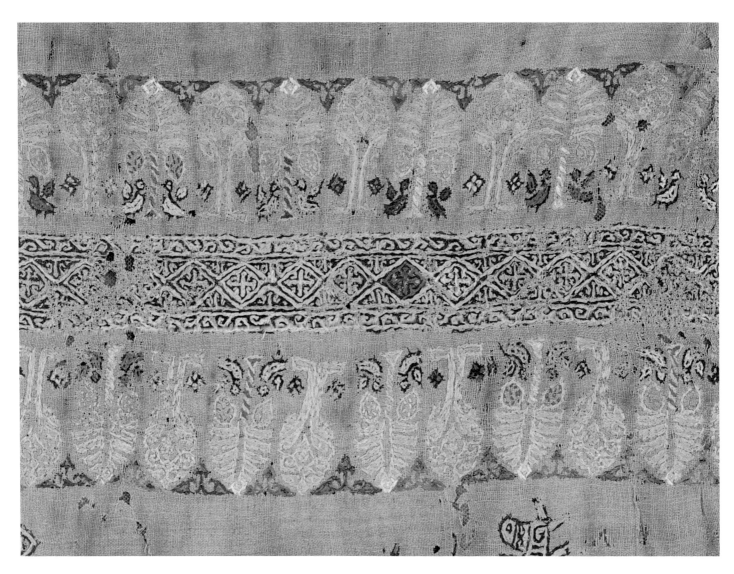

Few furnishing fabrics survive from the twelfth century. The motifs on this rare cushion cover (518 and 519) include inscribed medallions, trees, animals and seated human figures, made in stem stitch. They relate closely to paintings on ivory caskets and wooden ceilings in Egypt during this period. ACL

518 (LEFT) & 519 (ABOVE)
Cushion cover of plain weave linen with embroidery in silk
Egypt, 1100–1200

V&A 252-1890

The design of this cushion cover (520) is highly unusual. The central medallion appears to copy the design typical of silver-inlaid brass dishes made in fourteenth-century Mamluk Egypt. The motifs around it and in the border relate to those made in fifteenth-century carpets from Spanish workshops. ACL

520 (OPPOSITE)
Front and back of cushion cover of cut silk velvet with embroidery in silk and silver thread
Spain, 1400–1600

V&A 383-1894

This is a rare surviving example of a complete and unaltered sixteenth-century bedhead. Its pattern is predominantly achieved by applying cut-out motifs of golden yellow satin and taffeta to the blue satin ground. The costliness of the materials, the elegance of the fashionable design and the high quality work suggest that it adorned the residence of an affluent family. SB

521 (ABOVE) & 522 (OPPOSITE)
Bedhead of satin weave silk with appliqué and embroidery in silk
France, 1550–70

V&A T.405-1980

These two bed covers reveal
seventeenth-century cross-
cultural exchanges. The richly
embroidered Chinese coverlet
(523 and 524) is a perfect
example of the artistic fusion
in export textiles of a Chinese
phoenix with Indian motifs. The
red velvet is unusual in Chinese
production but the expertly
manipulated coloured floss
silks in satin stitch are typical
of early Chinese embroidery
for export. In contrast,
embroiderers in Bengal
adapted illustrations from
popular European books to
produce coverlets, first for the
Portuguese and later for a wider
European market. Narrative
scenes borrowed from the
Bible, classical Greek myths and
popular European prints were
embroidered in chain and back
stitch on cotton using India's
naturally golden indigenous
wild silks (525). HP/AF

523 (OPPOSITE) & 524 (RIGHT)
Coverlet of silk velvet with
embroidery in silk floss and
gilt-paper wrapped silk thread,
with silk cord
Probably Canton (now Guangzhou),
China, about 1600

V&A T.36-1911

525 (BELOW)
Detail of quilt of plain weave cotton
with embroidery in tasar silk
Possibly Hugli, West Bengal,
India, 1600–30

V&A 616-1886

Sumptuous materials, brilliant colours and exquisite design suggest that the valance opposite (527) was worked by the most skilful French embroiderers. A woodcut by Bernard Salomon (526), first published in 1557, served as a model for the central scene. It shows the death of Pyramus and Thisbe, the ill-fated lovers whose story forms part of the Roman poet Ovid's narrative poem *Metamorphoses*, completed around 5 CE. SB

526 (RIGHT)
Detail of *Death of Pyramus and Thisbe*
By Bernard Salomon, published in *La vita et metamorfoseo d'Ovidio* (Lyon 1584, first edition 1557), p. 63
Woodcut

National Art Library, V&A 38041800121295

527 (OPPOSITE)
Section of a bed valance of satin weave silk with embroidery in silk
France, 1560–70

V&A T.219B-1981

Morte di Pyramo & Tisbe. 51

Pyramo giunto al deſtinato loco,
Il velo in terra della Donna vede,
Ch'il feroce animal, ſatio di poco,
Macchiato hauea col ſanguinoſo piede.
Tienla per morta, e⁊ ſtato in forſe vn poco,
Con la ſpada à vn tratto il cuor ſi fiede,
Ritorna Tisbe, e'l petto anchor ſi punge,
Coſi l'un corpo all'altro ſi congiunge.

This devotional 'painting in embroidery' faithfully copies an engraving by Raphael Sadeler, who worked in the Netherlands and Germany. Silver-gilt and polychrome silk threads are complemented by tiny pieces of foil, which are applied to suggest reflective surfaces, such as the water in the cup. SB

528 (OPPOSITE)
Detail of *St Francis Consoled by the Musician Angel*, a panel of plain weave silk with embroidery in silk and silver-gilt threads
Italy, 1600–22

V&A T.246-1965

529 (RIGHT)
Saint Francis of Assisi in his Cell Having a Vision of an Angel Playing the Violin on a Cloud
Engraving by Raphael Sadeler after Paolo Piazza, Italy, 1600–30

Wellcome Collection, London, England

The embroiderer's great skill is most evident in the fashionable dress of the figures: fur, metal and differently textured fabrics are depicted realistically (530). The embroidery was probably made in the Netherlands, where the art of couching metal threads with coloured silks (*nué*) was particularly accomplished by the mid-fifteenth century. SB

530 (LEFT)
Tomyris, Queen of the Massagetae, Receiving the Head of Cyrus, picture of satin weave silk with embroidery in silk and metal threads
After an engraving by Paulus Pontius, Netherlands, 1630–50

V&A T.14-1971

531 (BELOW)
Detail of *Tomyris Receiving the Head of Cyrus*
By Paulus Pontius, after Peter Paul Rubens, Antwerp, Belgium, 1615–58
Engraving

Bequeathed by Rev. Alexander Dyce.
V&A DYCE.2220

Embroidery and Appliqué 415

Black silk thread embroidery on a linen ground, known as blackwork, was fashionable in sixteenth-century and early seventeenth-century England. A range of stitches was used to create motifs that often came from print sources, such as emblem books. Here, insects and flowers are executed in stem, double-running and back stitch (532). Black floss silk from Spain was particularly prized because of the fastness of the dye. CKB

532 (LEFT)
Under-sleeve panel of plain weave linen with embroidery in silk
Britain, 1610–20
V&A T.11-1950

In seventeenth-century England amateur embroidery flourished, decorating many household items from mirror frames (533) to caskets and cabinets. Embroiderers sometimes created their own patterns but often bought linen or silk satin panels with pre-drawn designs to work. They then customized the panels through their choice of coloured threads and stitches. EM

533 (OPPOSITE)
Unfinished mirror frame of satin weave silk with embroidery in silk
England, 1650–75
V&A T.142-1931

The three-dimensional figures on this picture and casket are typical of mid-seventeenth century raised work embroidery. Biblical stories and mythological tales provided ample inspiration to amateur embroiderers. The panel above (534) depicts the story of King Solomon and the Queen of Sheba from the Old Testament of the Bible, with the figures depicted in contemporary seventeenth-century fashions. EM

534 (ABOVE)
Picture of satin weave silk with embroidery in silk, seed pearls and coral
England, 1660–90

V&A 892-1864

535 (OPPOSITE)
Casket covered in satin weave silk with embroidery in silk, metal wrapped silk and bobbin lace
England, 1650–75

V&A T.223-1968

There is no technical reason for creating repeat patterns in embroidery designs. Nevertheless, the prestige of the woven designs of Ottoman silks and velvets with repeat patterns was so great that such repeating motifs dominated local embroidery production until the eighteenth century. Here the main field has seven parallel wavy stems set with tulips, carnations and other flowers (536). TS

536 (OPPOSITE)
Cover of satin weave silk with embroidery in silk in *atma* stitch
Turkey, 1600–1700
V&A 830-1902

The ground of this panel (537) indicates it may have once formed part of a royal tent, as red tents were traditionally reserved for rulers in India. Both the exterior and interior panels of such tents might be decorated, but the quality of the fine silk chain stitching and excellent condition suggest this set was made for use indoors. AF

537 (RIGHT)
Tent panel of cotton with embroidery in silk
Possibly Jaipur, Rajasthan, India, about 1700–30
V&A IM.62-1936

Shield knuckle pads were small cushions used to protect the hand while gripping an Indian shield. This piece (538) is one of a small group from the Jaipur court, all worked in extremely fine chain stitch. Despite its association with combat, it presents a tranquil scene of a prince and a lady in a palace garden. AF

538 (ABOVE)
Shield knuckle pad cover with cotton, embroidered in silk and silver wrapped thread
Probably Jaipur, Rajasthan, India, about 1730

Given by Mr Imre Schwaiger.
V&A IM.107-1924

This silk embroidery (539) – in split, stem, overcasting and chain stitch – was made for domestic use, drawing on local traditions in technique and design. Its symmetrical design of stylized birds and geometrical motifs belongs to the vocabulary of the Ottoman empire. The Greek islands sat on the boundary between eastern and western Europe at that time. LEM

539 (OPPOSITE)
Cushion cover of plain weave linen with embroidery in silk and silver thread and with drawn threadwork
Cephalonia, Ionian Islands, Greece, 1700–1800

Given by Professor R.M. Dawkins.
V&A T.207-1950

This detail of an elaborate valance (540) reveals the freedom that embroidery can offer a skilled needleworker, its densely couched silver threads providing a lustrous backdrop for the polychrome flowers. A valance hung along the canopy of a bed, as part of an ensemble that often included matching curtains, bed cover and a bedhead. SB

540 (OPPOSITE)
Detail of bed valance of canvas with embroidery in silk and metal threads
Italy, 1650–1700

V&A T.36-1946

Morocco has a rich embroidery tradition, with distinct techniques, colours, patterns and stitches being used in different centres for both dress and furnishings. The embroidered ends on this curtain (541) are characteristic of the embroidery of Tétouan, in the north of Morocco. Such rich and colourful textiles were part of a woman's trousseau and displayed during family gatherings, especially weddings. ACL

541 (RIGHT)
Detail of curtain of plain weave silk with unfinished embroidery in silk
Tétouan, Morocco, 1800–1900

V&A T.106-1925

This large and striking hanging (542) was produced in Japan to appeal to the western market. It depicts an eagle sweeping down through a pine forest and carrying away a mythical lion cub while two monkeys try to pull a terrified companion across a stream. The whole scene is meticulously executed in embroidery, with the stitches covering the entire surface of the fabric. AJ

542 (LEFT)
Hanging of plain weave cotton with embroidery in silk and gold wrapped threads
Probably Kyoto, Japan, 1870–95

V&A 167-1898

In Japan gifts were placed in a box on a tray, over which a *fukusa* (gift cover) was draped. Choosing a *fukusa* appropriate to the occasion was an important part of the gift-giving ritual. This example (543) is embroidered with a detailed and witty design of an elephant being washed. It suggests, perhaps, that the gift itself is a great rarity that has been carefully prepared. AJ

543 (OPPOSITE)
Gift cover of satin weave silk with embroidery in silk and gold wrapped threads
Probably Kyoto, Japan, 1800–50

Given by Mr T.B. Clarke-Thornhill.
V&A T.94-1927

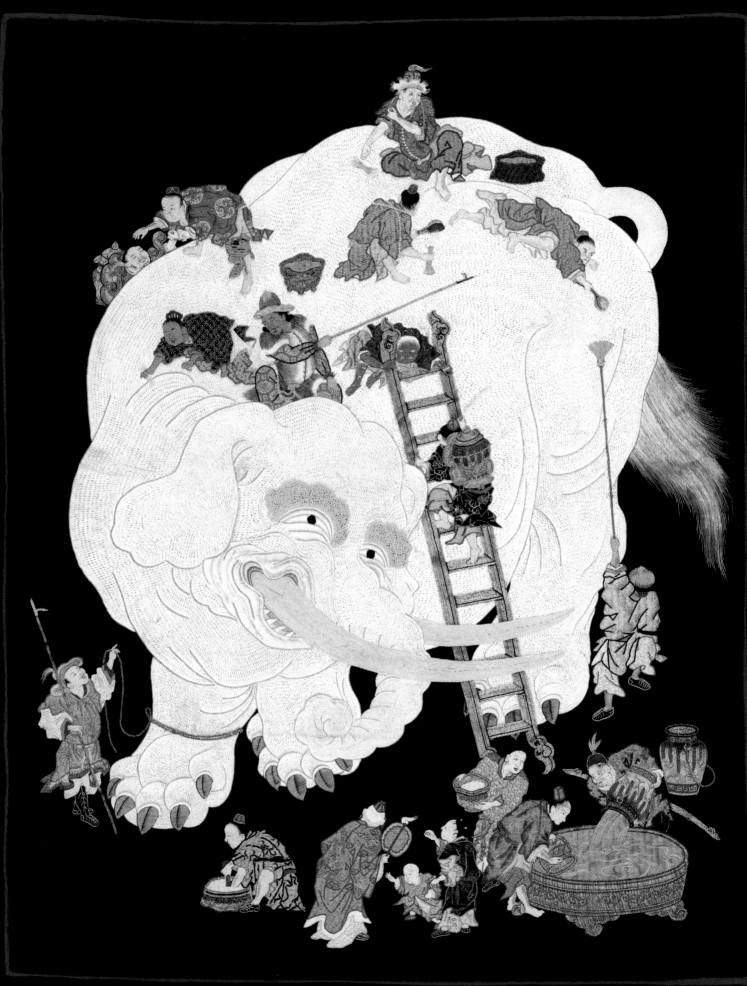

May Morris promoted silk embroidery as a fine art. She was a prolific designer, running the Morris & Co. embroidery workroom which produced kits for embroiderers to work at home. Stitched in glowing, soft shades of the company's specially dyed silk thread, this large hanging combines text from May's father William's poem 'The Flowering Orchard' (1891) with a repeating pattern of slender fruit trees and swirling acanthus leaves, inspired by medieval design. It is worked in stem, darning, satin, herringbone, buttonhole and pistil stitch with couching. JL

544 (OPPOSITE) & 545 (RIGHT)
Fruit Garden, portière or hanging of plain weave silk with embroidery in silk
Designed by May Morris and made by Theodosia Middlemore, England, 1894
V&A CIRC.206-1965

This coat is perhaps the finest known work of Mughal embroidery. The super-fine silk chain stitching on satin was likely to have been embroidered in an imperial workshop, probably to a design drafted by court artists. Its landscape pattern combines Iranian-style animal combats with Chinese-style rocky outcrops, plum blossoms and nimbus clouds, both worked alongside early Mughal experimentation with naturalistic flowers. AF

546 (OPPOSITE) & 547 (RIGHT)
Coat of satin weave silk with embroidery in silk
Probably Gujarat, India, about 1620–30

V&A IS.18-1947

This sample of magnificent embroidery (548) probably served as a model for the lavish train of a European court dress. Embroiderers such as the renowned Jean-François Bony made a variety of samples to show to distinguished clients who wished to make a selection for this most prestigious of garments. This rich, labour-intensive work reveals the effects achieved through the juxtaposition of different qualities of silk thread – floss and chenille – with swansdown. SB

548 (OPPOSITE)
Sample of satin weave silk with embroidery in silk
Attributed to Jean-François Bony, Lyon, France, about 1800

Given by the Royal School of Needlework.
V&A T.68-1967

The warm colours of this petticoat (549), which has a matching gown, are a variation of the mid-eighteenth-century fashionable palette. Shades of brown and green are embroidered on a golden beige ground, highlighted with the tawny (a popular shade between brown, red and orange) of the pomegranate seeds, and the purple and blue flowers. SN

549 (RIGHT)
Detail of woman's petticoat of plain weave silk with embroidery in silk thread
Britain, 1740–50

V&A 834A-1907

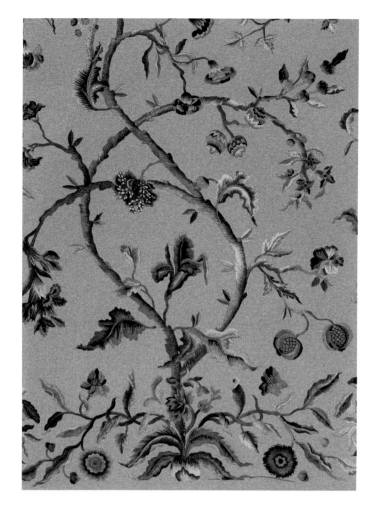

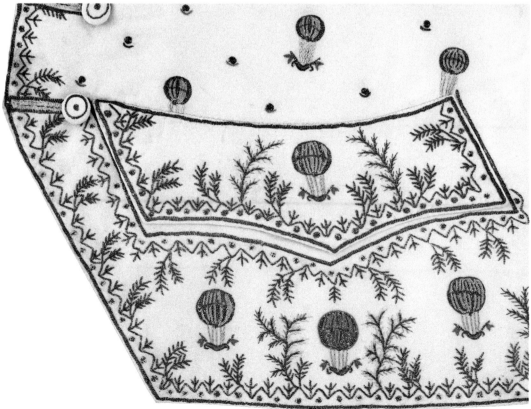

In the last quarter of the eighteenth century in Europe, men's waistcoats became the focal point of their suits, embroidery being the perfect technique for the quick delivery of a variety of decorative and topical designs. In this case (550), the design commemorates the first manned balloon flight, which took place at the Jardin des Tuileries in Paris in December 1783. KH

550 (LEFT)
Detail of waistcoat of ribbed silk, with tambour embroidery in silk and silver thread
Probably France, 1785–90

V&A T.200-2016

Embroidery and Appliqué 433

The luxurious suits worn at courts throughout Europe were often embroidered to shape. By the 1790s, the coat and breeches were usually a dark-coloured silk, often velvet, and the waistcoat white silk (551). Both were embroidered in the same floral design and colours of silk thread. The detail opposite (553) shows the decoration around the opening at the centre back. SN

551 (ABOVE LEFT), 552 (ABOVE RIGHT) & 553 (OPPOSITE)
Man's court coat of figured silk velvet and waistcoat of satin weave silk, both with embroidery in silk thread
France or Britain, 1795–1800

Given by Mrs George Shaw.
V&A T.29&A-1910

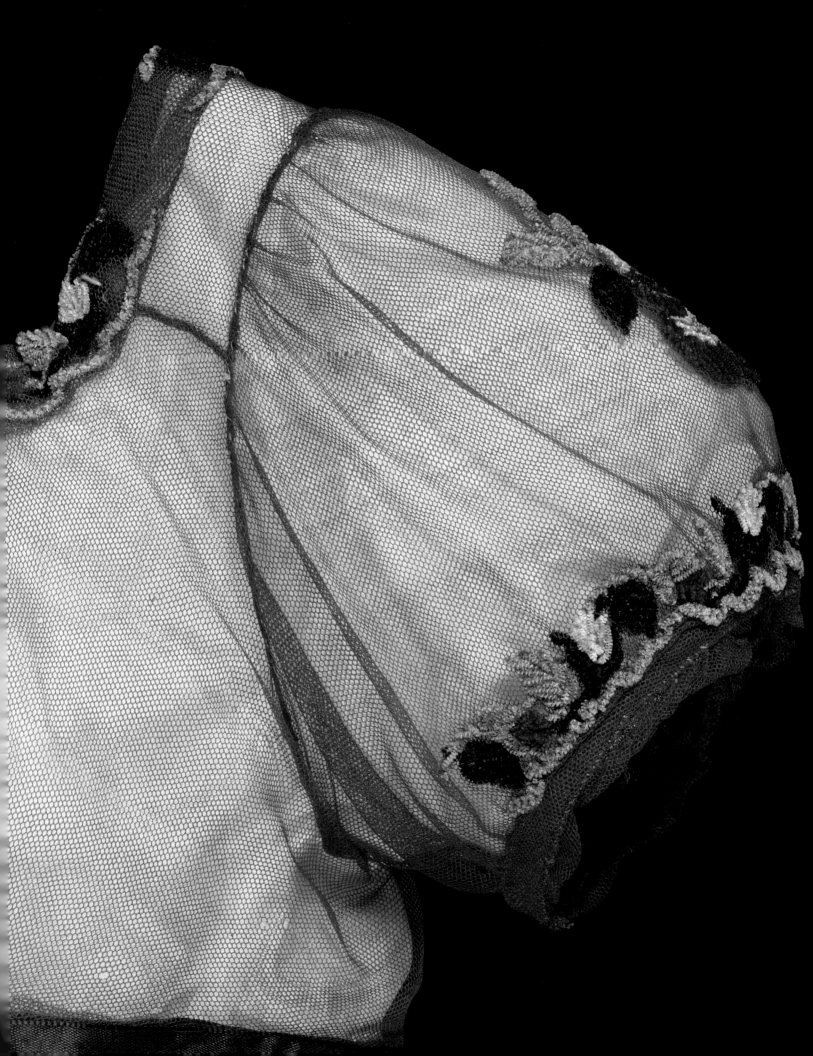

Dense chenille embroidered motifs often complemented the fashionable fine and transparent fabrics worn in early nineteenth-century Europe, such as this silk net made with a machine patented by the Englishman John Heathcote in 1809. The thick velvety threads were usually couched onto the base fabric to avoid damaging their pile. OC

554 (OPPOSITE) & 555 (RIGHT)
Gown of machine-made silk net with silk ribbon and embroidery in silk chenille thread
Britain, about 1810

Given by Mrs George Atkinson and Mrs M.F. Davey.
V&A T.194-1958

This panel, embroidered with decorative motifs symbolizing marital bliss and the inscription 'May the union of the two families be the source of ten thousand blessings', was once part of the back of a sumptuous traditional Korean bridal robe (*hwarot*). Similar panels adorned the front, sleeves and cuffs of the robe. Initially reserved for the nobility, such robes were worn throughout society by the late nineteenth century. RK

556 (OPPOSITE) & 557 (RIGHT)
Panel from a wedding garment of plain weave silk with embroidery and couching in silk
Korea, 1850–1900

V&A T.200-1920

In Japan, when embroidery was the sole decorative method, it was often executed on shimmering satin weave silk. The roundels of flowers on this kimono are skilfully embroidered in a wide variety of stitches. The garment has a large padded hem and was designed as an outer kimono for winter wear. It would have been worn without an *obi* (waist sash). AJ

558 (LEFT) & 559 (OPPOSITE)
Young woman's outer kimono of satin weave silk with embroidery in silk and gold wrapped threads
Probably Kyoto, Japan, 1800–50

V&A FE.11-1983

Produced in China for the western market, silk accessories became luxury fashion items for European women in the first half of the nineteenth century. The satin stitch embroidery is reversible, a useful trait in items seen from both sides, such as shawls (560), and some parasols. The graduating tonal colours of the embroidery together with voided areas between the design edges give a defined outline and carved three-dimensional effect. Motifs included chinoiserie scenes of couples in gardens among flowers, birds, insects and pagodas (562) and English garden flowers, such as pansies, roses and honeysuckle (563). YC/HF

560 (RIGHT)
Shawl of silk crêpe with embroidery in twisted silks and knotted fringes
China, 1810–50

Given by HRH the Princess Louise, Duchess of Argyll.
V&A T.131-1924

Double-sided silk fans were fashionable during the Ming and Qing dynasties (1368–1911). Matching satin stitch appliqué butterflies, pomegranates and floral motifs have been applied on both sides of this fan (561). With their many seeds, pomegranates symbolize abundance and fertility. Here the seeds are stitched using the 'Beijing knot', also called 'seed stitch'. YC

561 (RIGHT)
Fan of gilt thread silk gauze with embroidery of silk appliqués and silk tassels with decorative knot
China, 1800–1900

Given by Mrs E.L. Cockell.
V&A T.51-1939.

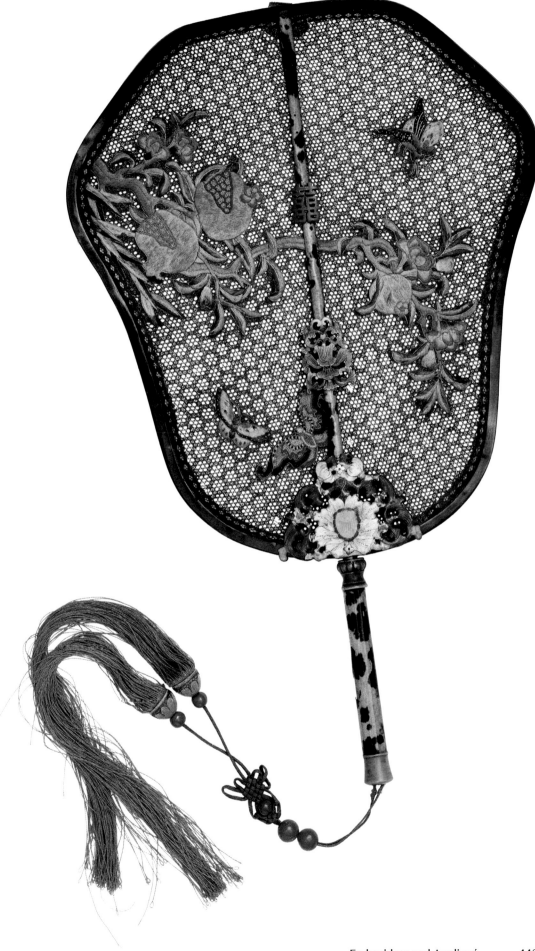

562 (OPPOSITE LEFT)
Parasol of plain weave silk with silk embroidery and hand-knotted silk fringe and ivory handle
China, 1840–60

Given by HM Queen Mary.
V&A T.18-1936

563 (OPPOSITE RIGHT)
Parasol of satin weave silk, with silk embroidery and fringe of knotted frost and ivory handle
China, 1860–70
Used by Queen Victoria

Given by Lord and Lady Cowdray.
V&A T.211-1970

This *jubla* (tunic; 564) is part of a traditional Parsi Indian ensemble for a young girl, to be worn with trousers and a cap. The work is in a Chinese style; the tunic is embroidered in satin stitch with high-twist silk thread, reflecting the trade connections many Parsi families in western India held with China. In Surat, Gujarat, immigrant Chinese embroiderers specialized in supplying the Parsi community with *chinai* embroidery of this type. AF

564 (OPPOSITE)
Tunic of satin weave silk with embroidery in silk
Probably Surat, Gujarat, India
about 1870
V&A 1426A-1874

This *chapan* (outer coat; 565) was part of the truly splendid dress of an Uzbek man. *Chapans* often have a woven-in pattern of stripes, but here the stripes are part of the embroidered decoration covering the entire outer surface of the robe. TS

565 (RIGHT)
Man's coat of plain weave cotton with embroidery in silk
Probably Shakhrisabz, Uzbekistan, 1850–1900
V&A T.61-1925

Silk embroidery adorns this cotton *kamis* (566). In Ethiopia silk thread was commonly obtained from unravelling imported cloth. The garment belonged to Queen Terunesh, or Empress Tiruwork Wube. It was sent to England after her death, a month after the British army's 1868 siege of Maqdala (Magdala) and given to the Victoria and Albert Museum. Items looted during the siege were also given to the museum. CAJ

566 (OPPOSITE)
Detail of dress of plain weave cotton with embroidery in silk thread
Ethiopia, about 1860

Given by the Secretary of State for India.
V&A 399-1869

Pashk, women's dresses from Baluchistan, are traditionally embellished with embroidery in four areas: the yoke, both cuffs and a large central pocket. The embroidery is typically worked in silk on a silk or cotton base, but formal *pashk* made for special occasions or for women of high rank might be embellished with couched silver-gilt wrapped thread. AF

567 (ABOVE)
Detail of dress of plain weave silk with embroidery in silk and silver-gilt wrapped thread
Shikarpur, Sindh, India (now Pakistan), about 1867

V&A 6050(IS)

A peacock spreads its tail feathers on both sides of this stylish *nukkadar* cap (568), which is simply constructed from two half-moon-shaped pieces of satin. The richness of this cap indicates it was designed for a wealthy, fashionable man as an informal alternative to a turban. AF

568 (ABOVE)
Cap of satin weave silk with embellishment of silver, silver-gilt and foil
Possibly Delhi, India, about 1840–60

V&A 5761(IS)

Western India and Pakistan are rich in domestic silk embroidery traditions. Often their embroideries are worked with untwisted floss silk, which lies very flat against the ground fabric to create dense designs. The embroiderer of this piece (569) used a straight needle to switch between chain, herringbone and Sindhi stitch (satin stitches radiating from a central point). AF

569 (RIGHT)
Child's dress of plain weave silk with embroidery in floss silk
Sindh, India (now Pakistan), 1900–30

V&A IS.139-1960

Phulkari, Punjabi flower-work embroideries, are characterized by counted thread surface darning stitches worked in shiny, untwisted floss silk. *Phulkari* is the technique used to embroider *bagh* (garden) shawls, made by women in advance of weddings and other special family occasions. Nearly the entire cotton ground has to be embroidered with silk – a process that can require a year or more of work. AF

570 (LEFT)
'Garden' shawl of plain weave cotton with embroidery in silk
Punjab, India or Pakistan, 1875–1900

Given by Dr W. Ganguly.
V&A IS.5-2017

The embroiderer of this woman's bodice (possibly the wearer herself) affixed hundreds of circular mirror pieces to the ground using decorative framing stitches (571). Silk satin was a popular choice of fabric for clothing in the Kachchh region, although sometimes it needed to be reinforced with harder-wearing cotton, as in the underarm gussets of this bodice. AF

571 (OPPOSITE)
Detail of bodice of satin weave silk with embroidery in silk and mirrors
Kachchh, Gujarat, India, 1850–1900

Given by Lady Ratan Tata.
V&A IM.256-1920

The simple cut of this plain silk gown (572) allows the exquisite chenille embroidery to take centre stage. The scrolling floral design was inspired by the embroidery on European eighteenth-century waistcoats and was worked by Lesage, a family firm, which had been under the creative direction and management of François Lesage since 1949. EM

572 (OPPOSITE)
Detail of an evening dress of silk zibeline with embroidery in silk chenille, sequins, beads and stones
Designed by Antonio del Castillo for Lanvin; silk by Staron; embroidery by Lesage, Paris, France, 1957
Worn by the Countess of Drogheda

Given by the wearer.
V&A T.284-1974

Highly skilled artisans in Mumbai embellished this cashmere scarf (573), which sports the classic Hermès cavalcade (*cavalcadour*) print of intertwined horse harness and bridles originally designed by Henri d'Origny in 1981. The fine hand embroidery of this recent version took 500 hours to complete. DP

573 (RIGHT)
Scarf of cashmere with screen printing and hand embroidery in silk
Designed by Henri d'Origny for Hermès, France; printed in Lyon and embroidered at Atelier 2M, Mumbai, India, 2014

Courtesy of Hermès.
V&A IS.72-2016

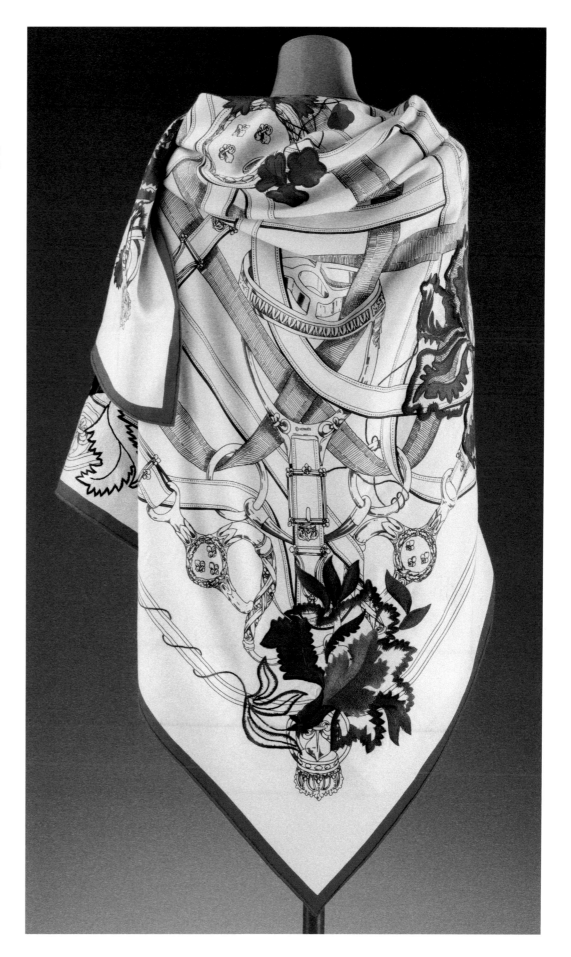

This long robe (574) is made from two different shades of tasar silk: panels of cream silk with a cut-away chevron design have been appliquéd by hand to a base of natural coloured silk. The decorative pattern has been skilfully arranged to fit perfectly onto the T-shaped structure of the garment. DP

574 (ABOVE)
Long coat of natural plain weave tasar silk with appliqué in tasar silk
Designed by Asha Sarabhai and made by Raag, Ahmedabad, Gujarat, India, 1994–5

V&A IS.9-1995

For this sari (575), the designer Swati Kalsi chose tasar silk as it was local to Bihar and therefore appropriate to showcase the embroidery skills of a group of women from the region. The women used *sujini*, a simple running stitch, to patch together old fabric into quilts. By transferring the technique to tasar silk they created a luxury garment. DP

575 (OPPOSITE)
Pebble Stream, sari of plain weave tasar silk with embroidery in cotton
Designed by Swati Kalsi for Jiyo! and embroidered by Guriya, Rani, Anisa and Khushboo Kumari, Bihar, India, 2011–12
Blouse of matching silk from India and tailored in London, 2011–12

Purchased with the assistance of the American Friends of the V&A through the generosity of Mr Perry Smith.
V&A IS.21-2012

The Chinese 'dragon robe' has now become emblematic of its imperial past, particularly those made in the distinctive yellow colour traditionally reserved for the emperor. They formed part of the court dress regulated by Emperor Qianlong (ruled 1735–96). The addition of sleeve-bands at elbow level and the absence of a centre front opening in the above robe (576) suggest it was intended for an imperial woman. YC

576 (ABOVE)
Woman's winter dragon robe of twill weave silk with embroidery in silk and gilt-metal thread
China, 1700–1800

V&A 870-1901

Fashion designer Laurence Xu has reinterpreted the dragon robe as contemporary couture (578). Xu combined traditional Chinese hand embroidery with western tailoring techniques including darts and shoulder-padding to construct a fitted mermaid-silhouette. A version of the dress was worn by the actor Fan Bingbing at the Cannes Film Festival in 2010 to critical acclaim. The dress was later reincarnated in a synthetic fabric on a special edition Barbie doll (577). YC

577 (RIGHT)
Fan Bingbing Barbie doll by Linda Kyaw, Mattel Inc., of moulded plastic, synthetic printed fabric, printed card and acrylic
China, 2013–14

Given by Fan Bingbing.
V&A FE.60-2015

578 (OPPOSITE)
The Auspicious Cloud of the Orient, 'red carpet' dress of satin weave silk with embroidery in silk and raised metal threads
By Laurence Xu, China, 2010–11

Given by the designer.
V&A FE.3-2012

In Vietnam silk robes heavily embroidered in metal wrapped threads were reserved exclusively for court dress until the middle of the twentieth century. Creating stylized flowers using the technique of double couching was a tradition of Hue, the imperial capital of the Nguyen dynasty (1802–1945). This contemporary example combines tradition and modernity, as the softer pastel-coloured silk and knot stitches in the centre of the flowers display a French colonial influence. SFC

579
Detail of woman's jacket of satin weave silk with embroidery in silk and silver wrapped threads
By Victoria Roe for WRŐNG by FASHION4FREEDOM, Hue, Vietnam, 2016–17

V&A. IS.22:1-2019

STAMPING

Stamping was an effective and relatively inexpensive means of patterning plain cut velvets in use in Europe by the sixteenth century. Metal dies or embossed seals were engraved with the desired motif, heated to the right temperature and impressed on the pile. The resulting patterns resembled those of voided and *cisé* velvets. In these examples the technique has been applied to a chasuble and the lining for a box that would have stored the owner's small precious objects. VB/SB

580 (BELOW)
Casket covered with gilt leather and lined with silk velvet with stamping
Italy, 1580–1620

V&A 479-1899

581 (OPPOSITE)
Detail of chasuble of cut silk velvet with stamping
Probably Italy, 1600–25

V&A 146-1895

Satin weave silks were embellished with pinking, patterning with decorative holes, as well as stamping. A heated metal stamp made decorative motifs by creating a contrast of light and dark. The stamped ribbon (584) features the royal arms flanked by scrolling banners and the words 'GLORIOUS WILLIAM' and 'REBELLION CRUSH D'. It commemorates King George II's triumphant victory that ended the House of Stuart's dreams of gaining the throne of Great Britain and Ireland in 1746. SN/SB

582 (OPPOSITE) & 583 (RIGHT)
Man's doublet and breeches of satin weave silk, with stamping, pinking and applied woven silk braid
England, 1630–40

V&A 348-1905

584 (BELOW)
Ribbon of plain weave silk with stamping
Britain, about 1746

V&A T.115-1999

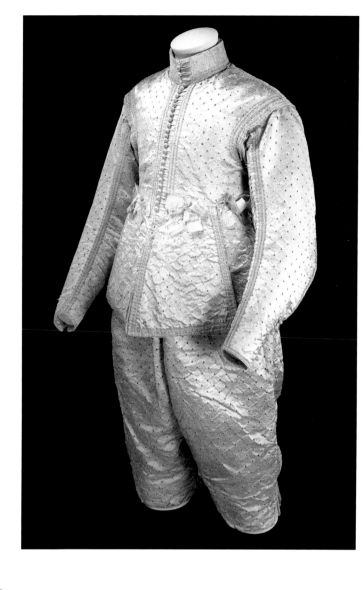

SLASHING, PUNCHING AND BURNING

Slashing was a popular method of decoration in sixteenth- and seventeenth-century Europe. It was a much faster technique than embroidery. The fabric needed to be densely woven – silk satin was the best. A small pointed tool with a shaped, sharpened edge made the cuts, usually on the diagonal to reduce fraying. SN

585 (BELOW) & 586 (OPPOSITE)
Woman's bodice of satin weave silk with slashing
England, 1630–40

V&A 172-1900

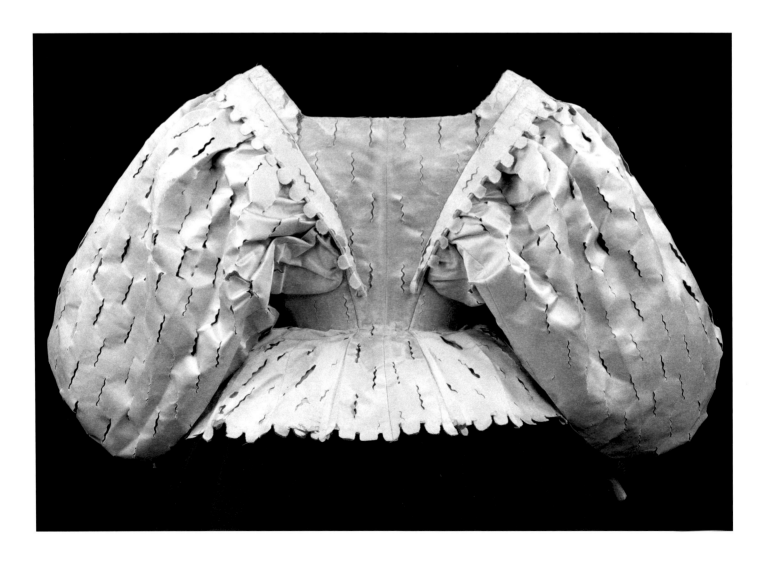

These two woven silks show before and after cutting or slashing. The diagonal bars created by the floats of the ground weft on the terracotta silk (587) have not yet been cut, while those on the olive silk have (588). The contrasting fabric of either the lining or undergarment showed through the slits creating further three-dimensional decoration. SB

587 (OPPOSITE)
Detail of fragment of *gros de Tours* plain weave silk with brocading
Italy, 1625–50

V&A T.226-1910

588 (ABOVE)
Detail of length of satin weave silk with slashing
Possibly Italy, about 1600

V&A 835-1901

Punching was done with a tool bearing rounded teeth to separate rather than sever the threads of the weave. In the waistcoat opposite (590), the tiny holes in concentric lines and scrolls around the embroidered rosebud were created by punching through the densely woven taffeta. In contrast, the silk scarf (589) has holes that have been burnt out of the fabric using chemicals, small ones forming a border around the edge and larger ones forming rings in the centre. The imprecise nature of some of the holes indicates the unique handmade quality of this scarf. SN/DP

589 (RIGHT)
Detail of scarf of plain weave silk with burnt out holes
Designed by Asha Sarabhai and made by Raag, Ahmedabad, Gujarat, India, 1994–5

V&A IS.23-1995

590 (OPPOSITE)
Detail of man's waistcoat of plain weave silk with punching and embroidery in silk thread and silver spangles
Britain 1780–90

V&A T.286-1982

WATERING

This suit is too small for a boy and too luxurious to be a masterpiece made by an apprentice to demonstrate skills acquired during his training. It was probably made by a tailor as an advertisement for his flair in making European men's court attire. The textured watered (moiré) silk complements the smooth taffeta beautifully. LEM

591
Miniature suit of plain weave silk (green) with watered *gros de Tours* (white)
France or England, about 1765
Given by Miss H. Prescott-Decie.
V&A T.262 to B-1978

The colour and texture of the silk used for these stays (592) suggest that they were intended to be seen, at least informally. The body of the stays is finely stitched with channels for the baleen (whalebone) strips that provide its shape, so the sleeves show off the rippled surface of the watered (moiré) silk more clearly. SN

592 (OPPOSITE)
Detail of woman's stays, exterior of plain weave silk with watering
England or the Netherlands, 1660–80
Given by Miss C.E. Gallini.
V&A T.14&A-1951

The striking colour, Prussian blue, enhances this lustrous watered (moiré) silk (593). It was the first synthetic pigment, preceding the vibrant aniline dyes that became widespread after William H. Perkins discovered synthetic mauve in 1856. CKB

593 (OPPOSITE)
Detail of a day dress of grosgrain silk with watering
Britain, about 1858

Given by Miss Janet Manley.
V&A T.90&A-1964

This *aba* (594), a sleeveless outer robe, is part of Bedouin male dress. Such a fine example probably originated in the 'robes of honour' commissioned by nineteenth-century shahs of Iran for presentation to nomad chiefs. They were also awarded to Iranian officials, some of whom are depicted wearing them draped over their other clothes in nineteenth-century portraits. TS

594 (ABOVE)
Man's robe of plain weave silk with tapestry weave metal thread and watering
Kashan, Iran, about 1870

V&A 1303-1874

Abraham Ltd supplied the watered (moiré) silk for this wedding dress. Based in Zurich, the firm specialized in high quality fabrics for couture houses. From the Autumn/Winter collection 1962/1963, Victor Stiebel chose a length of moiré silk. The same silk was used for this wedding dress the following Spring/Summer season. EM

595 (OPPOSITE)
Wedding dress of watered silk
Designed by Victor Stiebel, London, England; silk from Abraham Ltd, Zurich, Switzerland, Summer 1963
Given by the designer.
V&A T.169-1963

These ribbons (596–9) were all woven as *gros de Tours*, with one silk thread for the warp and one for the weft. The colour scheme in the striped, multicoloured ribbons is achieved by changing the single warp thread. The watered (moiré) effect was created by subjecting the woven fabric to heat and pressure, with ribbed rollers being used to flatten parts of the weave. It comes to life when light reflects off the uneven surface. HF

596, 597, 598 & 599 (THIS PAGE, LEFT TO RIGHT)
Ribbons of *gros de Tours* weave silk with watering
(596 & 597) Britain, 1800–50 and 1875–1914
(598 & 599) Britain, 1890–1910

(596 & 597) Given by Miss Juliet Reckitt & Messrs G.F. & A.L. Reckitt.
V&A T.147B-1923 & T.147:26-1923
(598 & 599) Given by Mrs Rosalie Sinclair.
V&A T.574-1996 & T.573-1996

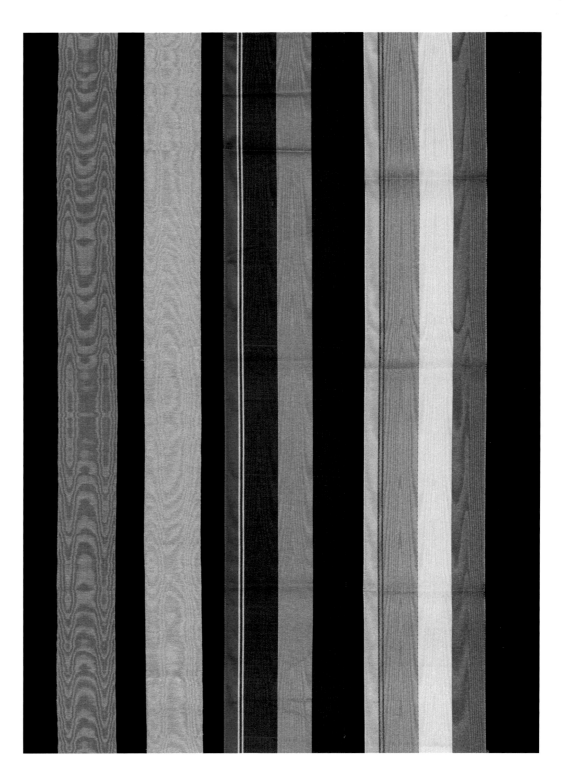

PLEATING AND SMOCKING

It remains a mystery how Mariano Fortuny achieved the tight permanent pleats which allowed his renowned *Delphos* dresses to cling to the body. These green iterations of the style, inspired by ancient Greek chitons, tunics that fastened at the shoulder, were owned by Italian actor Eleanora Duse, a great friend of the designer and one of various performer clients. CAJ

BELOW (600 & 601)
Delphos, dresses of plain weave silk with pleating
Designed by Mariano Fortuny, Italy and retailed by Babani, France, about 1920

Given by Fr Sebastian Bullough.
V&A T.740-1972 & T.739-1985

601 (RIGHT)
The designer Natacha Rambova wearing a *Delphos* gown by Fortuny
Photograph by James Abbe, 1924

The fabric for this jacket is referred to as *khadi*, which means that it is made from yarn that has been handspun and then handwoven. In this instance undyed mulberry silk yarn has been used. Asha Sarabhai favours the natural shades of silk and creates visual and textural interest through surface decoration such as fine pin pleating. DP

603 (ABOVE) & 604 (RIGHT)
Jacket of plain weave mulberry silk with pleating and stitching
Designed by Asha Sarabhai and made by Raag, Ahmedabad, Gujarat, India, 1994–5

V&A IS.4-1995

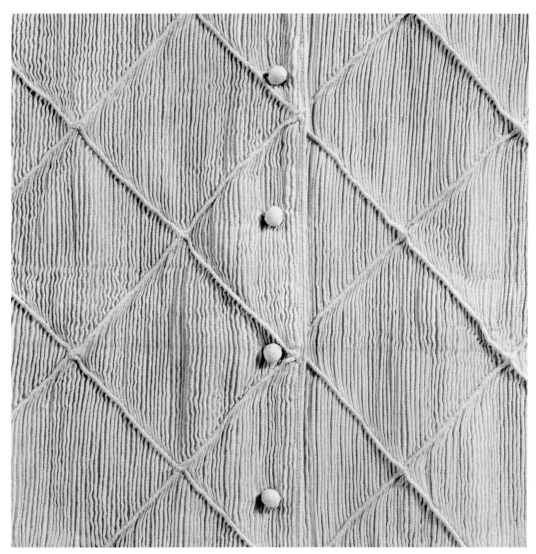

Following the opening of Liberty's costume department in 1884, many artistically minded middle- and upper-class British women embraced what was known as aesthetic dress reform. Their gowns contrasted with the rigidly boned and voluminous fashionable dresses worn over crinolettes or bustles, often in crisp silks. In many instances smocking in softer silks created the comfortable and flowing line sought by these unconventional dressers. CAJ

605 (OPPOSITE)
Dress of plain weave pongee silk with smocking in silk
Liberty & Co. Ltd, London, England, about 1895

V&A T.17-1985

607 (ABOVE)
Girl's dress of plain weave silk with hand smocking
Canada, about 1953

Given by Miss Caroline Goodfellow on behalf of her mother, Mrs J.M.A. Goodfellow.
V&A MISC.98-1980

Smocking – often associated in Britain with rural or folk dress – became a hallmark of children's clothing from the nineteenth century. Usually stitched into cotton, it appears in the illustrations of Kate Greenaway (606). By the time this party dress (607) was made by the wearer's mother in the 1950s, smocking was a classic design feature. The use of silk, however, makes this dress special. JR

606 (LEFT)
Three girls in white dresses in a garden, sitting at a table and drinking tea
Coloured wood engraving illustration by Kate Greenaway, London, 1880s–90s

Given by Guy Tristram Little.
V&A E.2446-1953

THE DANGERS OF DRINK, DANCE AND DIRT

It is not unusual to find dark yellow/brown stains on light-coloured silk evening gowns or wedding dresses that were most likely caused by champagne or similar colourless drinks. Seemingly inconsequential at the time, these accidental spillages darken with age as the sugars oxidize.

Couturier Paul Poiret's iconic *Sorbet* satin overdress (609), worn by his wife Denise, is an example. There is extensive staining on the cream silk bodice with distinct yellow tide-lines where the staining agent eventually dried (610). An accident with a drink seems most likely, given that there is only minor staining on the underarm area of the inner bodice from perspiration and the black silk sleeve is in good condition.

The combination of the silks, beading, wire hoop and fur would have made this a difficult garment to clean, and splash marks on the skirt suggest that it may never have received this attention.

In contrast, a costume from the Ballets Russes from the same decade testifies to the physical exertions of performers (following pages: 611 and 612). Constructed from red satin with yellow silk appliqué, heavily padded silver tissue decoration and a thick cotton lining, the jacket for the Chinese Conjuror must have been hot to wear on stage. The yellow silk appliqué is abraded at the neck and underarm from wear, the red silk is stained and fragmentary on the front and there are many losses on the back around the shoulders. The lining is heavily soiled and patched and the collar marked with greasy make-up.

The ballet company toured extensively and the costumes were occasionally dry cleaned – as time and money allowed – yet in the long run the weight of the silver decoration, the impact of the choreography and the costume's reputed burial to preserve it during the Second World War have all damaged it considerably.

Both soiled and clean garments attract pests. Moth casings were found in the red silk floss embroidery on the sleeve of a late eighteenth-century kimono (p. 484: 613). Silk is a protein, but pests seldom favour it as a food source. In this case, however, the moths have eaten the embroidery, the cream silk fabric, silk padding and the red silk sleeve lining (p. 485: 614). EAH

LAQUELLE ?

Robe de soirée de Paul Poiret

608 (OPPOSITE LEFT)
Laquelle? Robe de soirée de Paul Poiret, by Georges Lepape, published in *La Gazette du Bon Temps*, Paris, France, September 1913. Hand-coloured print

V&A CIRC.28-1974

609 (OPPOSITE RIGHT)
Sorbet, overdress of satin weave silk embroidered with glass beads and trimmed with fur, with silk chiffon sash, by Paul Poiret, Paris, France, 1913

V&A T.385-1976

610 (RIGHT)
Detail of damage to *Sorbet* overdress

The Dangers of Drink, Dance and Dirt   483

613 (ABOVE)
Woman's kimono of figured satin
weave silk with hand-painting in
ink, stencil-imitation tie-dyeing
and embroidery in silk and gold
wrapped threads, Japan, 1780–1820

V&A FE.19-1986

614 (OPPOSITE)
Detail showing damage on
the kimono

EMBROIDERY FIT
FOR A QUEEN

The soft, heavily padded structure of the case opposite (617) made it a secure holder for delicate accessories such as handkerchiefs, gloves or fans. Its six pairs of wide silk ribbons would have tied it firmly closed to keep its contents safe. Both sides, made of ivory plain weave silk edged with a stripe of light green taffeta, are embroidered with garlands of roses, pansies and lilacs, executed in satin stitch with their colours masterfully shaded, as are three peacock feathers springing from each corner.

These motifs, their arrangement and colours bear a strong resemblance to the summer furnishings of Queen Marie-Antoinette's bedchamber at Versailles, made in 1786 after designs by Jean-François Bony. The patterns for these new hangings and upholstery comprised ribbons and the same decorative repertoire as on the case.

This becomes particularly evident when comparing it with the design for the queen's bed cover (616) on which bouquets with three peacock feathers emerge from the corners, their tips gently bowing.

The Queen's Bedchamber at Versailles has been furnished with faithful reproductions of the charming silks by Bony.[11] Their luxuriance is emphasized by cascades of silk passementerie and tassels greatly resembling those adorning the handkerchief case. These eye-wateringly expensive trimmings consist of a myriad of rosettes and spirals, made of parchment strips and wire, twisted into a configuration of petals and wrapped in silk threads and knotted together. The silks used in making them match the colour palette of the embroideries, a convention evident in interior decoration as well as dress (615). SB

615 (BELOW)
Marie Antoinette, Queen of France by François-Hubert Drouais, Paris, France, 1773. Oil on canvas

Bequeathed by John Jones.
V&A 529-1882

616 (BELOW)
Design for the embroidery of the bed cover for the summer furnishings for Queen Marie-Antoinette's bedchamber at the Château of Versailles, France, by Jean-François Bony, about 1786. Gouache on paper

617 (OPPOSITE)
Handkerchief case of ivory and light green plain weave silks with embroidery in silk threads, trimmed with silk passementerie, France, about 1787

V&A T.43-2018

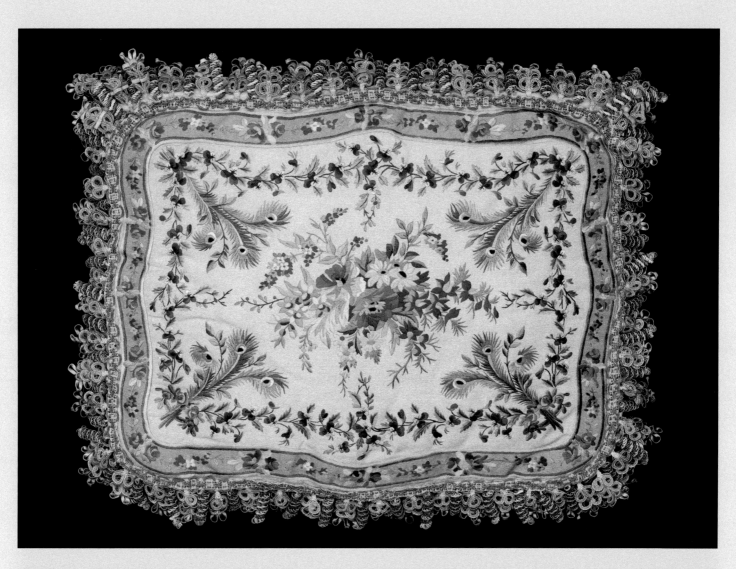

STITCHED MESSAGES FROM KOREA

Ham Kyungah, a South Korean artist, creates politically charged works whose content and making process focus on the political division of the Korean peninsula between North and South. Embroidery has been her medium of choice since 2008. Her designs are cut up and smuggled to and from North Korea, where anonymous embroiderers work on individual sections.

Ham's works conceal cryptic messages in English or Korean that are drowned in abstract or psychedelic patterns long suppressed by the communist government in the North. The final reconstituted embroidered panel based on her work is not always faithful to the original design as embroiderers modify colours or motifs to their liking or to avoid censorship. The direction of the satin stitches and silk threads is not always consistent as more than one embroiderer works on each piece.

As some sections are lost or confiscated on their way out to the South, Ham still patiently awaits their return in order to complete the piece. The Victoria and Albert Museum's embroidery reads 'Big Smile' (618 and 619), a North Korean motto rousing people to convey their pride and happiness to the leader during celebratory mass events.

During the Joseon dynasty (1392–1910), sewing and embroidery were a rare source of creative expression for women as they were encouraged to cultivate skills useful for the household in the confines of their home. Two embroidery styles developed in parallel: *gung-su* (court embroidery) and *min-su* (folk embroidery). *Gung-su* utilized pastel-tone twisted silk threads to embroider elegant patterns drawn by professional painters from the *Dohwaseo*, the Paintings Bureau of the Royal Court (620 and see 5 on p. 19). By contrast, *min-su*'s vibrant colours and spontaneous motifs were designed by and made for consumers of lowlier social status (621).

By the late nineteenth century a growing demand for embroidery saw the blooming of *min-su* into a lucrative business with one of its main production centres in Anju in South Pyeongan province (now in North Korea). Embroideries from this region in particular were renowned for being made by men.

Ham's work highlights the socio-cultural discrepancies between North and South Korea by revealing through embroidery the effect of divisive politics on daily life. Its place of production and makers' gender are unknown, but it echoes the fine, longstanding tradition of embroidery on the Korean peninsula. RK

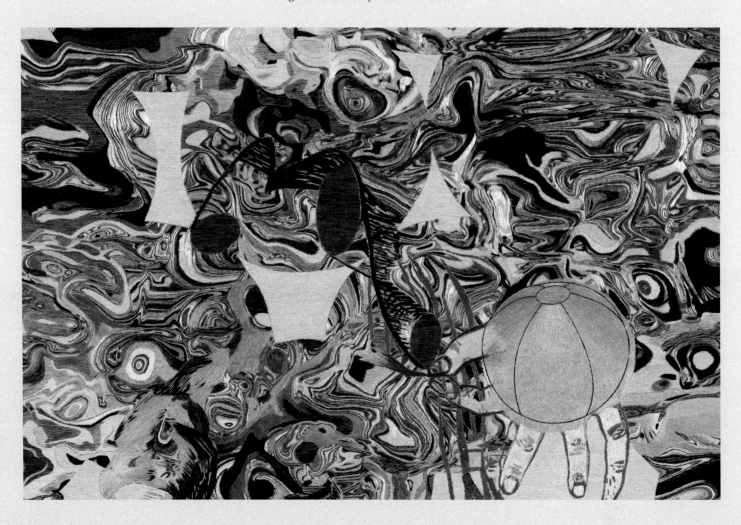

618 (ABOVE)
Needling Whisper, Needle Country/
SMS Series in Camouflage/Big
Smile RO1-01-01, cotton panel with
embroidery in silk, designed by Ham
Kyungah, Seoul, South Korea and
embroidered in North Korea, 2015

Purchase funded by Samsung.
V&A FE.24-2016

619 (OPPOSITE)
Detail of plain and satin stitch

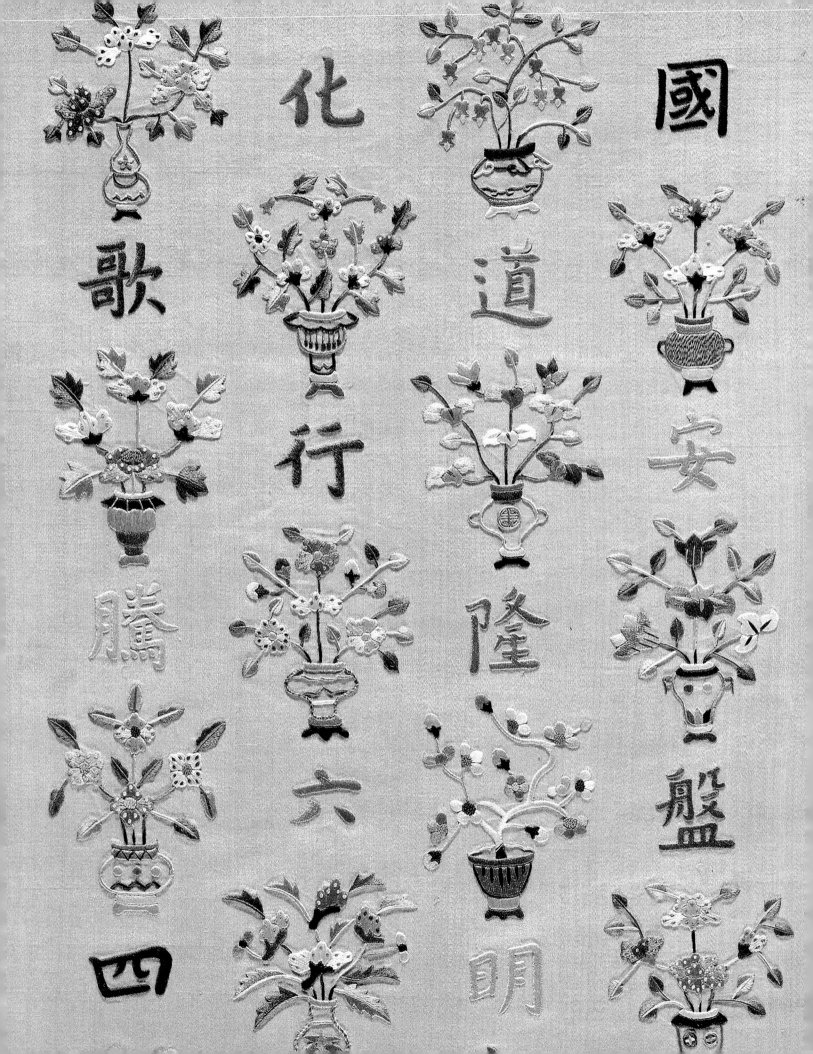

GLOSSARY

Bast: plant fibre collected from the inner bark surrounding the stem of certain plants, such as flax, hemp or ramie.

Batik: Indonesian word commonly used in Europe and English-speaking countries to describe a form of resist-dyeing.

Brocade: a general and imprecise term used for any rich figured textile, and by extension applied to any textile with a woven pattern, especially one with a pattern in gold or silver.

Cannelé: ribbed texture created by regular floats of warp threads, in most cases restricted to the ground of the silk.

Chenille: fancy yarn that has small tufts of fibre protruding all around its central core so that it resembles a caterpillar.

Chiffon: lightweight, sheer fabric with a dull finish, made with tightly twisted yarn.

Chiné: French term for a cloth with patterns resist-dyed on the yarn prior to weaving (similar to ikat) and from the 1830s onwards often also used for a cloth with a printed warp; the resulting pattern generally has an indeterminate or cloudy outline.

Cords: threads of the figure harness on the drawloom that control the pattern in the width of the fabric. The greater the number, the finer and more elaborate the design.

Count, thread: number of warp and weft threads in a specified linear measurement, such as a centimetre or inch.

Crêpe: medium or lightweight fabric with a textured surface achieved by using hard twisted yarns, textured yarns, chemical treatment or special weaves.

Discontinuous weft: weft thread that is not carried across the full width of the textile, as used in brocaded or tapestry-woven fabrics.

Drawloom: loom that uses a double harness, one of which is used to create the ground weave and the other the patterning.

Faille: a type of *cannelé* (see above) with ribs of equal width on face and reverse.

Figured: general term used for any textile with a repeat pattern achieved during weaving.

Filament: fibre of continuous length.

Floss: silk thread with no visible twist.

Foot-figured: fabric with simple, often geometrical pattern made on a treadle loom.

Frost: a curled metal thread (*frisé* in French).

Gauze: weave in which the warps are crossed and uncrossed between the wefts at intervals to create a transparent openwork fabric. The name is also given to plain weave fabrics in which the warps do not cross but are often 'paired', creating uneven spacing in the weave between the series of warp threads.

Gazar/super gazar/zagar: family of firm plain weave silk fabrics.

Gimp: an openwork trimming made of plaited or twisted strands of fibre.

Gros de Tours (French): a type of taffeta with warp and weft doubled to make a sturdier fabric.

Grosgrain: woven fabric with prominent horizontal ribbed effect on the surface, usually made of silk.

Ikat: Indonesian term, now widely used to describe all patterns created by resist-dyeing the warp and/or weft.

Jacquard: punch-card pattern-selecting device for handlooms or power looms, originally invented to replace the drawboy or drawgirl who worked with the weaver on the drawloom.

Kasuri: hand-woven Japanese fabric made by tie-dyeing yarns in the same method as for ikat.

Katazome: Japanese method of dyeing fabrics using a resist paste applied through a stencil.

Lampas: a compound weave fabric with two warps (main and binding) and at least two wefts for the ground and another one for the pattern.

Macramé: art of knotting string, cord, wool or other yarns and arranging these knots in different sequences to create different patterns.

Moiré: a wavy, rippled effect on the surface of the fabric, created by applying pressure to parts of ribbed fabrics after weaving.

Nishiki: Japanese silk brocade made in the Nischijin weaving district of Kyoto, often woven with supplementary gold and/or silver thread.

Or nué: a form of couching in silks over gold threads, in which the couching threads vary to achieve shading, thus changing the emphasis between gold and colour.

Organza: fine, lightweight plain weave sheer fabric made of silk or synthetic fibre yarns, crisp and lustrous.

Organzine: thrown silk twisted to increase its strength.

Passementerie: trimmings, especially braids, cords and gimp (see above).

Plain weave: an over-one, under-one weave structure that achieves an even, balanced weave. Also called 'tabby weave'.

Pinking: a decorative cutting of the edges.

Pongee: lightweight, plain weave fabric woven from wild silk, usually with a warp that is finer than the weft; its surface appearance is characteristically slubbed (see slub).

Power loom: loom powered by steam or electricity.

Purl: metal thread made from a very fine wire wound around a single core, which is either tubular or triangular in shape.

Qipao: style of Chinese dress, also known as *cheongsam*, whose prominent features are a high neck, side closure, long side-slits and a figure-hugging shape.

Raw silk: silk from which the gum (sericin) has not been removed.

Reeling: process by which silk filaments are unwound from their cocoons and wound into a circular contraption, called a reel.

Samite: fabric with two warps and at least two wefts, a weft-faced compound twill. The ground of the inner warp is invisible.

Satin: weave and fabric with a smooth shiny surface, in which the warp threads cover the wefts completely or vice versa.

Selvage/selvedge: outer edge of textile parallel to the warp, made by the weft threads wrapping round the outermost warp threads, often more densely set than the rest of the fabric.

Shibori: Japanese resist-dyeing technique, usually translated as tie-dyeing, which involves the binding, stitching, folding or clamping of fabric prior to immersion in the dyebath.

Shuttle: tool designed to store the holder carrying the thread of the weft yarn, thrown or passed back and forth between warps.

Slub: lump or thick place in yarn or thread.

Spooling: transferring reeled silk from large hanks onto small spools to facilitate the preparation of warp and weft threads.

Sprang: term applied to fabrics constructed by twisting yarns together.

Supplementary warp or weft: thread added to a single set of warp and weft threads during the weaving process.

Tanchoi: an Indo-Chinese style of satin-faced silk characterized by small scale patterns woven with two warps and multiple wefts in each pass.

Taffeta: plain and closely woven silk with a warp and weft with equal number of threads.

Taqueté (French): weave with two warps and two wefts, a weft-faced compound plain weave.

Tie-dye: resist-patterning created on a woven textile by tying selected sections of cloth with thread, thus preventing dye from entering the tied areas.

Tissue: generic term for a silk with two warp and two weft systems.

Tsuzuri-ori: Japanese tapestry weave.

Twill: weave and fabric in which the warp and weft interlace at one or more removes as the textile progresses.

Velvet: weave and fabric with pile made with one or more additional warps that are looped during weaving and then cut or left uncut to form the pile.

Velvet, *ciselé*: velvet whose pattern is formed by cut and uncut pile.

Velvet, voided: form of velvet that has areas of ground that have no pile but are instead in plain or satin weave, so contrast with the texture of the pile.

Warp: threads secured to the loom to run the length of the fabric.

Waste silk: silk from broken or defective cocoons or from the waste from reeling silk; sometimes spun into threads.

Weft: threads that are passed through the warps by the weaver using a shuttle.

Wild silk: semi-domesticated silks such as tasar, muga and eri (endi) with flat and spiral filaments.

Yarn-dyed: made with yarn dyed before weaving.

Yūzen: a Japanese freehand method of paste resist-dyeing, by which the outlines of a design are drawn in a thin ribbon of paste extruded from a small cloth tube. Dyes are then brushed within the paste boundaries.

Zibeline: originally used to describe a woollen cloth, this term was also applied to certain stiff medium- to heavy-weight twill weave silks by the 1950s.

NOTES

INTRODUCTION

1   Schäfer et al. 2018, p. 1.

2   Crill 2015, p. 120.

3   Ibid., pp. 20–3.

4   Denis Diderot and Jean Le Rond d'Alembert, *Encyclopédie, ou Dictionnaire raisonné des sciences, des arts et des métiers*, 28 vols (Paris 1751–72; Diderot and d'Alembert hereafter), vol. 15 (1765), pp. 303–6.

5   Peer 2012; Kassia St Clair, *The Golden Thread: How Fabric Changed History* (London 2018), pp. 271–86.

6   Donald Coleman, 'Man-made fibres before 1945' and Jeffrey Harrop, 'Man-made fibres since 1945', in Jenkins 2003, vol. 2, pp. 933–71.

7   Sea silk (*byssus*) does not have a continuous filament, though it is lustrous like silk. Felicitas Maeder, 'The project Sea-silk – Rediscovering an Ancient Textile Material', *Archaeological Textiles Newsletter*, 35 (Autumn 2002), pp. 8–11.

8   Faragò in Schoeser 2007, p. 64.

9   Douglas Page (ed.), *Mountaineers: Great Tales of Bravery and Conquest* (The Royal Geographical Society and the Alpine Club 2015), pp. 41–3.

10 Faragò in Schoeser 2007, p. 64; Brandon Gaille Small Business and Marketing Advice, *20 Silk Industry Statistics, Trends & Analysis*, 26 February 2019.

11 Watt and Wardwell 1997, p. 23; Susan Whitfield, *Silk, Slaves and Stupas. Material Culture of the Silk Road* (Oakland 2018), pp. 190–218.

12 Vainker 2004, pp. 46–8; Watt and Wardwell 1997, p. 23.

13 J.P. Wild in Jenkins 2003, vol. 1, p. 108; Muthesius 1995, pp. 255–314.

14 Crill 2015, p. 22.

15 W.O. Blanchard, 'The Status of Sericulture in Italy', *Annals of the Association of American Geographers*, 19:1 (1929), pp. 14–20.

16 Alison Philipson, 'Luxury of silk woven in Italy to return after decades-long absence', *Telegraph*, 19 March 2015.

17 Musée de la soie, Saint-Hippolyte-du-Fort; Seryicyn: https://www.sericyne.fr/en/sericyne-la-fibre-of-reves/ (accessed 25 November 2019).

18 Tessa Morris-Suzuki, 'Sericulture and the Origins of Japanese Industrialization', *Technology and Culture*, 33:1 (1 January 1992), pp. 101–21; Debin Ma, 'Why Japan, Not China, Was the First to Develop in East Asia: Lessons from Sericulture, 1850–1937', *Economic Development and Cultural Change*, 52:2, (01/2004), pp. 369–94.

19 The Silk Association of Great Britain, http://www.silk.org.uk/history.php (accessed 20 July 2019).

20 Feltwell 1990, pp. 26–33.

21 Mairead Dunleavy, *Pomp and Poverty. A History of Silk in Ireland* (New Haven and London 2011), pp. 43–5, 183–8.

22 Ben Marsh, '"The Honour of the Thing": Silk Culture in Eighteenth-century Pennsylvania', in Schäfer et al. 2018, pp. 264–80.

23 Bernard Webber, *Silk Trains: the Romance of Canadian Silk Trains or 'The Silks'* (Kelowna 1992), ch. 1 and 2, pp. 39 and 62. We are grateful to Susan North for this reference.

24 Vicki Hastrich, 'Making silk', *RAS* [Royal Agricultural Society of New South Wales] *Times* (25 October 2015).

25 J.G. Dingle, *Silk Production in Australia*. A Report for the Australian Government Rural Industries Research and Development Corporation (May 2000).

26 J.G. Dingle, *Silk Production in Australia*. A Report for the Australian Government Rural Industries Research and Development Corporation (November 2005).

27 José Luis Gasch-Tomás, 'The Manila Galleon and the Reception of Chinese Silk in New Spain, *c.* 1550–1650', in Schäfer et al. 2018, pp. 251–64.

28 Leslie Grace, '460 Years of Silk in Oaxaca, Mexico', *Textile Society of America Symposium Proceedings* (2004), 482, pp. 462–4.

29 'Artesanía textil de Oaxaca encuentra aliados: los gusanos de seda', *Forbes México* (21 January 2019).

30 Oswaldo da Silva Pádua, 'A Origem da sericicultura', *Nova Esperança* (4 April 2005).

31 Vinínicius Kleyton de Andrade Brito and Fabiane Popinigis, 'O Estabelecimento Seropédico de Itaguaí', Universidade Federal de Rio de Janeiro (June 2016); Aniello Angelo Avella, *Teresa Cristina de Bourbon: uma imperatriz napolitana nos trópicos 1843–1889* (Rio de Janeiro 2014), pp. 127–8.

32 'Cultura do bicho-da-seda vota a atrair produtores paranaenses', *Gazeta do Povo* (22 July 2016).

33 International Sericultural Commission (August 2019); Alessandro Maria Giacomin et al., 'Brazilian silk production: economic and sustainability aspects', *Procedia Engineering* 200 (2017), pp. 89–95.

34 International Sericulture Commission (August 2019).

35 Ole Zethner and Rie Koustrup, 'Sericulture Abroad: Africa: Wild Silkmoth Culture for Income and Eco-Conservation', *Fibre2Fashion*, about 2007: https://www.fibre2fashion.com/industry-article/5035/sericulture-abroad-africa-wild-silkmoth-culture-for-income-and-eco-conservation (accessed 1 August 2019).

36 Datta and Nanavaty 2005, Chapter 3; New Cloth Market, *The Global Silk Industry: Perceptions of European Operators toward Thai Natural & Organic Silk Fabric and Final Product* (December 2011).

37 Alternatively, if they are boiled, then the gum dissolves as they are reeled. Karolina Hurtková in Schäfer et al. 2018, pp. 281–94; Patrizia Sione, 'From Home to Factory: Women in the Nineteenth-Century Italian Silk Industry', in Daryl Hafter (ed.), *European Women and Preindustrial Craft* (Indiana 1995; Hafter 1995 hereafter), pp. 137–52; Debin Ma, 'Between Cottage and Factory: The Evolution of Chinese and Japanese Silk-Reeling Industries in the Latter Half of the Nineteenth Century', *Journal of the Asia Pacific Economy*, 10:2 (2005), pp. 195–213.

38 Rothstein 1990, p. 291.

39 Charles Germain de Saint-Aubin, *Art of the Embroiderer (1770)*, translated and annotated by Nikki Scheuer (Los Angeles and Boston 1983).

40 Crill 2015, pp. 23–5.

41 Vainker 2004, pp. 76–7.

42 Cited in John J. Beer, 'Eighteenth-Century Theories on the Process of Dyeing', *ISIS*, 51, (1960) pp. 21–3.

43 Dominique Cardon, *Natural Dyes. Sources, Tradition, Technology and Science* (London 2007; Cardon 2007 hereafter); Joyce Storey, *Dyes and Fabrics* (London 1978, reprinted 1992).

44 Cardon 2007, pp. 553–65.

45 Ibid., pp. 335–54.

46 'Teinture de soie', in Diderot and d'Alembert, vol. 16, (Paris 1765), pp. 29–30.

47 On Central and South American logwood and cochineal, Cardon 2007, pp. 263–74, 619–35. Amy Butler Greenfield, *A Perfect Red: Empire, Espionage, and the Quest for the Color of Desire* (New York 2005).

48 Cardon 2007, pp. 374–6.

49 'Colour in the Coal-Scuttle', *Leisure Hour*, 12 (1863), p. 375, cited in Charlotte Crosby Nicklas, 'Splendid hues: colour, dyes, everyday science, and women's fashion, 1840–1875', unpublished PhD thesis, University of Brighton 2009, p. 263. Subsequently, it became clear that such dyes were more durable than natural dyes.

50 Alison Matthews David, *Fashion Victims. The Dangers of Dress Past and Present* (London 2015), pp. 72–101, 102–25; Dilys Williams, 'Traceability and Responsibility', in Ehrman 2018, pp. 149–73.

51 Mary Lisa Gavenas, 'Who Decides the Color of the Season? How a Trade Show Called Première Vision Changed Fashion Culture', in Regina Lee Blazcyk and Uwe Spiekermann (eds), *Bright Modernity: Color, Commerce and Consumer Culture* (London 2017), pp. 251–69.

52 Yan Yong in Wilson 2010, p. 100.

53 Maria P. Zanoboni, 'Female labour in silk industry', in Chiara Buss (ed.), *Silk, Gold and Crimson. Secrets and Technology at the Viconti and Sforza Courts* (Milan 2010), p. 33; Daryl Hafter, 'Women who Wove in the Eighteenth-Century Silk Industry of Lyon', in Hafter 1995, pp. 42–65.

54 Dagmar Schäfer, 'Peripheral Matters: Selvage/Chef-de-pièce Inscriptions on Chinese Silk Textiles', *UC Davis Law Review*, 47: 2 (December 2013), pp. 705–33.

55 Amy DelaHaye and Shelley Tobin, *Chanel. The Couturière at Work* (London 1994), pp. 24–6 and 36.

56 Stanley Chapman, 'Hosiery and knitwear in the twentieth century', in Jenkins 2003, pp. 1024–9; Elizabeth Currie, 'Knitwear', in Sonnet Stanfill (ed.), *The Glamour of Italian Fashion since 1945* (London 2014), pp. 116–18.

57 Deborah Hofmann, 'Washed Silk Takes on New Guises', *New York Times* (21 April 1991), Section 1, p. 50.

58 Bernard Morel Journel, President of the ISA, *Report of the International Silk Association XVIIIth Congress, Taormina/Italy*, November 1991 (Lyon 1992), p. 19.

59 Callava 2018, p. 146.

60 The Saloon, Brighton Pavilion: https://brightonmuseums.org.uk/royalpavilion/whattosee/saloon/ (accessed 30 August 2019).

61 Stella McCartney: www.stellamccartney.com (accessed 30 October 2019); 'Pulling, not pushing, silk could revolutionise how greener materials are manufactured', University of Sheffield (University of Sheffield, 19 September 2017): https://www.sheffield.ac.uk/news/nr/silkworms-silk-greener-materials-1.731163 (accessed 5 February 2020).

62 'A filament fit for space', University of Oxford Press Release (3 October 2019): https://www.eurekalert.org/pub_releases/2019-10/uoo-aff093019.php (accessed 5 February 2020).

CHAPTER 1
PLAIN AND SIMPLE

1   Natalie Rothstein, 'Silk: The Industrial Revolution and After', in Jenkins 2003, vol. 2, pp. 790–808.

2   *Dior by Dior* (London 1954), p. 40.

3   Christian Dior, *The Little Dictionary of Fashion: A Guide to Dress Sense for Every Woman* (London 2008; first edn 1954), pp. 99, 115.

CHAPTER 2
WARPS AND WEFTS

1   Dorothy Burnham, *Warp and Weft* (Toronto 1980), pp. 199, 201.

2   Geoffrey Smith, *The Laboratory of the Arts* (London 1756), p. 44.

3   Kuhn 2012, pp. 55–8; Fotheringham 2018, p. 23.

4   Lesley E. Miller, 'Between Engraving and Silk Manufacture in late Eighteenth-century Lyon,' *Studies in the Decorative Arts*, vol. 3:2 (Spring 1996), pp. 52–76.

5   Natalie Rothstein, 'Silk in the Early Modern Period, c. 1500–1780', in Jenkins 2003, vol. 2, pp. 528–61; Rothstein, 'Taste and Technique, the Work of an 18th-Century Silk Designer', *Bulletin du CIETA*, 70 (1992), p. 148.

6   In Japan the word *nishiki* is used to describe polychrome figured silks. This term is translated in English as 'brocade', but in fact covers a wide range of silks woven with supplementary warps or, more frequently, wefts of coloured silk and/or gold or silver threads.

7   Eva Basile, handloom-weaving expert who taught cataloguing of historical textiles and Jacquard fabric design at Fondazione Lisio, Florence; personal communication with the author, March 2009.

8   Silk tapestry weaving (*tsuzuri-ori*) was introduced to Japan from China in the sixteenth century. Large scale works, made for export, were produced in the late nineteenth century. See Hiroko T. McDermott and Clare Pollard, *Threads of Silk and Gold: Ornamental Textiles from Meiji Japan* (Oxford 2012), pp. 170–4; Fotheringham 2018, p. 22.

9   Kuhn 2012, pp. 286–8.

10 Else Janssen, *Richesse de Velours* (Brussels 1995), p. 11.

11 Monnas 2012, p. 14.

12 Catherine Pagani, 'Europe in Asia: The impact of Western art and technology in China', in Anna Jackson and Amin Jaffer (eds), *Encounters* (London 2004), pp. 296–309.

13 Wilson 2010, pp. 14–15.

14 Cheng Weijing, *History of Textile Technology of Ancient China* (New York 1992), p. 443.

CHAPTER 3
TWINE AND TWIST, NET, KNOT AND KNIT

1   Chandramani Singh, *Textiles and Costumes from the Maharaja Sawai Man Sing II Museum* (Jaipur 1979).

2   Yuko Yoshida, 'Infinite Possibilities of Marudai Braiding', *Braids, Bands and Beyond* (The Braid Society 2016), pp. 21–4; Makiko Tada, 'Karakumi and Hirao', *Threads that Move* (The Braid Society 2012), pp. 23–8.

3   These were the functional and decorative elements of the small containers worn by Japanese men in the Edo period (1615–1865), suspended from their belts (*obi*).

4   Irene Emery, *The Primary Structures of Fabrics* (Washington 1966; Emery 1966 hereafter), p. 40; Richard Rutt, *A History of Hand Knitting* (London 1987), pp. 32–6.

5   Sandy Black, *Knitting: Fashion, Industry, Craft* (London 2012), p. 66.

6   Ibid., pp. 66, 233.

7   Emery 1966, pp. 43–4; Cary Karp, 'Defining Crochet', *Textile History*, 49:2 (2018), pp. 208–23.

8   Hongqi Lu, *Antique Carpets of China* (Beijing 2003), p. 192.

9   Jon S. Ansari, 'Chinese Carpets: The Modernization of an Ancient Craft', *Hali*, 5:2 (1982), pp. 160–2.

10 Verity Wilson, *Chinese Textiles* (London 2005), p. 72, fig. 80; Jonathan Spence, *The Search for Modern China* (New York 1990), pp. 574–83.

11 Terry Stratton (ed.), *Antique Chinese Carpets* (London 1978), p. 18.

CHAPTER 4
PAINT, RESIST AND PRINT

1   Harris 1993, pp. 36–42.

2   Some writers have considered this a printed Indian cotton, but the pattern is consistent with Chinese painted silks.

3   'Making ikat cloth': http://www.vam.ac.uk/content/articles/m/album-with-nested-carousel18/ (accessed 4 December 2019).

4   'Yohji Yamamoto: Shibori': http://www.vam.ac.uk/content/videos/y/yohji-yamamoto-shibori/ (accessed 4 December 2019).

5   Giorgio Riello, 'Asian knowledge and the development of calico printing in Europe in the seventeenth and eighteenth centuries', *Journal of Global History*, vol. 5 (2010), pp. 1–28.

6   Harris 1993, p. 37.

7   Linda Parry (ed.), *William Morris* (London 1996), p. 259, cat. M.52.

8   Field et al. 2007, p. 199.

9   Mary Schoeser, 'A Secret Trade: Plate Printed Textiles and Dress Accessories, *c.* 1620–1820', *Dress*, 34:1 (2007), pp. 49–59.

10 Harris 1993, pp. 37–8.

11 Datta and Nanavaty 2005, p. 67. Roller printing should not to be confused with the rolling-print press.

12 'Design repeats', Première Vision Paris, 12 December 2018, citing Textile addict, 7 October 2016: https://www.premierevision.com/en/news/spotlight-on/news-fabrics/design-repeats/ (accessed 18 April 2020).

13 Cardon 2007; Judith H. Hofenk de Graaff, *The Colourful Past: The Origins, Chemistry and Identification of Natural Dyestuffs* (Riggisberg 2004).

14 'Caracterización de las producciones textiles de la Antigüedad Tardía y Edad Media temprana: tejidos coptos, sasánidas, bizantinos e hispanomusulmanes en las colecciones públicas españolas' (HAR2008-04161), directed by Dr Laura Rodríguez Peinado, Department of Art History I (Medieval), Complutense University of Madrid, with analysis by Dr Enrique Parra at the Alfonso X El Sabio University, Madrid.

CHAPTER 5
STITCH, SLASH, STAMP AND PLEAT

1   Kuhn 2012.

2   Anne Wanner, 'The Sample Collections of Machine Embroidery of Eastern Switzerland in the St Gallen Textile Museum', *Textile History*, 23:2 (1992), pp. 165–76.

3   She then provided plates of 305 stitches. Mary Thomas, *Mary Thomas's Dictionary of Embroidery Stitches* (London 1938), p. v. Naturally, embroidery stitches have different names in different parts of the world. For Indian embroideries, see https://www.vam.ac.uk/articles/indian-embroidery (accessed 5 February 2020).

4   Maria João Pacheco Ferreira, 'Chinese textiles for Portuguese Taste', in Amelia Peck (ed.), *Interwoven Globe. The Worldwide Textile Trade, 1500–1800* (New York 2013), pp. 46–55.

5   Moira Thunder, *Embroidery Designs for Fashion and Furnishings from the Victoria and Albert Museum* (London 2011).

6   Astrid Castres, 'Les techniques de gaufrage : un champ d'expérimentation textile à Paris au XVIe siècle', in *Documents d'histoire parisienne*, 19 (2017), pp. 57–67.

7   Lesley Cresswell et al., *Textile Technology* (London 2002), p. 36.

8   Cesare Vecellio, *Habiti antichi et moderni di tutto il Mondo* (Venice 1590).

9   Joaquín Manuel Fos, *Instrucción metódica sobre los mueres* (Valencia 1790).

10 Patente nº 414119 *Genre d'étoffe plisée ondulée*, Paris, 10 June 1909.

11 Manufacture Prelle, *Catalogue des fabrications à caractère historique*: https://www.prelle.fr/files/pdf/cat_ref_hist.pdf (accessed 15 August 2019).

FURTHER READING

The literature on silk is vast and written in many languages. Below are some suggestions for books published in English on aspects of the subject.

Nurhan Atasoy et al., *Ipek: The Crescent and the Rose: Imperial Ottoman Silks and Velvets* (London 2001)

Carol Bier (ed.), *Woven from the Soul, Spun from the Heart: Textile Arts of Safavid and Qajar Iran, 16th-19th Centuries* (Washington, DC, 1987)

Luce Boulnois, *Silk Road: Monks, Warriors and Merchants on the Silk Road* (Hong Kong 2003)

Clare Browne, Glyn Davies and Michael A. Michael with Michaela Zöschg (eds), *English Medieval Embroidery: Opus Anglicanum* (New Haven, CT, and London 2016)

Trini Callava, *Silk through the Ages: The Textile that Conquered Luxury* (London 2018)

Ruby Clark, *Central Asian Ikats* (London 2007)

Peter Coles, *Mulberry* (London 2019)

Rosemary Crill, *The Fabric of India* (London 2015)

Rajat K. Datta and Mahesh Nanavaty, *Global Silk Industry: A Complete Source Book* (Boca Raton, FL, 2005)

Edwina Ehrman (ed.), *Fashioned from Nature* (London 2018)

Sharon Farmer, *The Silk Industries of Medieval Paris* (Pennsylvania 2017)

John Feltwell, *The Story of Silk* (Stroud 1990)

Jacqueline Field, Marjorie Senechal and Madelyn Shaw, *American Silk 1830-1930: Entrepreneurs and Artifacts* (Lubbock, TX, 2007)

Avalon Fotheringham, *The Indian Textile Source Book: Patterns and Techniques* (London 2018)

Jennifer Harris (ed.), *5000 Years of Textiles* (London 1993)

Anna Jackson (ed.), *Kimono: Kyoto to Catwalk* (London 2020)

David Jenkins (ed.), *The Cambridge History of Western Textiles*, 2 vols (Cambridge 2003)

Brenda King, *Silk and Empire* (Manchester and New York, NY, 2005)

Dieter Kuhn (ed.), *Chinese Silks* (New Haven, CT, and London 2012)

Xinru Liu, *Silk and Religion: An Exploration of Material Life and the Thought of People, AD 600-1200* (Delhi 1996)

Ben Marsh, *Unravelled Dreams: Silk and the Atlantic World 1500-1840* (Cambridge 2020)

Lesley Ellis Miller, *Selling Silks: A Merchant's Sample Book of 1764* (London 2014)

James A. Millward, *The Silk Road: A Very Short Introduction* (Oxford 2013)

Luca Molà, *The Silk Industry of Renaissance Venice* (Baltimore, MD, and London 2000)

Lisa Monnas, *Merchants, Princes and Painters: Silk Fabrics in Italian and Northern Paintings, 1300-1550* (New Haven, CT, and London 2008)

Lisa Monnas, *Renaissance Velvets* (London 2012)

Anna Muthesius, *Studies in Byzantine, Islamic and Near Eastern Silk Weaving* (London 2008)

Roberta Orsi Landini, *The Velvets in the Collection of the Costume Gallery in Florence* (Florence 2017)

Simon Peer, *Golden Spider Silk* (London 2012)

Natalie Rothstein, *Silk Designs of the Eighteenth Century* (London 1990)

Josephine Rout, *Japanese Dress in Detail* (London 2020)

Dagmar Schäfer, Giorgio Riello and Luca Molà (eds), *Threads of Global Desire: Silk in the Pre-modern World* (Woodbridge, Suffolk 2018)

Mary Schoeser, *Silk* (New Haven, CT, and London 2007)

Silk and Rayon Users' Association, *The Silk Book* (London 1951)

Chris Spring and Julie Hudson, *Silk in Africa* (London and Seattle, WA, 2002)

Shelagh Vainker, *Chinese Silk: A Cultural History* (London 2004)

James C.Y. Watt and Anne Wardwell, *When Silk was Gold: Central Asian and Chinese Textiles in The Cleveland and Metropolitan Museums of Art*, exhib. cat. (Cleveland, OH, and New York, NY, 1997)

Annabel Westman, *Fringe, Frog and Tassel: The Art of the Trimmings-Maker in Interior Decoration* (London 2019)

Ming Wilson (ed.), *Imperial Chinese Robes from the Forbidden City* (London 2010)

Verity Wilson, *Chinese Textiles* (London 2005)

Janet Wright, *Classic and Modern Fabrics: The Complete Illustrated Sourcebook* (London 2010)

Claudio Zanier, *Where the Roads Met: East and West in the Silk Production Processes (17th to 19th Century)* (Kyoto 1994)

Feng Zhao, *Treasures in Silk: An Illustrated History of Chinese Textiles* (Hong Kong 1999)

Feng Zhao (ed.), *Textiles from Dunhuang in UK Collections/in French Collections* (Shanghai 2007, 2011)

MUSEUMS AND HERITAGE SITES

CONTRIBUTORS

Many major museums have rich holdings of silks, especially those in cities where silks were manufactured or widely used. The museums and heritage sites below focus almost exclusively on silk production.

China
China National Silk Museum, Hangzhou. http://www.chinasilkmuseum.com/index_en.aspx

France
Maison des Canuts. Musée de la soie lyonnaise, Lyon. https://maisondescanuts.fr/

Musée de la Soie en Cévennes. http://www.museedelasoie-cevennes.com/

Great Britain
The Silk Museum and Paradise Mill, Macclesfield. https://macclesfieldmuseums.co.uk/venues/the-silk-museum

Whitchurch Silk Mill, Hampshire. http://whitchurchsilkmill.org.uk/mill/index.php

Italy
Museo Dittatico della Seta Como, Lake Como. https://www.museosetacomo.com/?lang_id=2

Japan
Okaya Silk Museum, Okaya City, Nagano. http://silkfact.jp/

Yokohama Silk Museum, Yokohama. No website

Spain
Colegio del Arte Mayor de la Seda, Valencia. https://www.museodelasedavalencia.com/

USA
The Paterson Museum, Paterson, New Jersey. https://www.facebook.com/ThePatersonMuseum

(All the above websites accessed 28 September 2020.)

Lesley Ellis Miller is Senior Curator in the Furniture, Textiles and Fashion Department at the Victoria and Albert Museum, London.

Ana Cabrera Lafuente is Curator of Fashion at the Museo del Traje, Madrid, and Marie Curie Fellow in the Research Department at the Victoria and Albert Museum, London.

Claire Allen-Johnstone is Assistant Curator, Furniture, Textiles and Fashion Department at the Victoria and Albert Museum, London.

ACL — Ana Cabrera Lafuente, Museo del Traje, Madrid/Research Department, V&A

AF — Avalon Fotheringham, Asian Department, V&A

AJ — Anna Jackson, Asian Department, V&A

CAJ — Claire Allen-Johnstone, Furniture, Textiles and Fashion Department, V&A

CKB — Connie Karol Burks, Furniture, Textiles and Fashion Department, V&A

DP — Divia Patel, Asian Department, V&A

EAH — Elizabeth-Anne Haldane, Textile Conservation Department, V&A

EL — Eunhae Lim, Asian Department, V&A

EM — Elisabeth Murray, Furniture, Textiles and Fashion Department, V&A

FHP — Francesca Henry Pierre, Asian Department, V&A

HF — Hanne Faurby, Sculpture, Metalwork, Ceramics and Glass Department, V&A

HP — Helen Persson, Independent curator and researcher

KH — Kirsty Hassard, V&A Dundee

JL — Jenny Lister, Furniture, Textiles and Fashion Department, V&A

JR — Julia Rank, Furniture, Textiles and Fashion Department, V&A

LEM — Lesley Ellis Miller, Furniture, Textiles and Fashion Department, V&A

MRO — Mariam Rosser-Owen, Asian Department, V&A

MZ — Michaela Zöschg, Sculpture, Metalwork, Ceramics and Glass Department, V&A

OC — Oriole Cullen, Furniture, Textiles and Fashion Department, V&A

RH — Ruby Hodgson, V&A East

RK — Rosalie Kim, Asian Department, V&A

SB — Silvija Banić, Furniture, Textiles and Fashion Department, V&A

SFC — Sau Fong Chan, Asian Department, V&A

SN — Susan North, Furniture, Textiles and Fashion Department, V&A

SS — Sonnet Stanfill, Furniture, Textiles and Fashion Department, V&A

TS — Tim Stanley, Asian Department, V&A

VB — Victoria Bradley, Furniture, Textiles and Fashion Department, V&A

YC — Yoojin Choi, Asian Department, V&A

ACKNOWLEDGEMENTS

PICTURE CREDITS

This book has been a true team effort, and the editors are extremely grateful to all contributors for generously sharing their expertise and pleasure in silk as the project progressed. We all learned much from the examination of objects from different cultures in the V&A collections. Many other colleagues participated in the project in different ways, including Edwina Ehrman, Joanne Hackett, Keith Lodwick, Elizabeth Miller, Will Newton, Angus Patterson, Josephine Rout, Suzanne Smith, Anna White, Christopher Wilk and Masami Yamada, while volunteers in the Furniture, Textiles and Fashion Department and the Asian Department worked conscientiously on a variety of tasks: Sophie Anagnostopoulou, Caroline Dourthe, Diana Haynes, Eunhae Lim and Julia Rank, who was an assiduous and faithful contributor to the project from the outset. External specialists responded generously to queries or read the text: Clare Bergkamp, Alison Carter, María J. Feliciano, Alexandra Jones, Lucina Llorente, Magdalene Miller, Mary Schoeser, Christopher Taylor, Guillaume Verzier and Annabel Westman. Claire Allen-Johnstone and Yoojin Choi undertook the major task of coordinating new photography of V&A objects, while Rob Auton, Pip Barnard and Richard Davies were eminently patient, enthusiastic and talented in capturing their lustre and luxury in evocative ways. In V&A Publishing, Coralie Hepburn and Hannah Newell were supportive throughout, while from Thames & Hudson Philip Watson offered wise advice, Roger Fawcett-Tang created a sumptuous and dynamic design suited to the many faces of silk and Caroline Brooke Johnson patiently and generously engaged with the intricacies of textile technique and aesthetics in her copy-editing. Thanks are also due to Trish Marx for her picture research of non-V&A images. To Clare Browne, we owe a massive debt as she read the text in various states, often at short notice. Her deep knowledge of textiles, eagle eye for inconsistencies and sharp pencil have surely much improved what she was offered. Family and friends endured endless conversations about silk, and the editors are exceptionally grateful to everyone who has listened to their obsession over many months.

INDEX

Page numbers in *italics* refer to illustrations.